어차피
제시카
G-TELP
실전 모의고사

어차피 제시카! G-TELP 모의고사 한권 완성

초판 1쇄 발행 2022년 1월 2일

지은이 제시카 황
디자인 지식과감성#
발행처 에어클래스
등록 제2018-000040호(2018년 2월 7일)
주소 서울시 서초구 반포대로 94 남양빌딩 2층 (서초동)
전화 (02) 745 1202
팩스 (02) 2274 7797
이메일 support@airklass.com

ISBN 979-11-963164-7-1(13740)
값 20,000원

에어클래스에서 '제시카지텔프'를 검색하세요!
www.airklass.com

 홈페이지 바로가기

이 책은 저작권법에 따라 보호받는 저작물이므로 무단복제와 무단전재를 금합니다.
이 책의 전부 또는 일부를 이용하려면 반드시 저작권자와 발행처의 동의를 받아야 합니다.

*파본은 구입하신 곳에서 교환해 드립니다.

Preface 머리말

"지텔프(G-TELP)는 방 탈출 게임과 같습니다."

지텔프(G-TELP) 시험은 실생활에서 영어를 잘 활용할 수 있는지 여부를 평가하는 시험이지만, 자신의 영어 실력이 부족하다고 해서 시험을 잘 보지 못할 것이란 두려움을 가질 필요는 전혀 없습니다. 지텔프 시험은 여러 힌트를 조합하여 빠르게 탈출하는 것이 목적인 "방 탈출 게임"과 같기 때문입니다.

따라서 시험을 앞두고 "나는 왜 영어를 못하지?" "나는 주어, 목적어도 모르는 영포자인데 어떻게 시험을 보지?"와 같은 걱정은 전혀 하실 필요 없습니다. 문제 출제 의도를 파악하고, 정답을 가리키는 힌트를 빠르게 찾는 방법을 아는 것만으로 이미 지텔프라는 방을 탈출하는 키를 쥔 것과 다름없으니까요.

저 제시카가 여러분에게 지텔프라는 방을 탈출하기 위한 '키'를 선물하겠습니다. 이 책을 통해 여러분은 반드시 '지텔프 합격'의 길로 향하는 문을 활짝 열게 될 것입니다!

저자 제시카 드림

G-TELP 시험 소개

1. 시험의 개요 및 목적

G-TELP는 청취(listening), 구술(speaking), 쓰기(writing), 읽기(reading) 평가 중심의 국제 공인 영어 평가 교육 시스템입니다. 88 서울 올림픽, 2008 베이징 올림픽의 공식 영어 평가 교육 툴(통역 안내, 자원봉사자 선발 교육)로서 지정 및 활용되어 영어 평가 교육 방법 체계의 객관성, 타당성, 우수성을 입증 받았습니다. 현재 국가고시(공무원, 군무원, 각종 자격증 등) 영어 대체 시험, 기업체의 신입사원 및 인사, 승진 평가 시험, 대학(원)교 졸업 자격 영어 대체 시험, 초중고 영어 교육 자료로 활용되고 있습니다.

2. 시험의 구성 및 출제 분야 (Level 2 기준)

G-TELP는 총 5개의 Level(Level 1~5)로 구성되어 있으며, 그중에서도 Level 2는 공무원, 군무원, 자격증 등 영어 대체 시험에 활용되는 급수로서 현재 가장 많은 수험생들이 응시하고 있습니다.

구분	출제 방식 및 시간	평가 기준	합격자의 영어 구사 능력
Level 2	문법: 26문항/20분 청취: 26문항/약 30분 독해 · 어휘: 28문항/40분 합계: 80문항/약 90분	다양한 상황에서 대화가 가능하며, 업무 상담 및 해외 연수 등이 가능한 수준	일상 생활 및 업무 상담 등에서 어려움 없이 의사소통이 가능하며 외국인과의 회의 및 세미나 참석, 해외 연수 등이 가능한 수준

	출제 분야
문법	- 가정법: 가정법 과거, 가정법 과거완료 등 - 시제: 진행형, 완료형, 완료진행형 등 - 조동사: 다양한 조동사의 쓰임 및 요구/제안/명령 동사와 should 생략 등 - to부정사와 동명사: 역할 및 목적어로 취하는 동사들 등 - 접속사: 종속접속사, 등위접속사, 접속부사 - 관계사: 관계대명사, 관계부사 등
청취	- 개인적인 이야기 - 어떤 결정에 이르고자 하는 비공식적인 협상 등의 대화 - 어떤 특정한 행동의 진행 상황을 설명하거나 특정한 상품을 추천하는 공식적인 담화 - 일반적인 어떤 일의 진행이나 과정에 대한 설명
독해 · 어휘	- 과거 역사 속의 사건이나 현시대의 이야기 - 최근의 사회적이고 기술적인 묘사에 초점을 맞춘 잡지나 신문의 기사 - 전문적인 것이 아닌 일반적인 내용의 백과사전 - 어떤 것을 설명하거나 설득하는 상업 서신

3. 시험 점수 비율 및 합격 기준

섹션	점수 비율
문법	100점 만점
청취	100점 만점
독해·어휘	100점 만점
총점	총 300점 만점
평균	100점 (성적표상 You have answered 00% of all the question in the test correctly 부분)

Mastery(합격) 기준

- 각 Section별 (문법·청취·독해 및 어휘) 75% 이상을 획득해야 해당 등급 Mastery
- 한 개 Section이 75% 미만인 경우 Near Mastery

4. 시험의 등급 (Level 2 기준)

점수	등급	등급의 정의
90% 이상	2-A	외국인과 대화해야 하는 실제 환경에서 영어를 다양하게 구사할 수 있으며, 국제 회의와 같은 상황하에서 동시 통역까지도 수행할 수 있는 고도의 영어 실력을 완성한 사람
75% 이상으로 Level 2의 합격자	2-B	외국인과 다양한 환경에서 의사소통을 수행할 수 있으며 일반적인 대화와 다소 복잡한 내용도 제한된 범위에서 자유롭게 대화할 수 있고 외국에서의 다양한 상담도 수행할 수 있는 사람
75% 이상으로 청취력 60% 이상 획득	2-C	외국인과 제한된 환경에서 일반적인 대화를 수행할 수 있는 수준으로, 해외에서 여러 가지 목적의 연수를 받을 수 있는 사람
60% 이상으로 청취력 40% 이상 획득	2-D	외국인과 간단한 의사소통을 수행할 수 있는 사람으로, 외국인이 비외국인을 의식해 비교적 간단한 일반적인 대화를 진행할 때 참여할 수 있는 사람
50% 이상	2-E	외국인과 최소한의 의사소통을 수행할 수 있는 기초적인 영어 능력을 가진 사람. 즉, 기초적인 일상 영어 의사소통 상황하에서 최소한의 영어를 사용해야 하는 사람에게 요구되는 수준

Features 교재의 구성

1

최신 기출 문제 완벽 반영!
문법·독해·청해 실전 모의고사
각 5회·5회·2회 수록!

따끈따끈한 최신 기출 문제를 완벽 분석하여 출제 의도를 그대로 살린 문항들로 실전 모의고사 구성! 점수 획득에 가장 유리한 '문법—독해—청해' 순서로 각 5회, 5회, 2회, 총 12회의 실전 모의고사를 수록하여 단기간 내 효과적으로 시험에 대비해 목표 점수를 얻을 수 있도록 하였습니다.

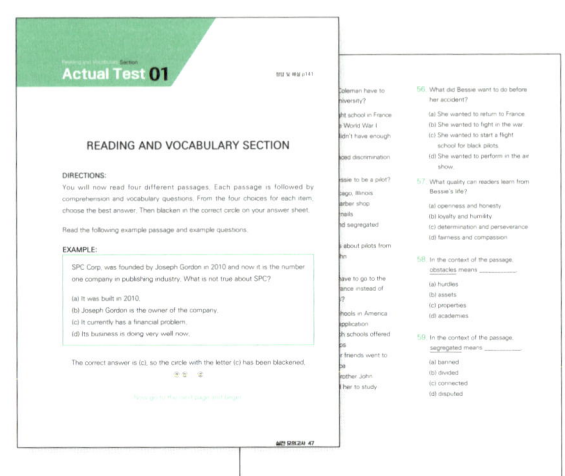

2

테스트 날짜 및 나의 점수
& 틀린 문항까지
꼼꼼하게 적고 체크하기!

각 모의고사를 풀어본 후엔 정답 및 해설을 확인하는 것뿐만 아니라 테스트를 치른 날짜 및 자신이 획득한 점수, 그리고 틀린 문항까지 꼼꼼히 적어볼 수 있는 공간이 수록되어 있어 보다 실전에 가깝게 문제를 풀어보고 자신의 부족한 점까지 완벽히 보완할 수 있습니다.

3

문항별 출제 유형 표기
& 핵심만 콕콕 집어 설명한
군더더기 없는 알짜배기 해설!

해설편엔 모든 문항별로 출제 유형 및 난이도를 표시하여 문제를 보다 정확히 파악할 수 있도록 하였고, 각 문항별 해설엔 쓸데없는 정보를 배제하고 핵심만 콕콕 집어 설명하여 짧은 시간 대비 효율적인 학습을 할 수 있도록 하였습니다. (모든 문항엔 한글 해석 및 어휘 소개 포함)

4

저자가 직접 해설하는
동영상 강의를
"에어클래스"에서 만나보자!

본 교재 모든 문항에 대해 저자가 직접 해설하는 동영상 강의를 에어클래스(www.airklass.com)에서 "제시카지텔프"를 검색하여 구매 가능합니다. 강의 구매 후, 표지 앞면에 수록된 QR코드를 스마트폰으로 스캔하면 문제 해설을 바로바로 편리하게 시청할 수 있습니다

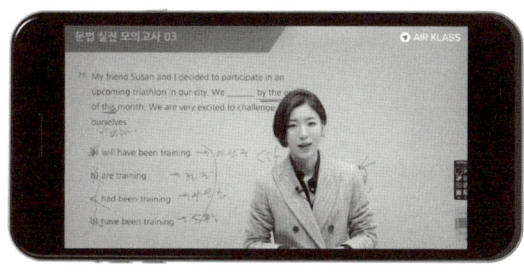

Contents 목차

G-TELP Level 2 : 실전 모의고사

Grammar 문법 실전 모의고사

Actual Test 01	13
Actual Test 02	19
Actual Test 03	25
Actual Test 04	31
Actual Test 05	37

Reading and Vocabulary 독해 실전 모의고사

Actual Test 01	47
Actual Test 02	57
Actual Test 03	67
Actual Test 04	77
Actual Test 05	87

Listening 청해 실전 모의고사

Actual Test 01	99
Actual Test 02	105

G-TELP Level 2 : 정답 & 해설

Grammar 문법 정답 & 해설

Actual Test 01 · 정답 & 해설	112
Actual Test 02 · 정답 & 해설	117
Actual Test 03 · 정답 & 해설	122
Actual Test 04 · 정답 & 해설	127
Actual Test 05 · 정답 & 해설	132

Reading and Vocabulary 독해 정답 & 해설

Actual Test 01 · 정답 & 해설	141
Actual Test 02 · 정답 & 해설	151
Actual Test 03 · 정답 & 해설	161
Actual Test 04 · 정답 & 해설	171
Actual Test 05 · 정답 & 해설	181

Listening 청해 정답 & 해설

Actual Test 01 · 정답 & 해설	194
Actual Test 02 · 정답 & 해설	208

어차피 제시카

G-TELP 모의고사

G-TELP | **Level 2**

Grammar
문법 실전 모의고사

Actual Test 01
Actual Test 02
Actual Test 03
Actual Test 04
Actual Test 05

Grammar Section
Actual Test 01

정답 및 해설 p112

GRAMMAR SECTION

DIRECTIONS:

The following items need a word or words to complete the sentence. From the four choices for each item, choose the best answer. Then blacken in the correct circle on your answer sheet.

EXAMPLE:

I _____ sushi for dinner last night.

(a) has
(b) have
(c) have had
(d) had

The correct answer is (d), so the circle with the letter (d) has been blackened.

ⓐ ⓑ ⓒ ●

Now go to the next page and begin.

01. Greg Coldwell the MLB pitcher was severely injured due to a lightning strike during the game. If he had been transported to the hospital earlier, he _____ the brain damage.

(a) will not suffer
(b) would not have suffered
(c) cannot suffer
(d) had not suffered

02. Earlier on Monday, the company posted a job opening for a digital currency and blockchain product lead, stirring questions among analysts. However, it denies _____ Bitcoin as payment, sending it tumbling.

(a) accepting
(b) to have accepted
(c) to accept
(d) accepted

03. UN Secretary General Anthony Grutters would post a video message to UN personnel in Afghanistan. He says they have his full support and solidarity. He also tells the media that their safety _____ soon.

(a) will be ensured
(b) ensured
(c) is being ensured
(d) had been ensured

04. Public health officials are aggressively amending claims by youtubers who _____ an anti-parasitic drug used for animals as a cancer treatment since February.

(a) will promote
(b) had promoted
(c) will have been promoting
(d) have been promoting

05. Federal and local governments extend business support packages to impacted businesses. However, the authorities notified that businesses _____ implement mandatory vaccine policy.

(a) must
(b) might
(c) could
(d) will

06. The sun is actually rather small in comparison to other stars, so it is unlikely to explode in a giant supernova. If the sun suddenly exploded, any death _____ at a much slower rate than expected.

(a) will progress
(b) would progress
(c) have progressed
(d) is progressing

07. The United States, the world's second-worst polluter after China, is preparing to adopt new energy policies _____ greenhouse emissions in half by 2035.

(a) reducing
(b) to be reduced
(c) to reduce
(d) having reduced

08. Intense heat and wildfires have struck Mediterranean countries. 12,000 firefighters have been struggling to contain a major blaze. Right now, thousands _____ the area.

(a) will flee
(b) flee
(c) are fleeing
(d) have been fleeing

09. Chris and his wife Anna Smith are operating a farm in northern Virginia that produces pasture-raised chicken, eggs, and grass-fed beef at affordable prices. They said if only 1 % could afford their food, it _____ sustainable.

(a) would not be
(b) would not have been
(c) will not
(d) is not

10. One of the key benefits of blood oranges is its high concentration of vitamin C, _____ present in plant-based foods. It also helps regulate inflammation that could lead to serious disease later on.

(a) that improves absorption of iron
(b) who improves absorption of iron
(c) where improves absorption of iron
(d) which improves absorption of iron

11. Since remote learning using laptops and tablets has become a mainstay in at-home learning, doctors suggest that children's eyes _____ regularly to protect their eyes and their overall health.

(a) will be checked
(b) has been checked
(c) are checked
(d) be checked

12. The letter from the Very Concerned Pleasantville resident claims that the mayoral candidate doesn't have correct paperwork on file and _____ prove his residency to receive tax exemption.

(a) will
(b) must
(c) might
(d) can

13. Anxiety disorders are the most common mental illnesses in the world. People with anxiety avoid _____ their lives and share symptoms like irritability and sleep trouble.

   (a) disrupting
   (b) to disrupt
   (c) to be disrupting
   (d) having disrupted

14. By next year, Ben Shultz _____ golf for 20 years. He recently came to the conclusion that traditional golf instruction simply won't work anymore.

   (a) is teaching
   (b) has been teaching
   (c) will have been teaching
   (d) will be teaching

15. If you had invested $1,000 in Netflix's IPO, you _____ 66 shares. Those shares would be worth more than $450,000.

   (a) obtain
   (b) would have obtained
   (c) obtained
   (d) will obtain

16. Even if the premature American military withdrawal had proceeded as smoothly as possible, we still _____ with various terrorist attacks.

   (a) face
   (b) had faced
   (c) will face
   (d) would have faced

17. Last Saturday at 10:00 p.m., Davis PD _____ a RIDE program on the road. A vehicle entered the checkpoint and was charged for operating without insurance and using plates not authorized for that vehicle.

   (a) is conducting
   (b) was conducting
   (c) will conduct
   (d) have conducted

18. An 8-year-old boy reportedly was charged with blasphemy punishable by death after urinating in the library in an Islamic religious school in Punjab. Amnesty International urged that the school _____ immediately.

   (a) will drop all charges
   (b) is dropping all charges
   (c) drop all charges
   (d) have dropped all charges

19. The latest research has revealed that thousands of pets have gained weight since March 2019. The severe health effects of obesity in our four-legged friends don't appear _____ among owners.

(a) to be recognized
(b) recognizing
(c) to recognize
(d) having recognized

20. Hawaii's governor made a plea to tourists to change their travel itinerary due to the sudden volcano eruption. _____, many are struggling with nonrefundable bookings, which can make canceling hard.

(a) Thus
(b) Eventually
(c) Moreover
(d) However

21. The telephone was such an integral part of the advances in the late 19th century. If the telephone had never been invented, some form of automated coding _____ to a greater extent.

(a) is developed
(b) would have been developed
(c) have developed
(d) was developed

22. Lake Monsters played a competitive first half against Forgers FC as people banged on drums and chanted. _____ his favorite team lost, Chris still considered the night a win for fans.

(a) As
(b) Although
(c) Because
(d) When

23. The Lord of the Rings is an epic fantasy novel by English author and scholar J.R.R. Tolkien, _____. It was eventually adopted as three big-budget blockbuster movies.

(a) that invented geography, and several languages for it
(b) who invented geography, and several languages for it
(c) where he invented geography, and several languages for it
(d) which invented geography, and several languages for it

24. My neighbor is trying to put together a simple will for himself. Lawyers advise that he _____ about websites that don't have any legal expertise.

(a) is careful
(b) will be careful
(c) be careful
(d) has been careful

25. Annie and Paul Goodwater ride their bicycle regularly along Villa Road, and they've noticed a lot of trash piling up in certain areas and reported it to News 1. The county admitted _____ it properly due to the budget cut.

(a) not taking care of
(b) not to take care of
(c) to not take care of
(d) not take care of

26. Romance scammers create fake profiles on popular social media like Instagram and Facebook and contact their targets. My friend Rosy _____ on Instagram, if there hadn't been a news story about it.

(a) probably believed a guy
(b) would probably have believed a guy
(c) was probably believing a guy
(d) would probably believe

Grammar Section
Actual Test 02

정답 및 해설 p117

GRAMMAR SECTION

DIRECTIONS:

The following items need a word or words to complete the sentence. From the four choices for each item, choose the best answer. Then blacken in the correct circle on your answer sheet.

EXAMPLE:

I _____ sushi for dinner last night.

(a) has
(b) have
(c) have had
(d) had

The correct answer is (d), so the circle with the letter (d) has been blackened.

ⓐ ⓑ ⓒ **ⓓ**

Now go to the next page and begin.

01. Areas along the Gulf Coast will start to experience the effects of Ida starting Sunday. The National Hurricane Center _____ an increasing risk of a life-threatening storm surge, right now.

(a) forecast
(b) is forecasting
(c) forecasted
(d) will forecast

02. If the Texas power grid had gone down, it _____ a black start. This requires incremental steps in different parts of the system and links together places in the system to restitch the grid into place.

(a) would have needed
(b) was needing
(c) would need
(d) needed

03. The Caldor Fire continued its march toward Lake Tahoe, burning cabins near Echo Summit. Jake Long, a Cal Fire division chief, urged that everyone _____ the region right now due to the extreme heat.

(a) to evacuate
(b) having evacuated
(c) to be evacuated
(d) evacuate

04. When interacting with teens, the best way to initiate a potentially difficult chat is to break the rules of adult conversation. One tactic is to avoid _____ directly what you're talking about.

(a) addressing
(b) to address
(c) to be addressing
(d) having addressed

05. The Ministry of Economy announced on Monday that it _____ revive dining coupons to citizens next month. Food delivery users can get $10 back via their credit card.

(a) might
(b) can
(c) will
(d) must

06. Scientists say heat waves occur naturally but if average temperatures increased everywhere, it _____ more intense heat events.

(a) has caused
(b) caused
(c) could cause
(d) was causing

07. I _____ a terrifying dream when the alarm clock went off at 6 o'clock this morning. It was hard to focus at the early morning meeting.

(a) had
(b) was having
(c) have had
(d) could have

08. When trying to lose weight, a general rule of thumb is to reduce your calorie intake. But you _____ consider nutritious eating and your lifestyle.

(a) would
(b) may
(c) will
(d) should

09. Discrimination still exists in the workplace. Companies are more than twice as likely to call applicants _____ for interviews.

(a) how don't reveal their ethnicity
(b) which don't reveal their ethnicity
(c) that don't reveal their ethnicity
(d) who don't reveal their ethnicity

10. Marcus Pirks, 38, who put off _____ a jab died in a hospital. He had displayed flu-like symptoms and later developed blood clots.

(a) getting
(b) to get
(c) to have gotten
(d) having gotten

11. My friend Hassan studied abroad for a year in the UK. We met up for dinner to catch up and he insisted that he _____ for the meal.

(a) will pay
(b) pay
(c) pays
(d) paid

12. Planning a trip with a group of unorganized people is challenging and stressful. I _____ it if they could at least confirm the date and time of the departure so that I can book my hotel.

(a) have appreciated
(b) appreciate
(c) am appreciating
(d) would appreciate

13. Researchers have shown that adequate housing has links to a person's physical and mental well-being. _____, Professor Bishop says governments should ensure decent housing for all that includes outside space.

    (a) Therefore
    (b) Moreover
    (c) Nonetheless
    (d) However

14. I share a car with my neighbor Bob because of the lack of parking space in the city. As I need to run a few errands today, I _____ the car this afternoon, so I have to text him.

    (a) drive
    (b) would have driven
    (c) will be using
    (d) have driven

15. We had an epic party last night at Saratoga Mansion to celebrate Jamie's 25th birthday. She _____ the plane if she had not gotten so drunk.

    (a) could be caught
    (b) could have caught
    (c) would catch
    (d) caught

16. Many parents can relate to the frustration of having a child refuse _____ anything. It may start off small, with them turning up their nose at the stinky broccoli.

    (a) to eat
    (b) eating
    (c) to be eating
    (d) having eaten

17. As a journalist, I usually find my writing materials around me. My daughter asks me not to write about her and I have to promise her that I _____ about her.

    (a) am not writing
    (b) never write
    (c) will never write
    (d) have never written

18. A group of local high school students are taking their science project further. They are attempting _____ the first to sail across the river on a raft entirely made of empty plastic water bottles.

    (a) becoming
    (b) to have become
    (c) having become
    (d) to become

19. Pharaohs in Egypt seem _____ the exception to the moral code that was highly regarded among the people.

(a) has been
(b) being
(c) having been
(d) to have been

20. Three winning lottery tickets were sold at the same SC store. If she hadn't lost the lottery tickets, Jennifer _____.

(a) would win
(b) would have won
(c) will be winning
(d) won

21. Initially, Ali was going to hire somebody professional, but he realized that he didn't have enough money, so Ali _____ the room himself for 2 hours. He's still painting it.

(a) is painting
(b) has been painting
(c) will paint
(d) painted

22. Scientists _____ often violate common sense and make seemingly absurd assumptions because existing theories simply do not explain newly observed phenomena.

(a) who are on the cutting edge of research
(b) which are on the cutting edge of research
(c) that are on the cutting edge of research
(d) whose are on the cutting edge of research

23. The natural disaster struck Haiti on 14 August, killing more than 2,000 people. Beth Davis and his team _____ a rescue mission on the south coast with local officials since the earthquake.

(a) had been running
(b) were running
(c) ran
(d) have been running

24. I just found out that this year, The Academy Awards will be held in a town near me. If I had gotten an invitation, I _____ there right now.

(a) might have gone
(b) can go
(c) would go
(d) will go

25. Little is known about the long-term impact of regular consumption on cardiovascular health, _____ coffee is among the most consumed beverages in the world.

(a) while
(b) even though
(c) since
(d) whenever

26. The accounting firm where David Kim is working has accepted numerous applications. He _____ more than 200 candidates by the time we are done for the day.

(a) has been interviewing
(b) has interviewed
(c) will interview
(d) will have been interviewing

Grammar Section

Actual Test 03

정답 및 해설 p122

GRAMMAR SECTION

DIRECTIONS:

The following items need a word or words to complete the sentence. From the four choices for each item, choose the best answer. Then blacken in the correct circle on your answer sheet.

EXAMPLE:

I _____ sushi for dinner last night.

(a) has
(b) have
(c) have had
(d) had

The correct answer is (d), so the circle with the letter (d) has been blackened.

ⓐ ⓑ ⓒ ⓓ

Now go to the next page and begin.

01. I _____ in Economics and Philosophy at a college now because I am interested in business ethics. I am planning to go to a graduate school after graduating college.

    (a) double major
    (b) will double major
    (c) am double majoring
    (d) will be majoring

02. If Rachel knew you were in hospital, she _____ to see you, but there is no way of reaching her right now since we lost touch a few years ago.

    (a) comes
    (b) would come
    (c) has come
    (d) is coming

03. Journalists got incredible inside tips on the corruption of the organization. The source for the story insisted that we _____ the name.

    (a) not reveal
    (b) don't reveal
    (c) won't reveal
    (d) aren't revealing

04. The 16-year-old was charged with both vehicle theft and mistreatment of animals. He admits _____ SUV with a dog inside, leaving it to die.

    (a) to steal
    (b) having stolen
    (c) stealing
    (d) to have stolen

05. Unless peace can be achieved on the ground in Darfur in the coming month, the situation for women and children _____ get worse.

    (a) may
    (b) should
    (c) shall
    (d) could

06. Some local folk originally wanted the site turned into a junkyard instead of Carhenge. If the local people had built one, people _____ the area.

    (a) were not visiting
    (b) would not have visited
    (c) didn't visit
    (d) should not visit

07. The audience _____ when the musical actor fell off the stage. Apparently, he lost his balance because he was intoxicated.

(a) was applauding
(b) applauded
(c) had applauded
(d) would applauded

08. Apple reportedly has delayed production of new Apple Watch models _____ it is encountering challenges manufacturing them.

(a) when
(b) while
(c) because
(d) if

09. KakaoTalk reported that the power outage in the area due to the incremental weather caused their system _____ for ten minutes, but the company was able to use the backup power.

(a) to shut down
(b) shutting down
(c) to be shutting down
(d) having shut down

10. Edgartown's 250th anniversary picnic has been months in planning, with live music and a beer garden. However, the town would consider _____ the picnic next year due to the rise of Covid-19.

(a) to hold
(b) holding
(c) having held
(d) to be held

11. Veterans Association (VA) has resources to help veterans transitioning from the military. It connects veterans with qualified representatives, _____.

(a) that walk through benefits available
(b) which walk through benefits available
(c) who walk through benefits available
(d) whose walk through benefits available

12. The New York City Marathon, the largest marathon in the world, is set for November 7th, 2021. Four-time Olympic winner Sarah Mill _____ in this historic event.

(a) runs
(b) would have run
(c) could run
(d) will be running

13. Jessie has been very busy with her new project since she is a famous journalist, so we didn't bother to invite her. Later, she told me that she _____ out for dinner with us if we had asked her since it was her day off.

    (a) would be gone
    (b) will be gone
    (c) had been gone
    (d) would have gone

14. Robert P. McCulloch bought the London Bridge and brought it to Arizona. Before builders took it down, each brick was numbered so they _____ know exactly where to put it.

    (a) will
    (b) would
    (c) shall
    (d) must

15. Maine Dental association urged that the state _____ their indoor mandatory mask wearing policy insisting that they should be excused for medical reasons.

    (a) revise
    (b) revises
    (c) to revise
    (d) will revise

16. I _____ the market all day ever since I started investing in cryptocurrency. I made some bad investment decisions and I want to make up for it.

    (a) have been watching
    (b) watch
    (c) was watching
    (d) will be watching

17. Sometimes, people keep the leftovers in the fridge too long. If I were him, I _____ the falafel that has been sitting in the fridge for more than a week.

    (a) would not eat
    (b) don't eat
    (c) wasn't eating
    (d) won't eat

18. Airbnb has published an update on the restrictions policy for bookings for guests under 25 in the United Kingdom. _____, the British government is working on a host registration system.

    (a) Therefore
    (b) However
    (c) Instead
    (d) Furthermore

19. Big data is often used to address population health concerns _____ large communities of people. However, before big data collection, there needs to be an understanding of risk involved.

(a) assisting
(b) will assist
(c) to assist
(d) having assisted

20. I was getting some help because I have a problem dealing with stress. For example, if I lost my job, I _____ what to do. I am doing some cognitive exercises with my therapist learning how to deal with stressful daily situations.

(a) will not know
(b) do not know
(c) would not know
(d) am not knowing

21. US Embassy ordered that everyone _____ Kabul airport immediately on Saturday because of a specific and credible threat just hours after the president said another attack was imminent.

(a) left
(b) would leave
(c) is leaving
(d) leave

22. Sam was famous for his great figure during his career as an actor, but he gained a lot of weight because he _____ since he retired. We think that he might have suffered from depression.

(a) was overeating
(b) had overate
(c) had been overeating
(d) overate

23. If the ambulance had arrived according to normal acceptable response time, dad _____. The average response time for life-threatening illnesses is usually seven minutes.

(a) would survived
(b) survived
(c) was surviving
(d) would have survived

24. The level of bad cholesterol, _____, can be increased by reusing cooking oil.

(a) which can increase the risks of heart disease
(b) where can increase the risks of heart disease
(c) that can increase the risks of heart disease
(d) who can increase the risks of heart disease

25. Retired Navy officer admits _____ $35,000 in bribe from Malaysian defense contractor in exchange for passing confidential information.

   (a) to take
   (b) taking
   (c) to have taken
   (d) will take

26. My friend Susan and I decided to participate in an upcoming triathlon in our city. We _____ by the end of this month. We are very excited to challenge ourselves.

   (a) will have been training
   (b) will be training
   (c) will train
   (d) have been training

Grammar Section

Actual Test 04

정답 및 해설 p127

GRAMMAR SECTION

DIRECTIONS:

The following items need a word or words to complete the sentence. From the four choices for each item, choose the best answer. Then blacken in the correct circle on your answer sheet.

EXAMPLE:

> I _____ sushi for dinner last night.
>
> (a) has
> (b) have
> (c) have had
> (d) had

The correct answer is (d), so the circle with the letter (d) has been blackened.

ⓐ ⓑ ⓒ ●

Now go to the next page and begin.

01. I will be busy organizing the meeting with our international clients. You can visit me during the first week of September. I _____ then.

(a) haven't been working
(b) am not working
(c) won't work
(d) won't be working

02. Apple's 2021 iPhone lineup _____ be unveiled in the fall of 2021, with the company returning to its traditional September launch timeline.

(a) can
(b) might
(c) shall
(d) will

03. After reviewing the comprehensive evaluation, Brynn got the promotion over four candidates _____ she knew the system best.

(a) since
(b) after
(c) so that
(d) although

04. A noun phrase is a group of words that work together _____ a person, place, thing, or idea. Like all nouns, a noun phrase can be a subject, object, or complement.

(a) naming
(b) having named
(c) to have named
(d) to name

05. Danny was left out of the promotion. If he hadn't insulted his boss, he _____ the position that he wanted for a long time.

(a) will get
(b) would get
(c) would have got
(d) was getting

06. My sister loves having people over, but she has been experiencing pain in her wrists. Now, she avoids _____ large dinners.

(a) cooking
(b) to cook
(c) having cooked
(d) to have cooked

07. Higher levels of education are associated with a wide range of positive outcomes. One of the positive aspects of education is that it contributes _____ one's identity.

(a) to confirm
(b) to confirming
(c) having confirmed
(d) to have confirmed

08. Mrs. Rosenberg took a maternity leave so we have Mrs. North as our substitute. Mrs. North is very strict. In the beginning of the class, she requested that everyone _____ their hands.

(a) to raise
(b) raise
(c) will raise
(d) raises

09. My uncle in Germany, _____, was a recluse. It means he lived a solitary life and avoided other people. He never showed up to the family gatherings.

(a) which I inherited a large sum of money
(b) where I inherited a large sum of money
(c) whom I inherited a large sum of money from
(d) that I inherited a large sum of money from

10. Many houses in my neighborhood recently got burglarized. I felt like I needed a more extensive security system. If burglars broke into my house, they _____ a multiple security system installed throughout the property.

(a) are facing
(b) face
(c) have to face
(d) would face

11. The kids from school _____ rocks at her window for five minutes before Sarah finally comes out of the house and yells, "leave me alone."

(a) would throw
(b) were throwing
(c) have been throwing
(d) threw

12. Hitting the bed late after considerable screen time ruins our sleep cycle. _____, many of us make the mistake of picking up their phones first thing in the morning to check messages.

(a) however
(b) therefore
(c) nevertheless
(d) moreover

13. Sarah has been having communication problems with her coworkers. If Sarah had known that her colleagues were going to be so difficult, she _____ the job.

    (a) would never have taken
    (b) will not take
    (c) took
    (d) is taking

14. Many students put things off and try to get things done last minute. Experts point out that procrastination is also a form of avoiding _____.

    (a) to take risks
    (b) taking risks
    (c) having taken risks
    (d) to have taken risks

15. Traditional forms of communication are dying out including face-to-face interaction. These days most people _____ email instead of writing letters.

    (a) are using
    (b) have used
    (c) used
    (d) will use

16. Jane and her husband found a place she likes. She _____ make a decision about that house before someone else buys it, but she feels a bit pressured.

    (a) will
    (b) should
    (c) can
    (d) may

17. If James had brushed his teeth more frequently, he _____ fillings. He realized that it costs a significant amount of money for his teeth to get treated.

    (a) wouldn't need
    (b) wouldn't have needed
    (c) didn't need
    (d) wasn't needing

18. The school is having a large-scale sporting event for the first time in its history. The principal has asked that all teachers _____ to respond to any emergencies that might arise.

    (a) will be available
    (b) are available
    (c) to be available
    (d) be available

19. Peter is a very popular instructor at his university. Peter _____ students at the university for more than a year by the time he leaves for Japan where he will take his sabbatical.

   (a) has been educating
   (b) will educate
   (c) will have been educating
   (d) has educated

20. The boy, _____, started a fire in the classroom endangering other children. The school board is hesitating pressing charges since everybody knows his parents and knows how devastated they are.

   (a) whose parents both work at the school
   (b) his parents both work at the school
   (c) which parents both work at the school
   (d) what parents both work at the school

21. Uncle Scott _____ the car while Christine looks for her new leather coat. They are eating at Scott's favorite restaurant today, Sunny's Pancake Diner.

   (a) is warming up
   (b) warms up
   (c) has been warming up
   (d) warmed up

22. We can see and observe other things with the help of our eyes. If there had been one eye of the man, then the image _____ three dimensional.

   (a) would not have been appeared
   (b) was not appearing
   (c) did not appear
   (d) would not have appeared

23. David and his team are introduced to a digital surveillance platform called Sneek. While they _____, the program will capture a live photo of David and his workmates via their company laptop webcams.

   (a) were working
   (b) had worked
   (c) are working
   (d) work

24. Nearly one third of young people in Latin America and the Caribbean live in poverty. It is imperative that the UN and ECLAC _____ comprehensive social protection.

   (a) are calling for
   (b) will call for
   (c) call for
   (d) called for

25. Humanitarian rescue ships have pulled 396 migrants from a dangerously overcrowded wooden boat. If it hadn't been for the rescue ships, they _____ like many refugees in the Mediterranean Sea.

(a) would drown
(b) drowned
(c) will drown
(d) would have drowned

26. Amy Glenn, 34, is devoted to her five-year-old. However, when discussing motherhood, she confessed that she regrets _____ children.

(a) to have
(b) having
(c) having had
(d) to have had

Grammar Section

Actual Test 05

정답 및 해설 p132

GRAMMAR SECTION

DIRECTIONS:

The following items need a word or words to complete the sentence. From the four choices for each item, choose the best answer. Then blacken in the correct circle on your answer sheet.

EXAMPLE:

I _____ sushi for dinner last night.

(a) has
(b) have
(c) have had
(d) had

The correct answer is (d), so the circle with the letter (d) has been blackened.

ⓐ ⓑ ⓒ ●

Now go to the next page and begin.

01. A driver received a $20 fine for driving through Birmingham, despite never driving his car there. Ben Costello said he _____ the $120 penalty charge notices since June.

   (a) will be getting
   (b) gets
   (c) had been getting
   (d) getting

02. The local zoo is getting quite run-down over the years, so the city is looking for an idea for the renovation. If I owned a zoo, I _____ people interact with the animals more.

   (a) am letting
   (b) let
   (c) would let
   (d) will let

03. A Kansas City, Missouri board ordered that the bar's liquor license _____ because it failed to comply with COVID-19 health orders. John Burk, the owner of the bar, was very defiant in his stance not to follow the Mayor's emergency order.

   (a) is revoked
   (b) be revoked
   (c) will be revoked
   (d) revoked

04. Canada would consider _____ in additional Afghan refugees on behalf of the United States or other allies if asked to do so, Immigration Minister Marco Mendicino said on Friday.

   (a) taking
   (b) to take
   (c) be taking
   (d) having taken

05. Natural gas is pumped through wells just like crude oil and is found near oil deposits underneath the earth surface. Coal, _____, is a solid fossil fuel.

   (a) therefore
   (b) as long as
   (c) moreover
   (d) on the other hand

06. The university is planning to provide a variety of classes for the graduate students. Total of ten classes, most of _____, will be offered next semester.

   (a) which will be taught in English
   (b) whose will be taught in English
   (c) whom will be taught in English
   (d) that will be taught in English

07. Police and healthcare providers should never explicitly express their doubts about a crime survivor's story. They deserve _____ with dignity.

(a) had been treated
(b) being treated
(c) having treated
(d) to be treated

08. A young man had stabbed a stranger 20 times in different parts of the body last week. Prosecutors had requested that the maximum sentence _____ to the accused.

(a) be given
(b) to be given
(c) was given
(d) gave

09. People who are missing several types of cone cells tend to be very sensitive to light. They _____ also have difficulty seeing clearly, especially in bright light.

(a) should
(b) need
(c) ought to
(d) may

10. My friend Jess spent a lot of time teaching English abroad. After coming back to the United States, Jess landed on a great job. The company _____ her if she hadn't had some experience abroad.

(a) hadn't hired
(b) wouldn't have hired
(c) wouldn't hire
(d) wasn't hiring

11. While Earth's biodiversity is so rich that many species have to be discovered, many species _____ with extinction due to human activities right now.

(a) had been threatened
(b) will be threatened
(c) were threatened
(d) are being threatened

12. Martha was planning to run in the historic Boston Marathon. Martha _____ almost 40 miles a day every day before she broke her leg. She is pretty devastated right now.

(a) was running
(b) has been running
(c) would be running
(d) had been already running

13. Marion Jones was a great track star from the United States who won five medals at the 2000 Summer Olympics. She had to return all her medals when she admitted _____ drugs to run faster.

    (a) using
    (b) to use
    (c) to have used
    (d) used

14. We are still accepting registration for the qualification exam. If you decided to take it, you _____ by 31 March.

    (a) register
    (b) registered
    (c) should register
    (d) will register

15. Celebrity photographer Andy Grotts, _____, refuses to photoshop movie icons. His pictures of the late Tony Curtis stand out as the most significant of his career.

    (a) that has snapped numerous stars
    (b) whoever has snapped numerous stars
    (c) who has snapped numerous stars
    (d) when he snapped numerous stars

16. My wife and I are still settling in at our new apartment. We haven't decided where to place our sofa and our interior designer recommended that it _____ in front of the window.

    (a) went
    (b) go
    (c) to go
    (d) had gone

17. While Jonathan _____, someone stole his gray Chrysler 300 from his garage. The County Sheriff's Office said the thief loaded up the car with other things from his home, including a chainsaw.

    (a) was sleeping
    (b) had slept
    (c) will sleep
    (d) is sleeping

18. I wanted to learn Japanese when I was younger, but I didn't have the opportunity. Years later, I was offered a university scholarship in Tokyo. If I had taken it, I _____ fluent.

    (a) got
    (b) would get
    (c) will have gotten
    (d) could have gotten

19. There are three types of cone cells. One type absorbs blue light, one green light, and one red light. Combining these three main colors allows us _____ thousands of colors.

(a) seeing
(b) to be seeing
(c) to see
(d) to have seen

20. I am sorry to bother you, but I didn't expect that traffic in the city would be this bad. My friend may arrive before I get home. _____, please ask her to call me.

(a) In fact
(b) In that case
(c) However
(d) Yet

21. I have to call my previous accountant, Anthony. I recently had to eliminate a contract with an accounting firm. If they hadn't raised their fee so much, I _____ working with them.

(a) would have kept
(b) kept
(c) will keep
(d) would kept

22. Kelly said that he _____ at the library tonight for his midterms, so he will not see Ellie when she arrives. I am worried that that will make them argue.

(a) will be studying
(b) is studying
(c) studies
(d) would study

23. The traffic in the city is a nightmare. It took me three hours to get home from downtown. If I didn't have to waste my time commuting, I _____ more stuff at work.

(a) accomplish
(b) would accomplish
(c) will accomplish
(d) accomplished

24. Go straight for three blocks and then turn left, then go two more blocks and it's right across the street from a Quickie Mart. You _____ miss it.

(a) can't
(b) needn't
(c) mustn't
(d) won't

25. You can practice _____ English online with us. It is the fastest way to fluency. Learn with certified English tutors, and experience tailored lessons and personalized tuition. Book now.

(a) to speak
(b) speaking
(c) having speaking
(d) to be speaking

26. NASA is getting ready to send astronauts to explore more of the Moon as part of the Artemis program. Astronauts _____ on the Moon by the year 2025.

(a) have been landing
(b) will have landed
(c) are landing
(d) would have landed

어차피 제시카

G-TELP 모의고사

G-TELP | Level 2

Reading and Vocabulary
독해 실전 모의고사

Actual Test 01
Actual Test 02
Actual Test 03
Actual Test 04
Actual Test 05

Reading and Vocabulary Section
Actual Test 01

정답 및 해설 p141

READING AND VOCABULARY SECTION

DIRECTIONS:

You will now read four different passages. Each passage is followed by comprehension and vocabulary questions. From the four choices for each item, choose the best answer. Then blacken in the correct circle on your answer sheet.

Read the following example passage and example questions.

EXAMPLE:

> SPC Corp. was founded by Joseph Gordon in 2010 and now it is the number one company in publishing industry. What is not true about SPC?
>
> (a) It was built in 2010.
> (b) Joseph Gordon is the owner of the company.
> (c) It currently has a financial problem.
> (d) Its business is doing very well now.

The correct answer is (c), so the circle with the letter (c) has been blackened.

ⓐ ⓑ ● ⓓ

Now go to the next page and begin.

PART 1.

Read the following biography article and answer the questions. The underlined words in the article are for vocabulary questions.

BESSIE COLEMAN

Bessie Coleman was the first female African American and Native American pilot ever to hold an international pilot license. Known for performing flying tricks, Coleman's nicknames were; "Brave Bessie," and "Queen Bess." She fought discrimination to follow her dream of becoming a pilot. As a Black woman in the 1920s, she faced many **obstacles** because of her race and gender.

Bessie was born in Atlanta, Texas, in 1892. Her parents were Black and her father was of Native American descent as well. Bessie grew up helping her mother pick cotton and wash laundry to earn extra money. She attended **segregated** schools, but had to drop out of university because she couldn't afford to continue her study.

She eventually moved to Chicago, Illinois in 1915 and worked in a barber shop painting fingernails. When her brother John returned from fighting in France during World War I, he told Coleman stories about war. Hearing stories about the brave pilots sparked Bessie's new dream: to be a pilot.

She applied to U.S. flight schools, but every school rejected her because she was Black and a woman. Famous African American newspaper publisher Robert Abbott told her to move to France where she could learn how to fly. In 1920, Coleman traveled on a ship to France. She found a school run by the Cauron brothers. She earned her international pilot's license on June 15, 1921, within a year of enrolling.

When she returned to the United States in 1922 as an aerial acrobat, Coleman amazed Back and White audiences with her daredevil feats. She would do loops, barrel rolls, and figure eights in her plane. She'd even walk on the wings and parachute out.

In 1923, Coleman survived a bad accident that left her with a broken leg and ribs, but she recovered and started doing stunts at air shows again. Her goal was to open a school for Black pilots, but she never completed that dream. She died a few years later in another plane accident, but her courageous feats of flight have inspired a fleet of Black women pilots who came after her.

53. Why did Bessie Coleman have to drop out of the university?

(a) to go to the flight school in France
(b) because of the World War I
(c) because she didn't have enough money
(d) because she faced discrimination

54. What inspired Bessie to be a pilot?

(a) moving to Chicago, Illinois
(b) working at a barber shop painting fingernails
(c) having to attend segregated schools
(d) hearing stories about pilots from her brother John

55. Why did Bessie have to go to the flight school in France instead of the United States?

(a) because no schools in America accepted her application
(b) because French schools offered her scholarships
(c) because all her friends went to school in France
(d) because her brother John recommended her to study abroad.

56. What did Bessie want to do before her accident?

(a) She wanted to return to France.
(b) She wanted to fight in the war.
(c) She wanted to start a flight school for black pilots.
(d) She wanted to perform in the air show.

57. What quality can readers learn from Bessie's life?

(a) openness and honesty
(b) loyalty and humility
(c) determination and perseverance
(d) fairness and compassion

58. In the context of the passage, obstacles means _____.

(a) hurdles
(b) assets
(c) properties
(d) academies

59. In the context of the passage, segregated means _____.

(a) banned
(b) divided
(c) connected
(d) disputed

PART 2.
Read the following magazine article and answer the questions. The underlined words in the article are for vocabulary questions.

WHAT DOES TOO MUCH SCREEN TIME DO TO CHILDREN'S BRAINS?

Nearly half of all children 8 and under have their own tablet device and spend an average of about 3 hours a day on screen. What is all this screen time doing to kids' brains?

For young children, especially those under the age of 5, development is happening rapidly. Young children learn by exploring their environment and watching the adults in their lives and then imitating them.

However, excessive screen time may **inhibit** a child's ability to observe and experience the typical everyday activities they need to engage with in order to learn about the world, leading to a kind of tunnel vision, which can be harmful to overall development.

Children who are often playing on smartphones or tablets don't pay attention to anything else around them. They will not learn about the world around them if all they're doing is looking at a smartphone. This will not just affect their ability to learn new things, but also how they interact with others and how language develops.

Language development expands rapidly between 1 to 3 years of age, and studies have shown that children learn language best when engaging and interacting with adults who are talking and playing with them. There is also some evidence that children who watch a lot of television during the early elementary school years perform less well on reading tests and may show deficits in attention.

According to the recent National Institutes of Health (NIH) study, children who spent more than two hours a day on screen-time activities score lower on language and thinking tests, and some children with more than seven hours a day of screen time experience weakening of cortex, the area of the brain related to critical thinking and reasoning.

Dr. Joseph Cross, an assistant professor at Cornell University, says, "if young children spend most of their time engaging with an iPad, smartphone, or the television, all of which are highly entertaining, it can be hard to get them **engaged** in non-electronic activities, such as playing with toys to foster imagination and creativity, exploring outdoors, and playing with other children to develop appropriate social skills."

Dr. Cross recommends that parents keep bedtime, mealtime, and family time screen-free. She also says that parents consider setting a curfew or an agreed-upon time because balancing online and offline time is extremely important.

60. According to the article, how do young children learn about the world?

    (a) by watching educational tv shows like sesame street
    (b) by observing and copying grown-ups in their lives
    (c) by interacting with one another at a nursery
    (d) by engaged in activities designed by teachers

61. How does the increased screen time affect children?

    (a) It gives more opportunities to connect with other kids.
    (b) It makes children more violent and impulsive.
    (c) It stunts the proper brain development that could affect their language ability.
    (d) It helps them learn new information they can't learn at school.

62. What happens to the kids who spend a lot of time on their digital devices?

    (a) They lose interest in playing with their friends.
    (b) They are eager to participate in school activities.
    (c) They want to spend more time with their family.
    (d) They learn to communicate with other people.

63. According to Dr. Cross, what should families do to reduce screen time?

    (a) leave it to the kids to decide
    (b) have the kids write their screen time on their journal
    (c) take their smartphones and give them only when they behave
    (d) turn their smartphones and iPads off during certain times of the day

64. What can parents do to limit their children's screen time?

    (a) decide their screen time and notify them
    (b) regulate their screen time but get their consent
    (c) let them use their digital devices whenever they want
    (d) consult experts and decide their screen time

65. In the context of the passage, inhibit means _____.

    (a) assist
    (b) block
    (c) encourage
    (d) permit

66. In the context of the passage, engaged means _____.

    (a) entertain
    (b) inform
    (c) dismissed
    (d) participated

PART 3.

Read the following article and answer the questions. The underlined words in the article are for vocabulary questions.

STORM CHASERS

Some storm chasers are photographers trying to capture spectacular images of a tornado. But most storm chasers are scientists and meteorologists who study the weather. They put themselves in the paths of dangerous storms to collect more information than they could get from far away. How fast is a tornado moving? Will a hurricane hit the coast? Questions like these are hard to answer without getting close to a storm. Storm chasers gather data, take photos, and shoot videos to convince people to prepare for the storm.

Storm chasers have to find a storm before they can chase it. They watch for weather patterns that usually lead to dangerous storms. By looking at all the features of weather such as wind speed, a sudden change in temperature, humidity, storm chasers can predict when and where a storm might form. When the storm chasers have located a forming storm, radar maps guide the team to the storm's location. Storm chasers living in coastal areas often specialize in hurricanes, also called typhoons or cyclones. Hurricanes form over the open ocean near the equator. They are powered by warm, moist air. Hurricanes become most damaging as they move toward a coast.

The central United States is nicknamed Tornado Alley. Cold and dry air from the north **collides** with warm, moist air from the south. Large temperature differences create strong winds. This pattern leads to thunderstorms that may become tornadoes.

They drive in **armored** trucks filled with weather instruments. They place sensors called turtles on the ground in the path of the storm. The turtles will gather data from inside the storm. The truck is equipped with side armor that blocks the wind from getting under trucks and flipping it over. Strong spikes attach the truck to the ground. Even with safety precautions and special vehicles, storm chasing is very dangerous. Tornadoes can quickly change direction and destroy everything in their path. Hurricanes can cause huge waves that wipe out buildings. Even experienced storm chasers have been hurt or killed by monster storms.

If we are near a storm, we need to get indoors to stay safe. We also should listen to the weather report. Sometimes a battery-powered radio will still work if cell phones go out during a bad storm. Storm chasers urge people to leave the storm chasing to the expert.

67. What are storm chasers most likely to be engaged in?

(a) measuring the speed of the wind inside a tornado
(b) talking to the media about the upcoming storm
(c) trying to take as many pictures as possible near the storm
(d) trying to get people to evacuate the area

68. Why do storm chasers follow dangerous storms?

(a) to warn people of the dangers of the powerful storms
(b) to get amazing pictures for the media coverage
(c) to get information they can't obtain from far away
(d) to broadcast it on their Youtube channels and social media

69. How do storm chasers know where the storms will form?

(a) They get information from meteorologists.
(b) They look for the signs of the storms.
(c) They drive around trying to spot a storm.
(d) They just hope for storms to strike.

70. Based on the article, what is responsible for forming tornadoes in "Tornado Alley?"

(a) hot and humid air from south
(b) cold and dry air from the north
(c) the great temperature differences
(d) thunderstorms that are frequent to the area

71. According to the article, why do storm chasers use armored vehicles?

(a) to protect the truck from flying debris
(b) to drive fast in the storm
(c) to get dramatic footage of the storm
(d) to carry equipment needed to collect data

72. In the context of the passage, collides means _____.

(a) attach
(b) crash
(c) forecast
(d) train

73. In the context of the passage, armored means _____.

(a) protected
(b) predicted
(c) exposed
(d) forced

PART 4.

Read the following letter and answer the questions. The underlined words in the letter are for vocabulary questions.

Best tours,

711 Vermont Road

Berkeley CA

91471

Dear Sir/Madam,

My wife and I have just returned from one of your "Romantic city tours" in Bangkok (October 20 – 24) and I am writing to complain about the holiday we were given.

First of all, the hotel was not at all what we had been led to expect from your website. You advertised air-conditioned rooms with a mini bar and **private** bathroom, but what we got was a tiny room with none of the promised appliances. Worst of all, we had to share a bathroom with five other parties on our floor. I don't think having a stool with your room number in a shared bathroom isn't considered private. The temperature was 30 degrees Celsius inside everyday even at night, so you can imagine our discomfort. As for the hotel staff, whenever we called down to the reception, no one was around. There did not even seem to be any cleaning staff since our beds were made only once during the whole of our stay.

Moreover, the tourist guide included in your offer called in sick shortly after we arrived at the hotel and there was nobody in charge to organize a suitable **substitute**. We were disappointed to find out that the tour guide only spoke broken English and we had difficulties understanding him. The tour guide took us to various shopping malls where we could have gone by ourselves.

As you can see, we are highly dissatisfied with the holiday your company provided. We expect a letter of apology as well as a full refund. We are determined to take this matter a step further, if our demands are not met.

Sincerely,

M.J. Jones

74. What is the purpose of the M.J. Jones' letter to Best tours?

(a) to file a formal complaint
(b) to express their gratitude
(c) to inform them of some lost items during their stay
(d) to offer help in operating the business

75. According to the letter, what is M.J. Jones most concerned about?

(a) the inability of hotel staff to manage the place
(b) the untidy room condition
(c) the false advertisement
(d) the hot weather in a no air-conditioned room

76. Based on the letter, what is expected of the hotel reception?

(a) to provide translators and tour guides
(b) to organize the tour among their guests
(c) to clean the rooms once a day
(d) to be at reception at business hours

77. What happened when the tour guide called in sick?

(a) The tour guide made up for his absence.
(b) There was no tour that day.
(c) The company organized a different tour.
(d) The tour guide sent another person.

78. What was the main problem with the tour guide?

(a) his tardiness
(b) his inability to communicate
(c) his rude attitude
(d) his unsanitary behavior

79. In the context of the passage, private means _____.

(a) exclusive
(b) inclusive
(c) conclusive
(d) executive

80. In the context of the passage, substitute means _____.

(a) management
(b) involvement
(c) encouragement
(d) replacement

Reading and Vocabulary Section

Actual Test 02

정답 및 해설 p151

READING AND VOCABULARY SECTION

DIRECTIONS:

You will now read four different passages. Each passage is followed by comprehension and vocabulary questions. From the four choices for each item, choose the best answer. Then blacken in the correct circle on your answer sheet.

Read the following example passage and example questions.

EXAMPLE:

> SPC Corp. was founded by Joseph Gordon in 2010 and now it is the number one company in publishing industry. What is not true about SPC?
>
> (a) It was built in 2010.
> (b) Joseph Gordon is the owner of the company.
> (c) It currently has a financial problem.
> (d) Its business is doing very well now.

The correct answer is (c), so the circle with the letter (c) has been blackened.

ⓐ ⓑ ● ⓓ

Now go to the next page and begin.

PART 1.
Read the following biography and answer the questions. The underlined words in the article are for vocabulary questions.

JOHN MUIR

John Muir was an influential Scottish-born American naturalist, author, writer and the founder of an important organization. His words inspired many people to make an effort to protect wilderness. They also helped bring about the protection of many nature areas, including Yosemite Valley.

John Muir was born on April 21, 1838, in Scotland. When John was eleven, his family moved to Wisconsin, in the United States, so his father could start a farm. John's father was very **strict** and forced his children to work long hours doing farm labor. He only allowed them one small meal a day. The children's health suffered as a result.

John did not attend school, but he loved to learn. His father allowed him to wake up early to have time to read. He studied many different subjects on his own. If he had any free time during the day, he explored the woods and fields around the family farm. During John's teen years, he spent part of his early morning time working on inventions. In 1860, he displayed his inventions at the Wisconsin State Fair where his talent was recognized and awarded. He studied math and science at the University of Wisconsin, but soon left to travel on foot around parts of Canada and the Midwest. He took odd jobs to pay his way.

After traveling to Yosemite in 1889, Muir published two articles about the area's beauty. Other people worked with Muir by asking the government to protect Yosemite. The next year, Yosemite became the third U.S national park. In his later years, Muir spent more time writing about his travels. He also led a twelve-year fight to protect a valley in Yosemite from being flooded by a dam. Even though he couldn't stop the dam from being built, the fight raised awareness about the protection of wild places. John Muir died on December 24, 1914.

John Muir was a founding father of the **conservation** movement. He was one of the first people to call for taking action to protect wild places. His letters, essays and books of his adventures in nature, especially in the Sierra Nevada mountains of California, have been read by millions of people. For his outstanding accomplishments in preserving America's environment, he is known to many as the "Father of the National Parks" and "son of the wilderness."

53. What most likely is Muir's legacy?

    (a) organizing a group advocating immigrants' rights
    (b) promoting science and biology among young kids
    (c) writing about the beauty of the United States
    (d) raising awareness of the protection of nature

54. Why did Muir and his siblings' health suffer?

    (a) because Muir's father didn't make enough money
    (b) because Muir had too many siblings
    (c) because they were overworked and underfed
    (d) because their parents were too busy adjusting to the new life

55. Why did Muir wake up early at a young age?

    (a) to pursue his own academic projects
    (b) to know more about farm work
    (c) to go to state fairs around the states
    (d) to travel to the mountains in the area

56. How did Muir contribute to Yosemite becoming a national park?

    (a) by protesting against government policy
    (b) by writing article about Yosemite
    (c) by fighting with land developers
    (d) by sending letters to the president

57. Why is Muir called a founding father of the conservation movement?'

    (a) because he participated in the conservation movement in America
    (b) because he was the first to speak up for wilderness protection
    (c) because he had the most influence on the government policy
    (d) because he made the Yosemite as a national park

58. In the context of the passage, strict means _____.

    (a) inflexible
    (b) independent
    (c) generous
    (d) enjoyable

59. In the context of the passage, conservation means _____.

    (a) communication
    (b) freedom
    (c) tradition
    (d) preservation

PART 2.

Read the following article and answer the questions. The underlined words in the article for vocabulary questions.

TikTok IS NOW THE WORLD'S MOST DOWNLOADED APP

Originally called A.me and later Douyin, the app was launched by ByteDance in Beijing, China in September 2016. This led to the app's rebranding as TikTok in September 2017 and was later launched outside of China in international markets. By January 2018, it was already number one in several countries including Thailand. TikTok's software allows people to record videos, add favorite songs or audio already posted to the app, apply effects and edit them.

According to a global analysis compiled by Nikkei, TikTok has officially overtaken Facebook, Instagram, WhatsApp, and every other messaging platform to become the most downloaded social media app in the world. Until 2019, Facebook had held that title. However, TikTok has grown around the world at an **unprecedented** rate, so that now it's taken over social media.

The most popular videos on Youtube currently stretch around ten minutes – a lot shorter than traditional TV or video entertainment. TikTok has been paving the way for something completely new: very quick, snappy videos averaging between nine to fifteen seconds. In the beginning, most TikToks were quick, funny clips aimed at making you smile or laugh. However, its style has expanded to include educational clips, life hacks, mini cooking tutorials, and much more.

TikTok has even been inspiring other platforms to **mimic** its style, after seeing its popularity boom – such as instagram Reels, or YouTube Shorts. Both of these have been pushed as additional short-video platforms alongside the main platform.

For a while last year, people didn't really think TikTok was going to make it in the US, after Donald Trump, the president of America had threatened to get rid of the app from the United States due to a national security risk. He said that the Chinese government had access to its user data. The company repeatedly denied the allegations. Trump's executive order was later withdrawn by the next president of the US, Joe Biden.

The pandemic served to provide a massive boost to TikTok's popularity, as not only were most people stuck at home with limited means of entertainment, but also because many famous artists were forced to cancel shows and tours, and decided to take to this platform instead.

60. What did Nikkei recently investigate about popular Social Media Platforms?

(a) the growth of new social media platforms
(b) the management of fake news
(c) the age and gender of social media users
(d) the danger of leaking personal information

61. What is the notable feature of TikTok videos?

(a) their content
(b) their technology
(c) their openness
(d) their length

62. How did TikTok most likely influence other social media platforms like YouTube and Instagram?

(a) the launching of new ad campaigns
(b) coming up with a short video format
(c) changing the layout of the platform
(d) adding more interactive functions

63. What kind of problem did TikTok face in the United States?

(a) promoting illegal drug use
(b) increasing violence among teens
(c) posing a national security risk
(d) unregulated graphic contents

64. What will happen to TikTok in a pandemic situation?

(a) It is expected to expand even more.
(b) It will have to let people post longer videos.
(c) It is expected to work with a government agency.
(d) It will lose its current popularity and disappear.

65. In the context of the passage, unprecedented means _____.

(a) distant
(b) available
(c) present
(d) extraordinary

66. In the context of the passage, mimic means _____.

(a) continue
(b) protect
(c) allow
(d) imitate

PART 3.

Read the following encyclopedia article and answer the questions. The underlined words in the article are for vocabulary questions.

SINKHOLES

Sinkholes are pits in the ground that form in areas where water gathers without external drainage. A sinkhole forms in the ground when the dirt and rocks wash away and there is nothing underneath the ground anymore to support it. Sinkholes mainly occur as water drains below ground. It can **dissolve** subterranean caverns, particularly in areas where the bedrock is made of water-soluble evaporate rocks such as salt or limestone.

Sinkholes can be natural or man-made. Natural sinkholes occur due to erosion or underground water. They start developing a long time before it actually appears. There is water continually seeping in between the mud, rocks and minerals, as it makes its way down to the ground water reservoirs. As this happens, the water slowly erodes the rocks and minerals. Sometimes the flow of water increases to the point where it washes away the underground structure of the land. And when the structure becomes too weak to support the surface of the earth, it collapses and opens up a hole. This is how sinkholes are formed. Sometimes sinkholes can open suddenly and swallow buildings, cars, and people.

In 2010, one of the most **devastating** sinkholes in recent times hit Guatemala City. It was particularly bad because the sinkhole was formed in the middle of the busy city. It swallowed a three-story factory killing 15 people. The hole was more than 100 meters deep — deep enough to swallow two Statues of Liberty. The sinkhole was caused by a number of factors including an influx of water from storms and leakage from a local sewage pipe.

Underground mines can also cause sinkholes. Near one Russian city, underground water filled an old mine. The bedrock of salt began dissolving. In 1986, a huge sinkhole opened up. It grew to 238 meters deep and covered more than 25 football fields. It is still growing and new sinkholes are opening up. Hundreds of people have had to leave their homes. To be safe, the entire city may need to move. The deepest sinkhole in the world is located in China. It is Xiaozhai Tiankeng, which literally means 'heavenly pit.' This particular example in the Chongqing district is a staggering 662 meters deep and 626 meters wide.

The Sarisarinama sinkholes in Venezuela were discovered in 1961. Scientists have discovered plants and animals inside that are found nowhere else. A sinkhole can be stopped if it is found in time. If someone finds a sinkhole starting, people can put grout into the hole, and it can cause the sinkhole to be stopped. This can help to save areas from a lot of damage.

67. What is a sinkhole?

(a) a man-made tourist destination
(b) a natural and artificial geographical feature
(c) a geographical rock formation in a certain area
(d) a name of the natural phenomenon in Guatemala City

68. In which terrain are sinkholes most likely to form?

(a) in a place with water-soluble bedrock
(b) in a place with less topsoil
(c) in a place with glaciers
(d) in a place with poor drainage

69. What element is most responsible for forming a sinkhole?

(a) drilling in the ground in cities
(b) underground water with water soluble rocks
(c) unregulated waste disposal
(d) melting snow on mountain tops

70. Why was the sinkhole in Guatemala City particularly devastating?

(a) because it formed gradually over time
(b) because it lasted for a while without being filled
(c) because it happened in the middle of the city
(d) because it was left uncovered by workers

71. What is required to do when a person finds a sinkhole?

(a) fill it up immediately
(b) notify the authorities
(c) investigate by him or herself
(d) put some water to form a pond

72. In the context of the passage, dissolve means _____.

(a) solve
(b) prove
(c) depart
(d) melt

73. In the context of the passage, devastating means _____.

(a) distinctive
(b) represent
(c) increasing
(d) destructive

PART 4.

Read the following email and answer the questions. The underlined words in the letter are for vocabulary questions.

May 15, 2020
College Scholars Program
University of Tennessee
354 Jefferson Rd.
Danville, NC 34098
To Whom It May Concern,

It is with much enthusiasm that I recommend John B. Bloomberg for inclusion in the College Scholars Program at the University of Tennessee.

I had the pleasure of teaching John in his 11th grade honors English class at Morristown–Hamblen High school. From the first day of class, John impressed me with his ability to articulate difficult concepts and texts, his sensitivity to the nuances within literature, and his passion for reading, writing, and creative expressions – both in and out of the classroom. John displayed a level of creativity, wit, an analytical thought that is quite **rare** among high school students.

His writing and research skills are excellent. For his major essay project in AP English, he researched and wrote a remarkable study of visual imagery in the work of Ron Padgett, a contemporary American poet. John is ready to assume and excel in upper division classwork, and possesses the self-motivation to successfully create and **execute** an independent course of honors study.

Throughout the year John was an active participant in our discussions, and he always supported his peers. His caring nature and personality allowed him to work well with others in a team setting, as he always respects others' opinions even when they differ from his own.

John also demonstrated leadership skills in a school band and the Student Council. He was our band's drum major for two years and served as Vice President of the Student Council and Editor of our high school yearbook.

I am certain that John is going to continue to do great and creative things in his future. He is talented, caring, intuitive, dedicated, and focused in his pursuits. John is truly a stand-out individual who will impress everyone he meets.

Please let me know if I can provide any more information to strengthen John's candidacy for the College Scholars Program.

Sincerely,

Peter Evans

74. What is the purpose of this email?

    (a) to inquire about the College Scholars Program
    (b) to offer a position at University of Tennessee
    (c) to request more information on the program
    (d) to recommend a student to a program

75. What is John most praised for?

    (a) his creative research work on a poet
    (b) his pleasant attitude in the class
    (c) his persistent effort in the AP class
    (d) his respectful manners towards teachers

76. Why does Peter Evans think John will do well in the program?

    (a) because he is ready for the college level work
    (b) because he has enough credits to go to college
    (c) because he will graduate high school soon
    (d) because he is old enough to go to college

77. Why did Peter mention John's roles in a school band and a Student Council?

    (a) to show that John is good at playing drums
    (b) to show that John is a popular student
    (c) to show that John also possessed leadership
    (d) to show that John really worked on his resume

78. What is Peter willing do to support John?

    (a) He will ask his colleagues for further recommendations.
    (b) He will contact the University to make sure John got in.
    (c) He will write more emails to different schools.
    (d) He will provide more information on John's performance.

79. In the context of the passage, rare means _____.

    (a) slow
    (b) engaged
    (c) uncommon
    (d) undercooked

80. In the context of the passage, execute means _____.

    (a) set up
    (b) carry out
    (c) get rid of
    (d) take over

Reading and Vocabulary Section
Actual Test 03

정답 및 해설 p161

READING AND VOCABULARY SECTION

DIRECTIONS:

You will now read four different passages. Each passage is followed by comprehension and vocabulary questions. From the four choices for each item, choose the best answer. Then blacken in the correct circle on your answer sheet.

Read the following example passage and example questions.

EXAMPLE:

> SPC Corp. was founded by Joseph Gordon in 2010 and now it is the number one company in publishing industry. What is not true about SPC?
>
> (a) It was built in 2010.
> (b) Joseph Gordon is the owner of the company.
> (c) It currently has a financial problem.
> (d) Its business is doing very well now.

The correct answer is (c), so the circle with the letter (c) has been blackened.

ⓐ ⓑ ● ⓓ

Now go to the next page and begin.

PART 1.
Read the following biography article and answer the questions. The underlined words in the article are for vocabulary questions.

J.K. ROWLING

Joanne Rowling is the well renowned British author of the Harry Potter book series. The Harry Potter series has gained worldwide attention and critical acclaim, and has even been made into a film series by the production house Warner Bros. The books have sold more than 400 million copies.

Joanne was born to Peter James and Anne Rowling in Gloucester, England. From an early age, she was fond of making up stories that she narrated to her sister and grandmother. She wrote her first book at the age of six— a story about a rabbit, called 'Rabbit.' At just eleven, she wrote her first novel— about seven cursed diamonds and the people who owned them.

She attended St. Michael's Primary school whose headmaster at that time, Alfred Dunn, is said to be the basis for the character Albus Dumbledore in her books. Rowling claims that the **precocious** character Hermione Granger is modeled after herself and her years at Wyedean College and her old school friend Sean Harris, who owned a turquoise Ford Anglia like in the book, is the basis for the character Ron Weasley.

After graduating with a degree in French and Classics from the University of Exeter, Rowling moved to London to work as a bilingual research assistant for Amnesty International. Although she began work on the Harry Potter series in 1990 the first book wasn't published. She married the father of her child. After her marriage ended, Rowling moved to Scotland where she decided to spend all her energy writing the first Harry Potter book.

Rowling did not have an easy time becoming successful. She struggled with rejection at 12 different publishing houses. She found the time to write in between being a single parent to her young daughter and found **solace** in her writing. She was even dissuaded by her editor to find a full-time job other than writing to earn money. She proved everyone wrong with the success of her first book.

The book was first published in 1997, under the name J.K. Rowling in England and was published in the US under a different title, Harry Potter and the Sorcerer's Stone. Six further titles followed in the Harry Potter Series, each achieving record-breaking success.

J.K Rowling started a non-profit organization known as 'Lumos,' to aid orphaned children and children in trouble to find a loving home. Lumos is committed to making family care for all children a global reality by 2050.

53. What is the Harry Potter series?

(a) a big hit and adapted to movie series
(b) a flop and caused a lot of financial loss
(c) a masterpiece taught in schools
(d) a financial success but had no literary value

54. Based on the article, where did Rowling get motivation for her stories?

(a) from herself and people around her
(b) from books she read as a child
(c) from movies she watched
(d) from her imagination

55. Why did Rowling move to Scotland?

(a) to focus on her book series
(b) to work to support herself and her kid
(c) to write for a local newspaper
(d) to think about what to do next

56. Why did her editor tell her to get a different job?

(a) because he didn't like her writing at all
(b) because she wasn't good at writing articles
(c) because he hired another person for the job
(d) because she wasn't making money by writing

57. What was the purpose of 'Lumos?'

(a) to educate young magicians
(b) to encourage kids to read books
(c) to offer special deals for her books
(d) to help kids without parents

58. In the context of the passage, precocious means _____.

(a) focused
(b) intelligent
(c) indifferent
(d) stunt

59. In the context of the passage, solace means _____.

(a) comfort
(b) isolation
(c) loneliness
(d) solidarity

PART 2.

Read the following magazine article and answer the questions. The underlined words in the article are for vocabulary questions.

BLACK LIVES MATTER

Black lives matter, international social movement, formed in the United States in 2013, dedicated to fighting racism and anti–Black violence, especially in the form of police brutality. The name Black Lives Matter signals condemnation of the <u>unjust</u> killings of Black people by police. Supporters point to the fact that black people are much more likely to be shot by police in the US. They say that in the US and many other countries, they also suffer many other forms of discrimination. They want action to address unequal treatment and oppression that goes all the way back to the era of slavery, but which continues today.

BLM activists have held large and influential protests in cities across the United States as well as internationally. BLM was co-founded as an online movement using the hashtag BlackLivesMatter on social media by three Black community organizers – Patrisse Khan–Cullors, Alicia Garza, and Opal Tometi. They formed BML after Trayvon Martin, an unarmed Black teenager, in Sanford, Florida, was shot and killed by a Neighborhood–watch volunteer in February 2012.

The BLM movement expanded in 2014 after the police killings of an unarmed Black man, Eric Garner. Garner died after a white police officer held him in a prolonged illegal choke hold, which was captured in a video taken by a bystander. Large protests captured national and international attention.

In 2020, George Floyd, an unarmed Black man, was killed by a white police officer who knelt on his neck for several minutes. Following the death of Mr. Floyd, the term "defund the police" made headlines. Cities including Minneapolis, Portland, Philadelphia and Seattle have started shifting budgets away from police and into areas like schools and housing. It <u>triggered</u> massive demonstrations in cities throughout the United States and across the globe. In the UK, demonstrations drew attention to the UK's colonial past and saw statues of people linked to the slave trade removed.

The Black Live Matter movement seeks to draw attention to the many ways in which Black people are treated unfairly in society and the ways in which institutions, laws, and policies help to perpetuate that unfairness. The movement has fought racism through nonviolent protests.

60. According to the article, what is the main purpose of the BLM movement?

(a) to fight the violent and oppressive government
(b) to oppose the current policies towards minorities
(c) to point out unfair treatment of black people
(d) to get more followers on their social media

61. How did the BLM activists use to lead the online campaign?

(a) by getting people to follow their Instagram
(b) by posting police videos on their social media
(c) by sharing outrageous police videos
(d) by asking people to tag BlackLivesMatter

62. Based on the article, what was the problem in the Trayvon Martin case?

(a) He hid his face with his hoodies.
(b) He was armed and dangerous.
(c) He was defenseless.
(d) He broke out of the prison.

63. Why did the BLM movement in 2014 get a lot of national and international attention?

(a) because of the video evidence
(b) because of the testimony of a witness
(c) because of the death of an officer
(d) because of the large-scale protests

64. What is the main strategy for the BLM movement?

(a) flash mob in public spaces
(b) peaceful demonstration
(c) sharing postings on social media
(d) occupying government buildings

65. In the context of the passage, unjust means _____.

(a) gentle
(b) cruel
(c) unfair
(d) violent

66. In the context of the passage, triggered means _____.

(a) composed
(b) provoked
(c) rigged
(d) unprecedented

PART 3.

Read the following encyclopedia article and answer the questions. The underlined words in the article are for vocabulary questions.

BIODIVERSITY

Biodiversity, the diversity of life on Earth, is essential to the healthy functioning of ecosystems. Healthy ecosystems, interdependent webs of living organisms and their physical environment, are vital to all life on Earth. Our ecosystems provide us with clean air, fresh water, food, resources and medicine. Biodiversity, the variation of life on Earth, is a major factor in nature's strength.

While Earth's biodiversity is so rich that many species have yet to be discovered, many species are being threatened with extinction due to human activities, putting the Earth's magnificent biodiversity at risk. According to the Landmark United Nations—backed report, agricultural activities have had the largest impact on ecosystems that people depend on for food, clean water and a stable climate. The loss of species and habitats poses as much a danger to life on Earth as climate change does.

Some areas in the world, such as areas of Mexico, South Africa, Brazil, the southwestern United States, and Madagascar, have more biodiversity than others. Areas with extremely high levels of biodiversity are called hotspots. All of the Earth's species work together to survive and **maintain** their ecosystems. For example, the grassland feeds cattle. Cattle then produce manure that returns nutrients to the soil, which helps to grow more grass. This manure can also be used to fertilize cropland. Many species provide important benefits to humans, including food, clothing, and medicine.

Much of the Earth's biodiversity, however, is in **jeopardy** due to human consumption and other activities that disturb and even destroy ecosystems. Pollution, climate change, and population growth are all threats to biodiversity. These threats have caused an unprecedented rise in the rate of species extinction. Some scientists estimate that half of all species on Earth will be wiped out within the next century.

Helping people to understand what biodiversity loss means for them and their children, can be a very effective incentive for the positive change required to ensure more sustainable lifestyles and choices in energy, food and water consumption, which will in turn ease threats to biodiversity. In many ways, conservation is also good for business. According to the OECD, restoring 46 percent of the world's degraded forests could provide up to US $30 in benefits for every dollar spent, boosting employment and increasing community awareness of biodiversity's importance.

67. According to the article, what is 'biodiversity'?

(a) the diverse and complex ecosystem
(b) the large-scale plantation system
(c) the human activities in ecosystem
(d) the field of study at a university

68. Why is biodiversity in danger?

(a) because of losing of keystone species
(b) because of the natural cycle of life
(c) because of what people do
(d) because of the large number of predators

69. According to the article, what are hotspots?

(a) areas with a lot of human activities
(b) areas with beautiful sceneries
(c) areas that are protected by law
(d) areas with outstanding biodiversity

70. Based on the example of the grassland, what can be said about ecosystems?

(a) Ecosystems are beyond our grasp.
(b) Ecosystems are interdependent.
(c) Ecosystems need to be studied.
(d) Ecosystems are not protected enough.

71. According to the article, what is expected to happen to Earth's biodiversity in the next century?

(a) 50 % of species on Earth will extinct.
(b) 25% of species on Earth will extinct.
(c) Only 10% of species will survive.
(d) Everything will be wiped out.

72. In the context of the passage, maintain means _____.

(a) manage
(b) survive
(c) sustain
(d) overcome

73. In the context of the passage, jeopardy means _____.

(a) danger
(b) beauty
(c) complexity
(d) flexibility

PART 4.

Read the following business letter and answer the questions. The underlined words in the letter are for vocabulary questions.

Dear Dahyun Oh,

Thank you so much for all the information provided, it truly helps me understand your company a little further.

To get started, I have provided a link below to our image release as well as our policies so you can review them. I have also attached our first order form; this is simply to enter your first order and send it back to me when ready.

We only require that the first order is placed this way.

https://www.treasureusa.com/Indexasp?page
Below you will see a **temporary** online access to our site where you will be able to log on and view pricing and availability. Once your first order ships from our warehouse in the US, you will be provided with your own permanent log in where you will be able to place orders, view inventory and pricing, view your invoices, and obtain tracking numbers for your order.
We require a first time order of $500 (USD) and we require all accounts to maintain a yearly **quota** of $3,000 (USD) to keep the account in active status with us.
All pricing is in USD. Customs or import duties may apply. Please contact your local customs office for further information. We do offer a conversion chart which can be located on the website at the time of log in.
For the shipping to Korea, we use mainly UPS or FedEx, we do not have flat shipping rates as we are a wholesale company and we go with dimensional weight to determine the shipping cost, but we were able to negotiate excellent rates with our carriers on behalf of our customers given the volume that we do on a daily basis.
Online Temp User ID : EA #2
Temp User Name: POTENTIAL INTL CUS DEMO
Password has been changed to 12345
Effective : 3/12/2020 to 3/19/2020
https://www.treasureusa.com/Indexasp?pag
In the meantime please do not hesitate to contact me should you have any questions.
Kindest regards,

Karim Haggard
International Account Manager
105 S. Puente Street, Brea
CA 92821 USA

Sincerely,
Peter Evans

74. What is the purpose of the email?

(a) to introduce Dahyun their new products
(b) to notify delays in Dahyun's order
(c) to offer Dahyun a special deal
(d) to help Dahyun place the first order

75. If Dahyun wants to check the prices for the products, what does she have to do?

(a) She has to respond to this email to get an ID.
(b) She has to create ID on their website.
(c) She will use one-time ID to log on to the website.
(d) She has to call in and get a permanent ID.

76. When will Karim change Dahyun's temporary account to a permanent account?

(a) after they do a credit check on Dahyun
(b) after Dahyun logs on to their website
(c) after they send out her first order
(d) after Dahyun places her first order

77. What does Karim want Dahyun to keep her account active?

(a) Dahyun has to log on to their website once a day.
(b) Dahyun has to check with local customs office.
(c) Dahyun has to email back to Karim.
(d) Dahyun has to order a certain amount of price.

78. Why does Karim want Dahyun to contact the local customs office?

(a) because the company requires it
(b) because there is a problem
(c) because there might be tax
(d) because there might be a restriction

79. In the context of the passage, <u>temporary</u> means _____.

(a) short-term
(b) long-term
(c) distant
(d) permanent

80. In the context of the passage, <u>quota</u> means _____.

(a) indication
(b) allocation
(c) quotation
(d) collaboration

Reading and Vocabulary Section

Actual Test 04

정답 및 해설 p171

READING AND VOCABULARY SECTION

DIRECTIONS:

You will now read four different passages. Each passage is followed by comprehension and vocabulary questions. From the four choices for each item, choose the best answer. Then blacken in the correct circle on your answer sheet.

Read the following example passage and example questions.

EXAMPLE:

> SPC Corp. was founded by Joseph Gordon in 2010 and now it is the number one company in publishing industry. What is not true about SPC?
>
> (a) It was built in 2010.
> (b) Joseph Gordon is the owner of the company.
> (c) It currently has a financial problem.
> (d) Its business is doing very well now.

The correct answer is (c), so the circle with the letter (c) has been blackened.

ⓐ ⓑ ⓒ ⓓ

Now go to the next page and begin.

실전 모의고사 **77**

PART 1.

Read the following biography article and answer the questions. The underlined words in the article are for vocabulary questions.

I.M. PEI

Chinese-born American architect I.M. Pei was known for his strikingly contemporary, elegant, and functional buildings. They can be found throughout the United States and in other countries, including Canada, France, and Japan.

Leoh Ming Pei was born in Guangzhou, China, on April 26, 1917. He spent his summers in the countryside. He had an interest in rocks, nature, and history. He came to the United States in 1935, during a period of considerable political turbulence in China. He initially enrolled at the University of Pennsylvania in Philadelphia but then transferred to the Massachusetts Institute of Technology in Cambridge. He graduated from there in 1940 with a degree in architectural engineering.

In 1955, Pei formed his own firm, I.M. Pei and Associates, based in New York City. Pei's style of architecture is called modern or modernist. This style of architecture makes use of newer construction materials, such as concrete, glass, and steel. Modernist buildings are often designed with straight and simple lines, without a lot of decorations. One **distinctive** design that came out of his form is seen in many parts of the country-the five-sided control towers at many major American airports.

The Louvre Pyramid in Paris, the Bank of China Tower in Hong Kong and the East Building of the National Gallery of Art in Washington, D.C. are probably the most well-known projects in Pei's portfolio. However, Pei's projects, including arts facilities, university buildings, libraries and civic centers, are more diverse than the most well-known projects.

One of his most **controversial** projects was the design for a 71-foot (22-meter) steel-and-glass pyramid (1989) that was built in the courtyard of the world-famous Louvre Museum in Paris, France. It was heavily criticized because it is tempering with the Louvre's majestic old French Renaissance architecture. Glass and steel pyramid looked like an unlikely contemporary addition.

Not all of Pei's buildings were successes. The Hancock Tower in Boston is one example. The huge glass-covered skyscraper was nearly finished when disaster struck. Panes of glass began falling out of the building. They had to be replaced with plywood until a solution could be found. More than 10,000 panes of glass had to be replaced. Later on, though, the building wound up winning awards.

Pei received numerous honors during his career including the Pritzker Architecture Prize. He wanted his building to "stand the test of time." Pei died on May 16, 2019, at 102 years old.

53. What is I.M. Pei most famous for?

    (a) designing unique buildings around the world
    (b) being a successful Chinese American
    (c) traveling many countries at that time
    (d) going to famous universities in America

54. Why did Pei move to the United States?

    (a) because Chinese government exiled him
    (b) because there was a political unrest in China
    (c) because he saw more opportunities in America
    (d) because he wanted to study English in America

55. What did Pei study at Massachusetts Institute of Technology?

    (a) Chinese history and politics
    (b) airport traffic control
    (c) designing and constructing buildings
    (d) French art and art history

56. What was the Pei's design that is still used?

    (a) Louvre museum pyramid
    (b) university buildings and libraries
    (c) art facilities
    (d) the airport control tower

57. Why was the pyramid in the Louvre Museum controversial?

    (a) because it looked too modern
    (b) because the glass might shatter
    (c) because it shaped like a pyramid
    (d) because it was dangerous to construct

58. In the context of the passage, distinctive means _____.

    (a) common
    (b) ordinary
    (c) familiar
    (d) unique

59. In the context of the passage, controversial means _____.

    (a) viral
    (b) universal
    (c) disputed
    (d) faded

PART 2.

Read the following magazine article and answer the questions. The underlined words in the article are for vocabulary questions.

METAVERSE

The term metaverse is made up of the prefix "meta," which means beyond and the stem "verse," which means universe. The term is typically used to describe three-dimensional virtual spaces. It was coined by American writer Neal Stephenson in his 1993 sci-fi hit Snow Crash.

What is the metaverse? It's best explained as a collection of 3D worlds you explore as an avatar. Metaverse describes a non-physical world in which individuals can interact through different kinds of virtual technology. For example, a metaverse could permit people living on different sides of the world to meet up through technology and virtually go on a vacation, play sports or work together on projects. People linked to the metaverse would be connected at all times and physical distance would not limit their ability to interact. The main technologies that would drive such a world would be virtual reality, or VR and augmented reality, AR. Other, yet-to-be invented technologies would likely also be used to improve experiences within the metaverse. Today virtual worlds are formed, **populated**, and already generating serious money.

Because the metaverse brings a new dimension to the internet, brands and businesses will need to consider their current and future role within it. Some brands are already forging the way and establishing a new genre of marketing in the process: direct to avatar (D2A). Gucci sold a virtual bag for more than the real thing in Roblox; Nike dropped virtual Jordans in Fortnite; Coca-Cola launched avatar wearables in Decentraland, and Sotherby's has an art gallery that your avatar can wander in your spare time.

D2A is being supercharged by blockchain technology and the **advent** of digital ownership via NFTs, or tokens. More than $191 million was transacted on the "play to earn" blockchain game Axie Infinity in its first 30 days this year.

The companies are investing huge sums because they see the younger generations doing the same: 87% of Generation Z and 83% of millennials are playing video games and engaging with digital spaces on smartphones and computers at least weekly if not daily. Moreover, more than 65% of Gen Zers have spent money on in-game items.

60. What is metaverse?

(a) a virtual place your avatar can explore
(b) a sci-fi novel by an American writer
(c) online gaming service on your phone
(d) online shopping platform

61. How will metaverse change people's lives?

(a) working with others will be easier
(b) process information more effectively
(c) shopping will be easier and faster
(d) physical distance will matter less

62. Based on the article, why are brands and businesses interested in the metaverse?

(a) People can build houses and museums in the virtual space.
(b) People can explore the virtual world as avatars.
(c) People can buy goods and services with the virtual currency.
(d) People can play games with their friends in the metaverse.

63. What is D2A?

(a) virtual stores
(b) avatars
(c) virtual world
(d) digital currency

64. Why is Gen Z expected to spend money in the metaverse?

(a) They already play a lot of games on metaverse.
(b) They are already familiar with purchasing online.
(c) They have shown huge buying power.
(d) They tend to spend money recklessly.

65. In the context of the passage, populated means _____.

(a) indifferent
(b) inhabited
(c) interested
(d) situated

66. In the context of the passage, advent means _____.

(a) irregular
(b) disappear
(c) passive
(d) emergence

PART 3.

Read the following encyclopedia article and answer the questions. The underlined words in the article are for vocabulary questions.

ENTOMOPHAGY

Entomophagy, the consumption of insects as a source of nutrition by humans. Entomophagy is practiced in most parts of the world, though it is especially **prevalent** in the tropics, where more than 2,000 different species of insects are known to be consumed.

Eating insects is considered as disgusting or primitive in Western societies. Even though there was a substantial aversion to including insects in food, The Food and Agriculture Organization (FAO) of the United Nations (UN) has been making continuous efforts to popularize entomophagy as a healthy, sustainable, and environment-friendly practice.

There are more than 2,000 different kinds of edible insects in the world. Beetles are the most commonly eaten insect. For example, the larvae of the palm weevil that are enjoyed in parts of Africa and Asia. The number and type of insect species people eat varies in different parts of the world. Insects are surprisingly delicious. Stink bugs taste like apples, and termites taste like carrots. Many insects such as grasshoppers, crickets, and beetle larvae taste a bit nutty, especially if they've been roasted. This most likely because of their high fat content and crunchy mineral-rich outer skeletons. Insects often taste like what they eat. Honeypot ants select certain worker ants and feed them nectar until their bellies expand. They have a sweet flavor and are considered a delicacy in North America and Australia. Not only are insects tasty, but they're nutritious. Many insects, especially crickets and termites, are high in protein, an essential nutrient.

In comparison with livestock, insects have minimal resource requirements in terms of feed, land resources, and water. Apart from this, the carbon footprint of insects is **negligible**. Insect meat is rich in iron, calcium, and fat. Insects release minimal greenhouse gasses.

Even though there are many benefits of including insects into our diet, the aversion towards them still exists. Humans are taught to think about food beyond the nutritional quality it possesses. Accordingly, some food items are considered modern and are well accepted and some are considered primitive and face a general rejection. As a result, until recently, entomophagy was not a very common practice in the modern world. Yet, in many countries, there is now a growing appreciation of insects as food and feed.

67. What is entomophagy?

(a) consuming insects as food
(b) cooking insects as delicacy
(c) collecting insects for a project
(d) identifying edible insects

68. Why is there substantial aversion to eating insects in the west?

(a) because nobody eats them for food
(b) because it is considered gross and unsafe
(c) because they don't know how to cook properly
(d) because it is so rare and expensive

69. What do North Africans think of Honeypot ants?

(a) a common food
(b) a rare food
(c) a regional food
(d) an ethnic food

70. What are the benefits of eating insects?

(a) It strengthens immune system.
(b) It is nutritious and sustainable.
(c) it possesses medicinal values.
(d) It tastes great and feed many people.

71. How is the attitude towards entomophagy changing?

(a) positive
(b) negative
(c) undecided
(d) indifferent

72. In the context of the passage, prevalent means _____.

(a) unique
(b) moist
(c) dim
(d) common

73. In the context of the passage, negligible means _____.

(a) substantial
(b) neutral
(c) insignificant
(d) usual

PART 4.

Read the following business letter and answer the questions. The underlined words in the letter are for vocabulary questions.

Hello Mr. Yang

Hope this email finds you well.
We hope you are doing well along with your family. We sincerely hope that everyone remains safe and stays healthy.

To make things right, we've cancelled the Audible membership under the email yangtsu@gmail.com address and issued a refund in the amount of $16.44 back to your Visa credit card. Depending on your bank, a refund will typically take about 7–10 business days to appear in your account. An automated email with the subject "**confirmed**: Changes to your Audible Membership Plan" would also have been sent on that day confirming your cancellation as well. Note that we are not able to receive messages sent to this address.

However, you can still listen to any of your titles in your library even after your membership is cancelled.

There is a short survey below the email directly regarding the level of support provided by me and your feedback will be greatly appreciated.

Have you checked our new offering of free podcasts in which membership is not **compulsory**. I suggest you look into it by going through this link.

http://wwwaudible.com/search/keywords=free+podcast

Thank you again for contacting Audible. If you would like more help, contact us. We are here for you 24 hours a day, 7 days a week. Give us a call at 1–888–283–5051 and we'll do everything we can to ensure your next listen is a great one.

As a valued customer, your experience is important to us. Please answer the question below regarding your customer service experience. Your feedback will help us better serve your future needs.

To contact us about unrelated issue, please visit us at

www.audible.com

Sincerely,
Mohammead S.
Customer Service
Audible.com

74. What is the purpose of the email?

   (a) to terminate membership and refund money
   (b) to inform changes in the order status
   (c) to notify the membership fee hasn't charged
   (d) to offer podcast service on new titles

75. How will the money be refunded?

   (a) refund to the store credit
   (b) deposit to Mr. Yang's credit card
   (c) exchange with another audiobook
   (d) take off 50% penalty for ending service early

76. What email Mr. Yang would receive after this?

   (a) the confirmed refund
   (b) the confirmed cancellation
   (c) the complete new offer
   (d) the list of the new audiobook titles

77. What will happen to the audio books after the membership cancellation?

   (a) The books will be deleted forever.
   (b) He can access the books when he returns.
   (c) He can email them again about the books.
   (d) He can still access the purchased books.

78. What is needed to access the new offering podcast?

   (a) membership
   (b) store credit
   (c) subscription
   (d) nothing

79. In the context of the passage, confirmed means _____.

   (a) unknown
   (b) hidden
   (c) finalized
   (d) restricted

80. In the context of the passage, compulsory means _____.

   (a) mandatory
   (b) optional
   (c) voluntary
   (d) open

Reading and Vocabulary Section
Actual Test 05

정답 및 해설 p181

READING AND VOCABULARY SECTION

DIRECTIONS:

You will now read four different passages. Each passage is followed by comprehension and vocabulary questions. From the four choices for each item, choose the best answer. Then blacken in the correct circle on your answer sheet.

Read the following example passage and example questions.

EXAMPLE:

> SPC Corp. was founded by Joseph Gordon in 2010 and now it is the number one company in publishing industry. What is not true about SPC?
>
> (a) It was built in 2010.
> (b) Joseph Gordon is the owner of the company.
> (c) It currently has a financial problem.
> (d) Its business is doing very well now.

The correct answer is (c), so the circle with the letter (c) has been blackened.

ⓐ ⓑ ⓒ ⓓ

Now go to the next page and begin.

PART 1.

Read the following biography article and answer the questions. The underlined words in the article are for vocabulary questions.

STEVE WOZNIAK

Steve Wozniak invented the Apple computer and helped found the Apple Computer Company. He is one of the wealthiest and most famous inventors in the U.S. Wozniak left the world of business to spend his time teaching children about computers.

Stephen Gary Wozniak was born on August 11, 1950 in San Jose, California, to Margaret Wozniak, a homemaker, and Jerry Wozniak, an electrical engineer. Although he was never a star student in the traditional sense, Wozniak had an aptitude for building working electronics from scratch. Wozniak built his own radio transmitter and receiver from a kit. At 11, he built a machine he called a "ticktacktoe" computer.

Wozniak went to the University of California, at Berkeley. There, with the help of a high school friend named Steve Jobs, who was later to be his business partner at Apple Computer, Wozniak wanted to design an inexpensive personal computer, which was easy to program, **affordable**, and fun. When he completed his computer design, Jobs thought it could be a commercial success and wanted to market it. Jobs came up with the name "Apple." They sold personal possessions to raise money and worked in Jobs's family garage. Not long after Apple was founded, Wozniak created the Apple I. With Wozniak's knowledge of electronics and Jobs' marketing skills, the two were well-suited to do business together. Wozniak went on to **conceive** the Apple II. Priced at only $1,298, the computer was a great success.

By the end of its first year, the company had made almost three quarters of a million dollars in sales. The company grew and went public just four years after it started in 1980. The next two personal computers from Apple, the Apple III and the Lisa, were not very successful. Jobs put all his efforts into the development of the Macintosh. The Macintosh was introduced with much fanfare during the Super Bowl. It was a huge success. However, Apple was coming under increasing pressure from the PC designed by IBM. The PC was much cheaper than the Macintosh and Apple sales began to decline. Jobs took the blame and resigned from Apple in 1985.

Frustrated with Apple management, Wozniak also left the company and founded numerous ventures, including CL9, the company responsible for the first programmable universal remote control.

Wozniak was awarded, along with Jobs, a National Medal of Technology by the U.S. President Ronald W. Reagan and published his autobiography.

53. What is Steve Wosniak mostly famous for?

(a) for making universal remote control
(b) for helping establish a famous company
(c) for being friend with Steve Jobs
(d) for teaching children at school

54. What was Wozniak good at?

(a) getting good scores on tests
(b) playing tic tac toe on his computer
(c) coming up with working device
(d) teaching and helping young children

55. What kind of computer did Wosniak want to make?

(a) commercially successful
(b) complicated and specialized
(c) expensive and fancy
(d) cheap and easy to operate

56. What did Steve Jobs want to do with Wosniak's computer?

(a) He wanted to make them.
(b) He wanted to get funding.
(c) He wanted to change them.
(d) He wanted to sell them.

57. Why did Wosniak leave the Apple company?

(a) He felt unhappy with the management.
(b) He felt incapable to make new computers.
(c) He felt satisfied and retired from the company.
(d) He felt he was too old to do his job.

58. In the context of the passage, affordable means _____.

(a) afraid
(b) economical
(c) fancy
(d) durable

59. In the context of the passage, conceive means _____.

(a) miss
(b) avoid
(c) design
(d) destroy

PART 2.
Read the following magazine article and answer the questions. The underlined words in the article are for vocabulary questions.

GREEK IDEALISM

Ancient Greek civilization emerged around 1200 BC in a privileged place between the Mediterranean Sea and the Aegean Sea. This territory was made up of a peninsula and a group of islands. Ancient Greeks were settlers. They didn't just conform to staying in their territory. They wanted to look for and colonize new lands to expand their civilization. They reached many parts of the Mediterranean Sea extending their commercial activity and craftsmanship trade. Ancient Greek society was **devoted** to finding the highest standards of perfection. Some of these Greek ideas still have an influence on modern life and are the basis of what is referred to as the classical ideal.

Values
The ancient Greeks valued cooperation and sharing, personal achievement, hospitality, friendship, and hard work. These were the foundation for ancient Greek society. Men and women were expected to live up to these high ideals for a harmonious and orderly society.

Government
Ancient Greeks called their cities poleis and each one of them had its own government. The earliest form of democracy began in ancient Athens. The city was divided into ten tribes. Each tribe would send fifty men to a council of five hundred. They served for a month after which another fifty representatives were appointed. Only male citizens could serve. It was the first representative government, and it served as a model for many countries' systems of government around the world.

Athletics
In ancient Greece, physical beauty was seen as a direct link to mental beauty. The people of this time celebrated the body and had high standards for both men and women. An ideal male would be athletic and muscular as sports were highly important in that era. The classic athletic activities were boxing, wrestling, and track and field. Ancient Greeks held athletic games between city-states. These became the first Olympic Games.

Architecture and Art
The Greek ideal for art and architecture was order and harmony. States were idealized and created to show perfect human forms. The Parthenon is the ultimate example of order and harmony and a **feat** of engineering genius. The massive columns tilt inward slightly to hold up the heavy roof. It is also used to proclaim to the world the success of Athens in defeating the invading Persians and symbolizing the wealth and power the city possessed. Greek-inspired architecture is seen today throughout the world.

60. What is Greek Idealism?

(a) ideal form of men and women
(b) standards they strive to achieve
(c) idealistic government system
(d) ideas for art and architecture

61. Why did the Greek people value cooperation and sharing?

(a) to take over other city-states around Athens
(b) to hold Olympic games for city-states
(c) to distribute wealth and power Greeks had
(d) to maintain orderly and harmonious society

62. What is special about the Greek government?

(a) They have representatives.
(b) They have kings and queens.
(c) They have lords and knights.
(d) They had three elected kings.

63. Why did the Greeks promote athletics?

(a) because they wanted to prepare for wars
(b) because they wanted to win the Olympics
(c) because perfect body represents perfect mind
(d) because they were competing with Sparta

64. Why is Parthenon important?

(a) because it symbolizes the Greek idealism
(b) because it has many massive columns
(c) because the roof is very heavy to be supported
(d) because many people come to see it

65. In the context of the passage, devoted means _____.

(a) disloyal
(b) unfaithful
(c) different
(d) dedicated

66. In the context of the passage, feat means _____.

(a) courage
(b) achievement
(c) practice
(d) adventure

PART 3.
Read the following encyclopedia article and answer the questions. The underlined words in the article are for vocabulary questions.

COLOR BLINDNESS

White light has every color of the rainbow hidden inside it. Each color is a different wavelength. Things appear to be different colors because they absorb and reflect different wavelengths of light. A strawberry looks red because it reflects red wavelengths while absorbing most others.

People see colors because our eyes respond differently to different wavelengths of light. When light enters one of the eyes, it gets focused on the retina. The retina is a thin layer of tissue at the back of the eyeball. The light triggers rod cells and cone cells. These cells send signals to the brain, which uses the signals to make images. Rods detect only light and dark and are very sensitive to low light levels. Cone cells detect color and are concentrated near the center of our vision. There are three types of cones that see color: red, green and blue. The brain uses input from these cone cells to determine our color perception.

Color blindness can happen when one or more of the color cone cells are absent, not working, or detect a different color than normal. **Severe** color blindness occurs when all three cone cells are absent.

There are different degrees of color blindness. Some people with mild color deficiencies can see colors normally in good light but have difficulty in **dim** light. Others cannot distinguish certain colors in any light. The most severe form of color blindness, in which everything is seen in shades of gray, occurs when one has no working cone cell. It is uncommon. Color blindness usually affects both eyes equally and remains stable throughout life. Color blindness is usually something that you have from birth but you can also get it later in life.

Men are at much higher risk for being born with color blindness than women, who seldom have the problem. An estimated one in ten males has some form of color deficiency.

Color blindness can also cause safety issues. Fire hydrants and emergency equipment are often colored red or yellow to make them more visible. Someone who is color-blind may not notice bright colors that stand out to those with full-color vision.

There is no treatment for color blindness. It usually does not cause any significant disability. However, there are special contact lenses and glasses that may help.

67. What is Color blindness?

(a) not being able to see any colors
(b) not being able to distinguish shapes
(c) not being able to tell certain colors apart
(d) not being able to see in the dark

68. What is responsible for seeing colors?

(a) cone cells
(b) rod cells
(c) retina
(d) brain

69. What happens to people who have no working cone cells?

(a) Everything looks grayish in tone.
(b) They can't distinguish colors in the dark.
(c) Everything looks greenish in tone.
(d) They can't see any colors and shapes.

70. Who is more affected by color blindness?

(a) women
(b) children
(c) men
(d) adults

71. What can be used to correct color blindness?

(a) corrective surgery
(b) special glasses
(c) prescribed medicine
(d) certain home remedy

72. In the context of the passage, severe means _____.

(a) mild
(b) extreme
(c) gentle
(d) weak

73. In the context of the passage, dim means _____.

(a) faint
(b) vivid
(c) clear
(d) fancy

PART 4.

Read the following business letter and answer the questions. The underlined words in the letter are for vocabulary questions.

Dear Miss Kim,

After careful consideration, and based on guidance from the State of California, the California Department of Education, and the Student and Exchange Visitor Program (SEVP), we will be closing our school and canceling all school-related activities as of Tuesday, March 17, 2020, through Friday, April 3, 2020 for 3 weeks.

Here are steps we are taking to <u>**ensure**</u> a smooth operation during this public health crisis:

1. Classes will be held on our existing online platform, Canvas, on <u>http://qis.instructure.com</u>, starting Tuesday, March 17, 2020, through Friday, April 3, 2020.
2. We are closely monitoring information from the Center for Disease Control and Prevention (CDC), and federal, state and local agencies to help ensure actions we're taking are in line with the latest CDC recommendations and guidance and will monitor and update the school's closure accordingly.
3. We are in close contact with our host families to ensure students who are staying in a host family are in good health.
4. We are committed to helping when our partners and students need us.
   a. Teachers will be <u>**available**</u> online for all students during class hours and via email.
   b. Staff will be available for all agent partners and students both in person on a limited time schedule and via email/social media/phone.

If you have any urgent questions or requests, please contact Alvin, our Associate School Director, directly. His email is <u>alvinb@qschool.com</u>

We want you to know that you can continue to rely on us. We truly appreciate your patience and trust in Q international School. We are here to serve you, and we will be here when you need us.

Stay healthy and safe.

Sincerely,
Sarah Zimmer
Center Director
Q International School
1234 Fifth Avenue, San Diego CA
92090

74. What is the purpose of this letter?

(a) to inform class schedule changes
(b) to assign host families
(c) to notify the school closure
(d) to warn iliegal activities

75. Why did the school decide to close?

(a) because the school has some scheduling conflict
(b) because the school got some complaints
(c) because state government recommended
(d) because of the ongoing construction

76. How will the classes be taught?

(a) helping students one on one
(b) using their own online system
(c) communicating on social media
(d) submitting homework in person

77. Why is the school in close contact with the host family?

(a) to check up on their students
(b) to supervise illegal activity
(c) to ensure the students are fed
(d) to gather complaints about the students

78. What is recommended to do in case of emergency?

(a) talk with their host families
(b) come to the school immediately
(c) write an email back to Sarah Zimmer
(d) contact the designated person

79. In the context of the passage, ensure means _____.

(a) guarantee
(b) expose
(c) believe
(d) take

80. In the context of the passage, available means _____.

(a) edible
(b) doable
(c) foreseeable
(d) reachable

어차피 제시카

G-TELP 모의고사

G-TELP | Level 2

Listening
청해 실전 모의고사

Actual Test 01
Actual Test 02

Listening Section
Actual Test 01

정답 및 해설 p194

LISTENING SECTION

DIRECTIONS:

The Listening Section has four parts. In each part you will hear a spoken passage and a number of questions about the passage. First you will hear the questions. Then you will hear the passage. From the four choices for each question, choose the best answer. Then blacken in the correct circle on your answer sheet.

Now you will hear an example question. Then you will hear an example passage.

Now listen to the example question.

EXAMPLE:

(a) at 5 p.m.
(b) at 6 p.m.
(c) at 7 p.m.
(d) at 8 p.m.

Jessica got off work at 8 p.m., so the best answer is (d).
The circle with the letter (d) has been blackened.

ⓐ ⓑ ⓒ ●

Now go to the next page and begin.

PART 1.

You will hear a conversation between two people. First you will hear questions 27 through 33. Then you will hear the conversation. Choose the best answer to each question in the time provided.

27. (a) He wants her advice on how to manage his money.
    (b) He wants her to lend him some money.
    (c) He wants her to look for a new place to live.
    (d) He wants her to invest money in cryptocurrency.

28. (a) that he already borrowed money from her
    (b) that he was going to lend her some money
    (c) that he has a job that pays a lot
    (d) that he is investing money in cryptocurrency

29. (a) because he spent more than he made
    (b) because he just got a new job
    (c) because Mel lent him money to spend
    (d) because he made money by investing

30. (a) paying Mel back the money he owes
    (b) finding a new place in downtown
    (c) trying to eat meals by himself
    (d) tracking his expenses and income

31. (a) She thinks it is better than her own studio apartment.
    (b) She thinks he should find a cheaper place outside of downtown.
    (c) She thinks that it is very spacious and convenient to live downtown.
    (d) She thinks she should take over his apartment when he finds a new place.

32. (a) to consult professional to manage his money
    (b) to hire her as his financial planner
    (c) to create a budget and cut unnecessary expenses
    (d) to write everything down so that he knows how much he spent

33. (a) because Mel wants to pay back another person she owes money to
    (b) because Mel was mistaken how much money John actually owed her
    (c) because Mel wants to get some interest for her money
    (d) because Mel was charging him for her advice

PART 2.

You will hear an announcement by one person to a group of people. First you will hear questions from 34 through 39. Then you will hear the talk. Choose the best answer to each question in the time provided.

34. (a) to inform passengers of the entertainment features of the aircraft
    (b) to help passengers with in-flight shopping
    (c) to notify passengers of the safety features and procedures of the aircraft
    (d) to explain passengers where they are going and how long it will take

35. (a) because it has pretty pictures
    (b) because they'd need it for shopping
    (c) because it contains important information
    (d) because they need to fill it out

36. (a) when the cabin pressure suddenly changes
    (b) when the airplane is crashing
    (c) when the airplane is traveling through a turbulence
    (d) when the cabin is occupied by too many people

37. (a) help another person before you put yours on
    (b) put on yours first before you help another person
    (c) tell the flight attendant to help another person
    (d) show how to put the mask on

38. (a) You have to pay a fine if you get caught.
    (b) You will not be allowed to use the restroom.
    (c) You can get confined to your seat on the airplane.
    (d) You can face charges from the police.

39. (a) The plane will take off right after the announcement.
    (b) The crew will check people if they are ready for the take off.
    (c) The crew will have people look at the safety card.
    (d) The crew will allow people to use the restrooms.

PART 3.

You will hear a conversation between two people. First you will hear questions 40 through 46. Then you will hear the conversation. Choose the best answer to each question in the time provided.

40. (a) a doctor who was present in the group
    (b) the speaker who was raising her kids vegan
    (c) her friends who went to the workshop together
    (d) Steve, who is interested in Veganism

41. (a) because he doesn't know how to introduce vegan food to his kids
    (b) because he is worried that his kids would lack essential nutrients
    (c) because he believes that eating vegan is unhealthy
    (d) because he doesn't feel like he has enough information about being vegan

42. (a) because it is needed for forming muscles
    (b) because it is needed for brain growth
    (c) because it is needed for growing hair
    (d) because it is needed for keeping eyes healthy

43. (a) because you still could eat deep-fried and sugary junk food
    (b) because you might overeat to feel full
    (c) because you could eat multiple meals a day
    (d) because you don't get essential nutrients from vegan food

44. (a) They still have to eat meat from time to time.
    (b) They still have to take vitamins and other food supplements.
    (c) They still need to pay attention to what they eat.
    (d) They still have to check with their pediatricians.

45. (a) They are more active than non-vegan kids.
    (b) They have no signs of growth that is stunted due to their being vegan.
    (c) They are performing better at school than non-vegan kids.
    (d) They sometimes eat meat to get nutrients they can't get from vegan food.

46. (a) She will talk with one of her vegan friends.
    (b) She will talk about being vegan to her kids.
    (c) She will call her school and talk with the teachers.
    (d) She will take the kids to the hospital to check with the doctors.

PART 4.

You will hear an explanation of a process. First you will hear questions 47 through 52. Then you will hear the discussion. Choose the best answer to each question in the time provided.

47. (a) It helps people improve their test scores.
    (b) It helps people achieve their goals.
    (c) It helps people understand others.
    (d) It helps people reduce stress and focus better.

48. (a) practice meditation with a group of friends
    (b) don't expect to have a particular experience
    (c) set a goal and check the progress regularly
    (d) don't stop meditating once you get started

49. (a) finding a quiet place
    (b) setting as still as possible
    (c) meditating regularly
    (d) focusing on inner thoughts

50. (a) to practice sitting still everyday
    (b) to use a cushion and sit on a chair
    (c) to lean on the wall for the back support
    (d) to engage in other activities

51. (a) downloading apps
    (b) listening to the sound
    (c) eating a huge meal
    (d) getting professional help

52. (a) to see appropriate experts and consult them
    (b) to meditate to fix the problems
    (c) to learn more about therapeutic meditation
    (d) to make your meditation longer

Listening Section

Actual Test 02

정답 및 해설 p208

LISTENING SECTION

DIRECTIONS:

The Listening Section has four parts. In each part you will hear a spoken passage and a number of questions about the passage. First you will hear the questions. Then you will hear the passage. From the four choices for each question, choose the best answer. Then blacken in the correct circle on your answer sheet.

Now you will hear an example question. Then you will hear an example passage.

Now listen to the example question.

EXAMPLE:

> (a) at 5 p.m.
> (b) at 6 p.m.
> (c) at 7 p.m.
> (d) at 8 p.m.

Jessica got off work at 8 p.m., so the best answer is (d).
The circle with the letter (d) has been blackened.

ⓐ ⓑ ⓒ ●

Now go to the next page and begin.

PART 1.

You will hear a conversation between two people. First you will hear questions 27 through 33. Then you will hear the conversation. Choose the best answer to each question in the time provided.

27. (a) customer service
    (b) language instructor
    (c) human resources
    (d) payroll

28. (a) because her students are mainly cooks
    (b) because her former employer told her to do
    (c) because he feels like she needed to do that
    (d) because she completed a cooking program

29. (a) when they manage staff members
    (b) when they learn how to cook new food
    (c) when they open their own restaurant
    (d) when they communicate with foreign customers

30. (a) She completed her contract.
    (b) She had a new job opportunity.
    (c) She didn't get along with her employer.
    (d) She was fired from her job.

31. (a) to get back to teaching
    (b) to get more overseas experience
    (c) to build more extensive resume
    (d) to see if she could get paid more

32. (a) because she can use a variety of ways of helping students
    (b) because she can help students with their cooking
    (c) because she would work at a lower rate than other people
    (d) because she can communicate with people in foreign languages

33. (a) whether the position she applied is still available
    (b) whether she did a good job on the interview
    (c) whether she made it to the second round interview
    (d) whether she has been hired for the position

PART 2.

You will hear an announcement by one person to a group of people. First you will hear questions from 34 through 39. Then you will hear the talk. Choose the best answer to each question in the time provided.

34. (a) to introduce a travel destination
    (b) to give information about the state
    (c) to explain history of the state
    (d) to advertise a tour package

35. (a) people who enjoy shopping at the mall
    (b) people who enjoy socializing with others
    (c) people who enjoy outdoor activities
    (d) people who enjoy entertaining performances

36. (a) because there are good restaurants and cool cafes
    (b) because there is an international film fest
    (c) because there is a helicopter tour
    (d) because there are many national parks in Utah

37. (a) They can enjoy Native American culture.
    (b) They can enjoy the majestic mountains.
    (c) They can experience different kinds of weather.
    (d) They can watch famous indie movies.

38. (a) It is unpredictable and dangerous.
    (b) It is usually mild and pleasant.
    (c) It varies from place to place.
    (d) It is freezing cold, with a lot of snow.

39. (a) from British who occupied the area
    (b) from a Native American tribe
    (c) from animals that live in the area
    (d) from a geological feature

PART 3.

You will hear a conversation between two people. First you will hear questions 40 through 46. Then you will hear the conversation. Choose the best answer to each question in the time provided.

40. (a) which car brand she wants
    (b) what kind of car she wants to buy
    (c) how she can get a good used car
    (d) when she should get a new car

41. (a) because he recently bought an electric car
    (b) because he is thinking of buying a new car too
    (c) because he wants to sell his car to Julie
    (d) because he works for a car company

42. (a) It is cheaper than his old car.
    (b) It is a lot faster than his old car.
    (c) It is very quiet when driving.
    (d) It has a luxurious interior design.

43. (a) not having enough time to charge often
    (b) people complaining while charging a car
    (c) finding a charging station in rural areas
    (d) having to pay a lot of money to install a home charger

44. (a) free parking at the public parking lots
    (b) low maintenance cost in the long run
    (c) affordable charging cost compared to gas
    (d) the cheaper price of electric cars

45. (a) because the government money incentive will end soon
    (b) because it needs expensive parts
    (c) because it costs much more to maintain
    (d) because it costs a lot more than regular cars

46. (a) She will go test drive cars before making a decision.
    (b) She will talk to an expert before test driving a car.
    (c) She will do extensive research before going to a dealership.
    (d) She will discuss the matter with her family before buying a car.

PART 4.

You will hear an explanation of a process. First you will hear questions 47 through 52. Then you will hear the discussion. Choose the best answer to each question in the time provided.

47. (a) to teach people how to cook formal dinners
    (b) to suggest to people what to cook
    (c) to advertise the food products they sell
    (d) to make homemade food instead of store bought

48. (a) because many people have messed it up
    (b) because it is not very complicated
    (c) because it uses a good recipe
    (d) because it is featured on the show

49. (a) Mustard holds the ingredients together.
    (b) Mustard doesn't really do anything.
    (c) Mustard adds color to the mayonnaise.
    (d) Mustard gets rid of the strong flavor of oil.

50. (a) They have to be room temperature.
    (b) They have to be submerged in water.
    (c) They have to be kept in the fridge.
    (d) They have to be of a certain kind.

51. (a) because it would add a strong flavor
    (b) because it wouldn't thicken
    (c) because it wouldn't taste right
    (d) because it would break the food processor

52. (a) add it on salad and serve
    (b) put it in the food processor again
    (c) add more eggs to the mixture
    (d) taste and add more ingredients

어차피 제시카

G-TELP 모의고사

G-TELP | Level 2

Grammar
문법 정답 & 해설

Actual Test 01 / 정답 & 해설
Actual Test 02 / 정답 & 해설
Actual Test 03 / 정답 & 해설
Actual Test 04 / 정답 & 해설
Actual Test 05 / 정답 & 해설

Grammar Section
Actual Test 01

▶▶ 정답 & 나의 점수 확인

테스트 날짜: _____ 월 _____ 일 / 테스트 점수: _____

01 (b) 02 (a) 03 (a) 04 (d) 05 (a) 06 (b) 07 (c) 08 (c) 09 (a) 10 (d) 11 (d) 12 (b) 13 (a)
14 (c) 15 (b) 16 (d) 17 (b) 18 (c) 19 (a) 20 (d) 21 (b) 22 (b) 23 (b) 24 (c) 25 (a) 26 (b)

▶▶ 틀린 문제 체크해 보기

하단에 자신이 틀린 문항의 번호를 적고 해설을 보며 자신이 오답을 고른 이유를 정확히 파악하고,
같은 유형의 문제를 다시는 틀리지 않도록 재차 복습하도록 하세요.

▶▶ 문제별 정답 및 해설

01 가정법 문제

난이도 ★
정답 (b)

해설 MLB 투수인 그렉 콜드웰은 게임 중 벼락으로 인해 심각한 부상을 입었다. 만약 그가 병원에 좀 더 빨리 이송됐더라면, 심각한 뇌 손상을 입진 않았을 것이다.

해설 종속절의 동사가 'had+p.p.'이기 때문에 주절의 동사는 '조동사의 과거형+have+p.p.' 형태가 되어야 하므로 정답은 (b)이다.

어휘 pitcher 투수 lightning strike 낙뢰, 벼락 transport 수송하다 brain damage 뇌 손상

02 준동사 문제

난이도 ★
정답 (a)

해설 앞서 월요일에, 회사는 전자 화폐 및 블록체인 제품 담당직에 채용 공고를 내어 분석가들 사이에 의문을 불러일으켰다. 하지만, 회사는 텀블링을 허용하는 비트코인으로 결제하는 방식을 수용하길 거부한다.

해설 여기서 빈칸 앞 본동사 deny는 (동)명사 목적어를 취하는 타동사이므로 정답은 (a)이다.

어휘 post a job opening 채용 공고를 내다 digital currency 전자 화폐 analyst 분석가

03 시제 문제

난이도 ★
정답 (a)

해설 UN 사무총장인 앤쓰니 그루터스는 아프가니스탄에 있는 UN 직원들을 대상으로 비디오 메시지를 게재할 것이다. 그는 이들에게 전폭적인 지지와 연대 의식을 갖고 있다고 전한다. 또한 그는 언론에 이들의 안전이 조만간 보장될 것이라고 말한다.

해설 'soon(곧)'이라는 미래적 의미의 시간 표현이 나와 있으므로 빈칸엔 미래시제 동사 (a)가 적합하다.

어휘 Secretary General 사무총장 personnel 직원들; 인사과 solidarity 단결, 결속, 연대 (책임)

04 시제 문제

난이도 ★
정답 (d)

해설 공중 위생 공무원들은 2월 이후로 동물에 사용되는 구충제를 암치료에 장려해 온 유튜버들의 주장을 적극적으로 정정하고 있다.

해설 본동사(are amending)가 '현재진행시제'이고 뒤쪽에 'since February(2월 이후)'라는 시간 표현이 나왔으므로 빈칸엔 현재완료진행시제 동사 (d)가 적합하다.

어휘 public health 공중 위생 amend 수정[정정]하다 claim 요구, 청구; 주장 anti-parasitic drug 구충제

05 조동사 문제

난이도 ★★
정답 (a)

해설 연방 및 지방 정부들은 타격을 받은 기업들로 사업 지원 패키지를 확장한다. 하지만, 정부 당국은 기업들이 의무적인 백신 정책을 시행해야 한다고 발표했다.

해설 정부에서 정한 정책을 '시행해야 한다'는 당위의 뉘앙스로 말하는 것이 적합하므로 정답은 (a)이다.

어휘 extend 연장하다; (범위를) 넓히다 authorities (정부) 당국 implement 시행하다 mandatory 의무적인

06 가정법 문제

난이도 ★
정답 (b)

해설 태양은 사실상 다른 행성들과 비교했을 때 상당히 작기 때문에 거대 초신성으로 폭발할 가능성이 거의 없다. 만약 태양이 갑작스레 폭발한다면, 예상보다 훨씬 느린 속도로 죽음이 진행될 것이다.

해설 종속절의 동사가 '과거형(exploded)'일 경우 주절의 동사는 '조동사의 과거형+동사원형'이 되어야 하기 때문에 정답은 (b)이다.

어휘 in comparison to ~와 비교해 볼 때 explode 폭발하다, 터지다 supernova 초신성

07 준동사 문제

난이도 ★★
정답 (c)

해설 중국 다음으로 세계 두 번째 공해 유발 국가인 미국은 2035년까지 온실가스 배출량을 절반으로 줄이기 위해 신규 에너지 정책을 채택할 준비를 하고 있다.

해설 빈칸 이하는 '~하기 위해'라는 목적의 뜻을 가진 부사구가 되어야 하므로 정답은 to부정사인 (c)이다.

어휘 polluter 공해 유발 기업[국가] adopt 채택하다 greenhouse emission 온실가스 배출량

08 시제 문제

난이도 ★
정답 (c)

해설 맹렬한 열기와 화염이 지중해 국가들을 덮쳤다. 12,000명의 소방관들이 심각한 불길을 잡기 위해 고군분투해 오고 있다. 지금 현재, 수천 명이 이 지역에서 도망가고 있다.

해설 'right now(지금 현재)'라는 시간 표현이 나왔으므로 빈칸엔 현재진행시제 동사 (c)가 적합하다.

어휘 wildfire 도깨비불 Mediterranean 지중해의 contain 방지하다, 억제하다 blaze 불 flee 달아나다, 도망가다

09 가정법 문제

난이도 ★
정답 (a)

해설 크리스와 그의 부인은 초원에서 자란 닭과 계란 및 목초로 사육한 소고기를 알맞은 가격에 생산하는 농장을 운영 중이다. 이들이 말하길, 만약 1퍼센트만이 자신들의 음식을 먹을 수 있게 되면, 이는 지속 가능하지 않을 것이라고 한다.

해설 종속절의 동사가 '과거형(could)'일 경우 주절의 동사는 '조동사의 과거형+동사원형'이 되어야 하기 때문에 정답은 (a)이다.

어휘 pasture 초원, 목초지 afford (…을 살·할·금전적·시간적) 여유[형편]가 되다 sustainable 지속[유지] 가능한

10 관계사 문제

난이도 ★★
정답 (d)

해설 검붉은 오렌지의 주요 이점 중 하나는 식물 기반 식품에 든 철분 흡수를 향상시키는 비타민 C의 농도가 높다는 것이다. 이는 또한 나중에 심각한 질병으로 이어질 수 있는 염증을 조절하는 데 도움이 된다.

해설 선행사가 '사물'이고 콤마(,) 뒤에선 that 관계사절이 나올 수 없으므로 정답은 (d)이다.

어휘 concentration 농도 absorption 흡수 regulate 조절[조정]하다 inflammation 염증

11 should 생략 문제

난이도 ★
정답 (d)

해설 노트북과 태블릿을 이용한 원격 학습은 집에서 하는 학습에 있어 중심이 되었다. 의사들은 아이들의 눈과 전반적인 건강을 지키기 위해선 아이들의 눈이 정기적으로 검사되어야 한다고 권고한다.

해설 당위의 동사(suggest) 뒤 that절의 동사는 should가 생략된 동사원형이 되어야 하므로 정답은 (d)이다.

어휘 remote 먼, 원격의 mainstay 중심, 대들보 at-home 집에서 하는 regularly 정기적으로, 자주

12 조동사 문제

난이도 ★★
정답 (b)

해설 심히 우려를 표하고 있는 플레즌트빌 주민이 보낸 서신에 따르면 시장 후보가 서류 기록이 정확치 않으며 세금 면제를 받기 위해선 그의 거주 여부를 입증해야 한다고 주장한다.

해설 문맥상 'to receive ~(~을 받기 위해)'라는 목적을 이루려면 입증하는(prove) 행위를 '해야 한다'는 당위의 뉘앙스로 말하는 것이 적합하므로 정답은 (b)이다.

어휘 mayoral 시장의 residency 전속 (기간); 거주 tax exemption 세금 면제

13 준동사 문제

난이도 ★
정답 (a)

해설 불안 장애는 세계에서 가장 흔한 정신 질환이다. 불안이 있는 사람들은 자신들의 삶을 방해하는 것을 피하고 화를 잘 내는 습성 및 수면 장애와 같은 증상들을 공유한다.

해설 여기서 빈칸 앞 본동사 avoid는 (동)명사 목적어를 취하는 타동사이기 때문에 정답은 (a)이다.

어휘 anxiety 불안 disorder 장애 disrupt 방해하다, 분열시키다 irritability 화를 잘 냄, 성급함

14 시제 문제

난이도 ★★
정답 (c)

해설 내년이면, 벤 슐츠는 20년 동안 골프를 가르치고 있는 셈이 된다. 최근 그는 종래의 골프 지도가 더 이상은 효과가 없을 것이라는 결론에 도달했다.

해설 'by+미래 시점(~인 때가 되면)'과 'for+기간(~ 동안)'이라는 시간 표현이 나왔으므로 빈칸엔 미래완료진행시제 동사 (c)가 적합하다.

어휘 conclusion 결론, 결말 traditional 전통[인습]적인, 종래의 instruction 설명; 가르침, 지도

15 가정법 문제

난이도 ★
정답 (b)

해설 만약 당신이 넷플릭스 주식 신규 상장에 1천 달러를 투자했다면, 66주를 취득했을 것이다. 이 주식들은 45만 달러 이상의 가치를 지니게 된다.

해설 종속절의 동사가 'had+p.p.'이기 때문에 주절의 동사는 '조동사의 과거형+have+p.p.' 형태가 되어야 하므로 정답은 (b)이다.

어휘 invest 투자하다 IPO (주식의) 신규 상장 share 주(식)

16 가정법 문제

난이도 ★
정답 (d)

해설 미군의 조기 철수가 가능한 순조롭게 진행되었다 할지라도, 우린 여전히 각종 테러범들의 공격에 직면하게 됐을 것이다.

해설 종속절의 동사가 'had+p.p.'이기 때문에 주절의 동사는 '조동사의 과거형+have+p.p.' 형태가 되어야 하므로 정답은 (d)이다.

어휘 premature 너무 이른, 시기상조의 withdrawal 철회; 철수 proceed 나아가다; 계속[속행]하다

17 시제 문제

난이도 ★
정답 (b)

해설 지난 토요일 밤 10시에 데이비스 PD는 길거리에서 라이드 프로그램을 진행 중이었다. 차량이 검문소에 들어갔고 보험 없이 가동된 것과 해당 차량에 인가되지 않은 번호판을 사용한 것으로 인해 요금이 부과되었다.

해설 'last Saturday at 10:00 p.m.(지난 토요일 밤 10시에)'라는 과거 시점 표현이 나왔으므로 빈칸엔 과거진행시제 동사 (b)가 적합하다.

어휘 conduct (특정한 활동을) 하다, 실시하다 checkpoint 검문소 insurance 보험 plate 번호판

18 should 생략 문제

난이도 ★
정답 (c)

해설 전하는 바에 의하면 한 8살 남아가 펀자브의 이슬람 종교학교 내 도서관에서 소변을 본 후 사형에 준하는 신성 모독 혐의로 기소되었다. 국제 사면 위원회는 학교 측이 즉각 모든 기소를 취하해야 한다고 촉구했다.

해설 당위의 동사(urge) 뒤 that절의 동사는 should가 생략된 동사원형이 되어야 하므로 정답은 (c)이다.

어휘 reportedly 전하는 바에 의하면 blasphemy 신성 모독 punishable 처벌할 수 있는 urinate 소변을 보다

19 준동사 문제

난이도 ★★
정답 (a)

해설 최신 연구는 수천 마리의 애완동물들이 2019년 3월 이후 몸무게가 증가해 왔다고 밝혔다. 우리의 네 발 달린 친구들의 비만이 가진 심각한 건강상 영향은 주인들 사이에서 인식되고 있는 것 같아 보이지 않는다.

해설 보기 중 'appear to be 형용사(~한 것 같이 보이다)'라는 구문을 완성하기에 적합한 것은 (a)이다.

어휘 reveal 드러내다, 밝히다 gain weight 체중이 늘다 obesity 비만, 비대 recognized 알려진, 인식된

20 접속부사 문제

난이도 ★★
정답 (d)

해설 하와이 주지사는 갑작스럽게 발생한 화산 폭발로 인해 관광객들에게 여행 일정을 변경할 것을 간청했다. 하지만, 많은 이들이 환불이 불가한 예약으로 인해 고생하고 있으며 이는 취소가 힘들 수 있다.

해설 빈칸 앞뒤 두 문장이 '서로 대립되는 내용(여행 일정 취소를 간청 / 취소가 어려워 고생 중)'을 말하고 있으므로 빈칸엔 역접의 접속부사 (d)가 적합하다.

어휘 governor 주지사 make a plea 탄원[간청]하다 volcano eruption 화산 폭발 nonrefundable 환불이 안 되는

21 가정법 문제

난이도 ★
정답 (b)

해석 전화기는 19세기 후반의 발전에 있어 그야말로 필수적인 부분이었다. 만약 전화기가 발명되지 않았더라면, 일종의 자동화된 부호 형태가 더 크게 발달했을 것이다.

해설 종속절의 동사가 'had+p.p.'이기 때문에 주절의 동사는 '조동사의 과거형+have+p.p.' 형태가 되어야 하므로 정답은 (b)이다.

어휘 integral 필수적인 automated 자동화된 coding 부호화, 코딩 to a great extent 대부분은, 크게

22 접속사 문제

난이도 ★★
정답 (b)

해석 레이크 몬스터스는 사람들이 북을 두드리고 구호를 외치는 동안 포저스 FC와 치열한 전반전을 치렀다. 크리스는 자신이 가장 좋아하는 팀이 졌음에도 불구하고, 여전히 그날 밤은 팬들의 승리였다고 여겼다.

해설 종속절과 주절이 서로 '상반되는 내용(팀이 졌다 / 그래도 그날 밤은 팬들의 승리였다)'을 말하고 있으므로 빈칸엔 양보의 접속사 (b)가 적합하다.

어휘 first half 전반(전) competitive 경쟁의, 경쟁심이 강한 bang 치다, 두드리다 chant 구호를 외치다

23 관계사 문제

난이도 ★
정답 (b)

해석 반지의 제왕은 이 작품만을 위한 지형 및 여러 언어들을 발명한 영국인 작가이자 학자인 J.R.R. 톨킨이 쓴 웅장한 판타지 소설이다. 이 작품은 마침내 세 편으로 된 고 예산 블록버스터 영화에 차용되었다.

해설 선행사가 '사람'이고 콤마(,) 뒤엔 that 관계사절이 나올 수 없기 때문에 정답은 (b)이다.

어휘 epic 서사시의; 웅대한, 장대한 scholar 학자 geography 지리, 지형(도) adopt 채택하다, 차용하다

24 should 생략 문제

난이도 ★
정답 (c)

해석 나의 이웃은 본인을 위한 간단한 유언장을 작성하려 하고 있다. 변호사는 그에게 법률에 대한 전문 지식이 없는 웹사이트들을 주의하라고 조언한다.

해설 당위의 동사(advise) 뒤 that절의 동사는 should가 생략된 동사원형이 되어야 하므로 정답은 (c)이다.

어휘 will 유서, 유언장 legal 법률과 관련된, 합법적인 expertise 전문 지식[기술]

25 준동사 문제

난이도 ★
정답 (a)

해석 애니와 폴 굿워터는 빌라 로드를 따라 자주 자전거를 타는데, 특정 장소에 쓰레기가 많이 쌓인 것을 알아채곤 이를 뉴스 1에 알렸다. 주에선 예산 삭감으로 인해 이를 제대로 신경 쓰지 못했음을 시인했다.

해설 여기서 빈칸 앞 본동사 admit는 (동)명사 목적어를 취하는 타동사이기 때문에 정답은 (a)이다.

어휘 pile up (양이) 많아지다[쌓이다] report 알리다 county 주, 군 admit 인정[시인]하다 budget cut 예산 삭감

26 가정법 문제

난이도 ★
정답 (b)

해석 연애 사기꾼들은 인스타그램과 페이스북과 같은 유명한 소셜 미디어에 가짜 프로필을 만들어 이들의 목표 대상에게 접근한다. 만약 이에 대한 보도 기사가 없었더라면, 내 친구 로지는 인스타그램에서 한 남자를 믿었을 지도 모른다.

해설 종속절의 동사가 'had+p.p.'이기 때문에 주절의 동사는 '조동사의 과거형+have+p.p.' 형태가 되어야 하므로 정답은 (b)이다.

어휘 scammer 사기꾼, 난봉꾼 fake 가짜의, 거짓된

Grammar Section
Actual Test 02

▶▶ 정답 & 나의 점수 확인

테스트 날짜: _____ 월 _____ 일 / 테스트 점수: _____

01 (b) 02 (a) 03 (d) 04 (a) 05 (c) 06 (c) 07 (b) 08 (d) 09 (d) 10 (a) 11 (b) 12 (d) 13 (a)
14 (c) 15 (b) 16 (a) 17 (c) 18 (d) 19 (d) 20 (b) 21 (b) 22 (c) 23 (d) 24 (c) 25 (b) 26 (d)

▶▶ 틀린 문제 체크해 보기

하단에 자신이 틀린 문항의 번호를 적고 해설을 보며 자신이 오답을 고른 이유를 정확히 파악하고, 같은 유형의 문제를 다시는 틀리지 않도록 재차 복습하도록 하세요.

▶▶ 문제별 정답 및 해설

01 시제 문제

난이도 ★
정답 (b)

해석 멕시코만 해안을 따라 있는 지역들은 일요일에 아이다의 영향을 받기 시작할 것이다. 국립 허리케인 센터는 지금 현재 생명을 위협하는 폭풍 해일의 위험이 증가하고 있다고 예측하고 있다.

해설 'right now(지금 현재)'라는 시간 표현이 나왔으므로 빈칸엔 현재진행시제 동사 (b)가 적합하다.

어휘 Gulf Coast 멕시코만 해안 life-threatening 생명을 위협하는 storm surge 폭풍 해일

02 가정법 문제

난이도 ★
정답 (a)

해석 텍사스 전력망이 중단됐더라면, 이것은 '블랙 스타트'를 필요로 했을 것이다. 이것은 시스템의 다양한 부분에 있어 점진적인 조치를 요하며, 망을 제대로 다시 엮기 위해 시스템 내의 장소들을 연결한다.

해설 종속절의 동사가 'had+p.p.'이기 때문에 주절의 동사는 '조동사의 과거형+have+p.p.' 형태가 되어야 하므로 정답은 (a)이다.

어휘 power grid 전력망 incremental 증대하는, 증가의 restitch 다시 바느질하다[꿰매다/깁다]

03 should 생략 문제

난이도 ★
정답 (d)

해석 칼도르 화염은 에코 서밋 인근의 오두막들을 불태우며 타호 호수로 계속해서 진격해 나갔다. 칼 소방 부서장인 제이크 롱은 극심한 열기로 인해 지금 당장 모두 지역을 떠나야 한다고 촉구했다.

해설 당위의 동사(urge) 뒤 that절의 동사는 should가 생략된 동사원형이 되어야 하므로 정답은 (d)이다.

어휘 cabin 오두막 evacuate 떠나다, 피난하다

04 준동사 문제

난이도 ★
정답 (a)

해석 십대들과 소통할 때, 어려울 가능성이 있는 대화를 시작하는 가장 좋은 방법은 성인이 하는 대화의 법칙을 깨는 것이다. 한 가지 전략은 당신이 얘기하고 있는 것을 직접적으로 말하는 걸 피하는 것이다.

해설 avoid 뒤엔 (동)명사 목적어가 와야 하며, 여기서 동명사 목적어엔 특정 시제 개념이 내포될 필요가 없으므로 (d)는 오답, 따라서 정답은 (a)이다.

어휘 initiate 시작하다 potentially 잠재적으로 tactic 전략, 전술 address 말하다, 이야기하다

05 조동사 문제

난이도 ★★
정답 (c)

해석 경제부는 다음 달 시민들을 대상으로 식사 쿠폰을 재개할 것이라고 월요일에 발표했다. 음식 배달 이용자들은 신용 카드를 통해 10달러를 돌려받을 수 있다.

해설 '다음 달(next month)'에 무엇을 할 것인지 '발표했다(announced)'고 하는 것이 문맥상 적절하기 때문에 정답은 (c)이다.

어휘 Ministry of Economy 경제부 revive 부활시키다, 재개하다, 되살리다 citizen 시민

06 가정법 문제

난이도 ★
정답 (c)

해석 과학자들에 따르면 무더위는 자연적으로 발생하는 것이지만 모든 곳에서 평균 기온이 증가하게 되면 이것이 좀 더 혹독한 더위를 유발할 수 있다고 한다.

해설 종속절의 동사가 '과거형(increased)'일 경우 주절의 동사는 '조동사의 과거형+동사원형'이 되어야 하기 때문에 정답은 (c)이다.

어휘 heat wave 무더위, 열파 naturally 자연 발생적으로, 저절로 temperature 기온, 온도

07 시제 문제

난이도 ★★
정답 (b)

해석 자명종이 울렸던 아침 6시경 난 무서운 꿈을 꾸고 있었다. (그로 인해) 아침 일찍 있었던 회의에 집중하는 것이 힘들었다.

해설 '과거의 특정 시점(when+과거시제 문장)'에 어떠한 행위가 '발생 중이었다'고 해야 적합하므로 정답은 과거진행시제 동사 (b)이다.

어휘 terrifying 겁나게 하는; 무서운 alarm clock 자명종 go off (경보기 등이) 울리다

08 조동사 문제

난이도 ★★
정답 (d)

해석 체중을 줄이려고 노력할 때, 일반적인 방법은 바로 칼로리 섭취량을 줄이는 것이다. 하지만 영양가 높은 식사와 생활 방식을 고려해야 한다.

해설 문맥상 칼로리 섭취량을 줄이면서도 영양가 높은 식사와 생활 방식을 '고려해야 한다'는 당위의 뉘앙스로 말하는 것이 적합하므로 정답은 (d)이다.

어휘 a rule of thumb 경험에 바탕을 둔 방법 intake 섭취(량) nutritious 영양가가 높은 life style 생활 방식

09 관계사 문제

난이도 ★
정답 (d)

해석 차별은 여전히 직장 내에 존재한다. 회사들은 면접에서 자신의 인종을 밝히지 않은 지원자들에게 전화를 2배 이상 하는 경향이 있다.

해설 선행사가 '사람(applicants)'이므로 사람 선행사를 받는 관계사 who가 들어간 (d)가 정답이다.

어휘 discrimination 차별 workplace 직장 ethnicity 민족성 reveal 드러내다, 밝히다 interview 면접

10 준동사 문제

난이도 ★
정답 (a)

해석 예방 주사를 맞는 걸 미뤘던 38살인 마르쿠스 피르쿠스는 병원에서 사망했다. 그는 독감과 유사한 증상을 보였으며 이후 혈전이 나타났다.

해설 put off 뒤엔 (동)명사 목적어가 와야 하며, 여기서 동명사 목적어엔 특정 시제 개념이 내포될 필요가 없으므로 (d)는 오답. 따라서 정답은 (a)이다.

어휘 put off 미루다, 연기하다 jab 예방 주사 flu 독감 symptom 증상 blood clot 혈전

11 should 생략 문제

난이도 ★
정답 (b)

해석 내 친구 하산은 1년간 영국에서 유학을 했다. 우리는 서로 소식을 주고받기 위해 저녁을 먹으러 만났고 그는 자신이 밥값을 내겠다고 고집했다.

해설 당위의 동사(insist) 뒤 that절의 동사는 should가 생략된 동사원형이 되어야 하므로 정답은 (b)이다.

어휘 study abroad 해외에서 공부하다, 유학하다 meet up 만나다 catch up 따라잡다, 그 뒤의 소식을 듣다

12 가정법 문제

난이도 ★
정답 (d)

해석 조직화되지 않은 무리의 사람들과 여행을 계획한다는 것은 힘들고 스트레스가 많은 일이다. 만약 내가 호텔을 예약할 수 있도록 이들이 최소한 출발 날짜와 시간을 확정할 수 있다면 난 이를 감사히 여길 것이다.

해설 종속절의 동사가 '과거형(could)'일 경우 주절의 동사는 '조동사의 과거형+동사원형'이 되어야 하기 때문에 정답은 (d)이다.

어휘 unorganized 체계적[조직적]이 아닌 at least 적어도 confirm 확정하다 departure 떠남, 출발

13 접속부사 문제

난이도 ★★
정답 (a)

해석 연구자들은 알맞은 주거 공간이 사람의 신체적, 정신적 행복과 연관이 있음을 보여줬다. 따라서, 비숍 교수는 정부가 외부 공간을 포함한 모든 것에 있어 제대로 된 주거 공간을 보장해야 한다고 말한다.

해설 빈칸 앞뒤 두 문장이 '인과 관계'로 연결되어 있기 때문에 빈칸엔 인과의 접속부사 (a)가 적합하다.

어휘 adequate 적당한, 알맞은 decent 괜찮은, 제대로 된

14 시제 문제

난이도 ★★
정답 (c)

해석 도시에 주차 공간이 부족한 관계로 난 이웃인 밥과 차를 공유하고 있다. 내가 오늘 볼일을 보러 가야 해서, 오늘 오후에 차를 운전하게 될 것이기 때문에 그에게 문자를 보내야만 한다.

해설 문맥상 'today(오늘)' 볼일이 있어서 'this afternoon(오늘 오후)'에 '운전하게 될 예정'이라고 말하는 게 자연스러우므로 빈칸엔 미래시제 동사 (c)가 적합하다.

어휘 run an errand 심부름을 하다, 볼일을 보다

15 가정법 문제

난이도 ★
정답 (b)

해석 우린 어젯밤 제이미의 25번째 생일을 축하하기 위해 사라 토가 맨션에서 큰 파티를 열었다. 그녀가 심하게 취하지 않았더라면, 그녀는 비행기를 타러 갈 수 있었을 것이다.

해설 종속절의 동사가 'had+p.p.'이기 때문에 주절의 동사는 '조동사의 과거형+have+p.p.' 형태가 되어야 하므로 정답은 (b)이다.

어휘 epic 웅대한, 대규모의 get drunk 취하다

16 준동사 문제

난이도 ★
정답 (a)

해석 많은 부모들이 아이를 갖는 데 실패할 수 있고, 이러한 부모들은 그 어떤 것도 먹지 않으려 한다. 이러한 행동은 냄새가 나쁜 브로콜리를 먹지 못하는 작은 행동에서부터 시작될 수 있다.

해설 refuse는 to부정사 목적어를 취하는 타동사이며, 여기서 to부정사 목적어엔 특정 시제 개념이 내포될 필요가 없으므로 (c)는 탈락, 따라서 정답은 (a)이다.

어휘 frustration 좌절, 실패 start off 시작되다 turn up one's nose at ~을 경멸하다[멸시하다] sinky 악취가 나는

17 시제 문제

난이도 ★★
정답 (c)

해석 기자로서, 나는 보통 내 주변에서 글의 소재를 찾는다. 내 딸은 나에게 자신에 대해 글을 쓰지 말 것을 부탁하고 있고, 나는 그녀에 대해 절대 글을 쓰지 않을 것이라고 약속해야 한다.

해설 문맥상 자신에 대해 글을 쓰길 원치 않는 딸에게 '(향후) 글을 쓰지 않겠다'고 약속하는 것이 자연스러우므로 빈칸엔 미래시제 동사 (c)가 적합하다.

어휘 journalist 저널리스트, 기자

18 준동사 문제

난이도 ★
정답 (d)

해석 한 무리의 지역 고등학생들은 이들의 과학 프로젝트를 한층 진지하게 받아들이고 있다. 이들은 전체가 플라스틱 물병으로 된 뗏목을 타고 강을 건너는 최초의 사례가 되려는 시도를 하고 있다.

해설 attempt는 to부정사 목적어를 취하는 타동사이며, 여기서 to부정사 목적어엔 특정 시제 개념이 내포될 필요가 없으므로 (b)는 탈락, 따라서 정답은 (d)이다.

어휘 raft 뗏목 entirely 전적으로, 완전히

19 준동사 문제

난이도 ★★
정답 (d)

해설 이집트의 파라오는 사람들 사이에서 굉장히 중요시되었던 도덕적 규범에 있어 예외로 여겨져 오는 것처럼 보인다.

해설 보기 중 'seem to V(~하는 것으로 보인다/여겨진다)'라는 구문에 적합한 형태의 준동사는 (d)이다. (참고로 '과거부터 현재까지 그렇게 여겨져 왔기' 때문에 현재완료시제 개념이 내포된 to부정사가 쓰임)

어휘 exception 예외, 이례 moral code 도덕률 be highly regarded 높이 평가되다[중요시되다]

20 가정법 문제

난이도 ★
정답 (b)

해석 세 장의 당첨된 복권이 모두 같은 SC 상점에서 판매되었다. 만약 제니퍼가 복권을 잃어버리지 않았더라면, 그녀는 (복권에) 당첨되었을 것이다.

해설 종속절의 동사가 'had+p.p.'이기 때문에 주절의 동사는 '조동사의 과거형+have+p.p.' 형태가 되어야 하므로 정답은 (b)이다.

어휘 lottery ticket 복권

21 시제 문제

난이도 ★★
정답 (b)

해설 처음에, 알리는 전문 인력을 고용할 계획이었으나 자신에게 돈이 충분치 않다는 걸 깨닫게 되었고, 따라서 알리는 두 시간 동안 직접 방에 페인트칠을 해 오고 있다. 그는 아직까지도 페인트칠을 하고 있다.

해설 뒤쪽에 'for+기간(~ 동안)'이라는 시간 표현이 있고 'is still painting'이라는 현재진행시제 동사가 있으므로 빈칸엔 현재완료진행시제 동사 (b)가 적합하다.

어휘 initially 처음에, 당초에 professional 전문적인

22 관계사 문제

난이도 ★
정답 (c)

해설 연구의 최정상에 서 있는 과학자들은 종종 상식을 타파하고 보기에 터무니없는 추정을 하는데, 이는 간단히 말해 기존의 이론들이 새롭게 관찰된 현상들을 설명하지 못하기 때문이다.

해설 선행사가 '사람'이고 뒤에 콤마(,)가 없으므로 이 뒤엔 that 관계사절이 올 수 있다. 따라서 정답은 (c)이다.

어휘 cutting edge 최첨단 violate 위반하다 seemingly 겉보기에는 absurd 터무니없는 assumption 추정, 상정

23 시제 문제

난이도 ★
정답 (d)

해설 8월 14일경 2천 명이 넘는 사람들을 죽게 한 자연 재해가 아이티를 덮쳤다. 베쓰 데이비스와 그의 팀은 지진 후 지역 공무원들과 함께 남부 해안에서 구조 작업을 진행해 오고 있다.

해설 뒤쪽에 'since+과거 시점(~ 이후로)'이라는 표현이 나왔으므로 빈칸엔 과거부터 현재까지 쭉 진행 중인 행위를 나타내는 현재완료진행시제 동사 (d)가 적합하다.

어휘 rescue 구출, 구조 earthquake 지진 official 공무원

24 가정법 문제

난이도 ★★
정답 (c)

해설 올해, 내가 사는 곳 근처 시내에서 아카데미 시상식이 열릴 것이란 사실을 알게 됐다. 만약 내가 초대를 받았더라면, 난 지금 바로 그곳에 갈 것이다.

해설 빈칸 뒤쪽에 'right now(지금 바로)'라는 시간 표현이 있으므로 이것이 '혼합가정법' 문장임을 알 수 있고, 혼합가정법에서 주절의 동사는 '조동사의 과거형+동사원형'이 되어야 하므로 정답은 (c)이다.

어휘 be held 열리다 invitation 초대(장)

25 접속사 문제

난이도 ★★
정답 (b)

해설 커피가 세계에서 가장 많이 섭취되는 음료임에도 불구하고, (이것의) 규칙적인 소모량이 심혈관 건강에 미치는 장기적 영향에 대해선 알려진 바가 거의 없다.

해설 두 문장이 서로 '대조되는 내용(커피 소모량이 많다 / 그런데 커피 소모량의 영향에 대해선 거의 알려진 것이 없다'이므로 빈칸엔 양보의 접속사 (b)가 적합하다.

어휘 impact (강력한) 영향, 충격 consumption 소비[소모](량) cardiovascular 심혈관의 consume 먹다; 마시다

26 시제 문제

난이도 ★
정답 (d)

해설 데이비드 김이 일하고 있는 회계법인은 수많은 지원자들을 받았다. 우리가 하루 동안 일을 끝마칠 때쯤이 되면 그는 200명이 넘는 지원자들의 면접을 보고 있는 셈이 될 것이다.

해설 빈칸 뒤쪽에 'by+미래 시점(~일 때쯤)'과 'for+기간(~ 동안)'이라는 시간 표현이 나왔으므로 빈칸엔 미래완료진행시제 동사 (d)가 적합하다.

어휘 accounting firm 회계법인 applicant 지원자 candidate 후보자, 지원자[응시자]

Grammar Section
Actual Test 03

▶▶ **정답 & 나의 점수 확인**

테스트 날짜: _____월 _____일 / 테스트 점수: _____

01 (c) 02 (b) 03 (a) 04 (c) 05 (d) 06 (b) 07 (a) 08 (c) 09 (a) 10 (b) 11 (c) 12 (d) 13 (d)
14 (b) 15 (a) 16 (a) 17 (a) 18 (d) 19 (c) 20 (c) 21 (d) 22 (c) 23 (d) 24 (a) 25 (b) 26 (a)

▶▶ **틀린 문제 체크해 보기**

하단에 자신이 틀린 문항의 번호를 적고 해설을 보며 자신이 오답을 고른 이유를 정확히 파악하고,
같은 유형의 문제를 다시는 틀리지 않도록 재차 복습하도록 하세요.

▶▶ **문제별 정답 및 해설**

01 시제 문제

난이도 ★
정답 (c)

해설 나는 기업 윤리에 흥미가 있어서 현재 경제학과 철학을 전공 중이다. 나는 대학을 졸업한 후 대학원에 갈 계획이다.

해설 뒤쪽에 'now(지금, 현재)'라는 시간 표현이 나왔으므로 빈칸엔 현재진행시제 동사 (c)가 적합하다.

어휘 economics 경제학 philosophy 철학 ethic 도덕, 윤리 graduate school 대학원

02 가정법 문제

난이도 ★
정답 (b)

해설 레이첼이 당신이 병원에 있는 걸 안다면 당신을 보러 올 텐데, 우리가 몇 년 전부터 연락이 끊겨서 지금 바로 그녀에게 연락할 수 있는 방법이 없다.

해설 종속절의 동사가 '과거형(knew)'일 경우 주절의 동사는 '조동사의 과거형+동사원형'이 되어야 하기 때문에 정답은 (b)이다.

어휘 lose touch 연락[접촉]이 없다[끊어지다]

03 should 생략 문제

난이도 ★
정답 (a)

해석 기자들은 단체의 부패에 관한 믿을 수 없는 내부 정보를 얻었다. 이 이야기를 전한 사람은 우리에게 이름을 누설하지 말라고 강력히 요구했다.

해설 당위의 동사(insist) 뒤 that절의 동사는 should가 생략된 동사원형이 되어야 하므로 정답은 (a)이다.

어휘 journalist 기자 incredible 믿을 수 없는 corruption 부패, 타락, 오염

04 준동사 문제

난이도 ★
정답 (c)

해석 16세 소년이 차량 절도와 동물 학대 혐의로 기소되었다. 그는 개가 들어 있던 SUV 차량을 훔친 것을 시인했으며, 개가 사망하도록 방치했다.

해설 admit은 (동)명사 목적어를 취하는 타동사이며, 여기서 동명사 목적어엔 특정 시제 개념이 내포될 필요가 없으므로 (b)는 탈락, 따라서 정답은 (c)이다.

어휘 be charged with ~로 기소되다, ~의 혐의를 받다 vehicle theft 차량 절도 mistreatment 학대, 혹사

05 조동사 문제

난이도 ★★
정답 (d)

해석 다음 달 다르푸르 현지에서 평화가 실현되지 않는다면, 여성과 아이들의 상황이 점점 나빠질 수 있다.

해설 종속절(unless ~)의 조건이 충족되지 않을 경우 상황이 나빠질 '가능성'이 있다는 뉘앙스로 말하는 것이 적합하므로 정답은 (d)이다.

어휘 on the ground 현장[현지]에서 coming month 다음 달 get worse 점점 더 나빠지다

06 가정법 문제

난이도 ★
정답 (b)

해석 일부 지역 주민들은 당초 부지가 '카헨지' 대신 폐차장으로 바뀌길 원했다. 만약 지역민들이 그렇게 만들었더라면, 사람들은 그곳을 방문하지 않았을 것이다.

해설 종속절의 동사가 'had+p.p.'이기 때문에 주절의 동사는 '조동사의 과거형+have+p.p.' 형태가 되어야 하므로 정답은 (b)이다.

어휘 local folk 지역 주민 junkyard 폐품 처리장, 고물 집적소 Carhenge 카헨지(자동차로 만든 스톤헨지)

07 시제 문제

난이도 ★
정답 (a)

해석 뮤지컬 배우가 무대에서 떨어졌을 때 관중들은 박수를 치고 있었다. 분명, 그는 취한 상태였기 때문에 중심을 잃었다.

해설 '과거의 특정 시점(when+과거시제 문장)에 어떠한 행위가 '발생 중이었다'고 해야 적합하므로 정답은 과거진행시제 동사 (a)이다.

어휘 applaud 박수를 치다 apparently 보기에, 분명히, 명백하게 intoxicated (술·마약에) 취한

08 접속사 문제

난이도 ★★
정답 (c)

해석 전하는 바에 의하면 애플은 새로운 애플 워치 모델 생산을 연기했는데, 이들을 생산하는 데 있어 문제에 직면해 있기 때문이다.

해설 두 문장이 서로 '결과(제품 생산을 연기했다)-원인(생산에 문제가 있다)'와 같은 인과 관계로 연결되어 있기 때문에 빈칸엔 인과의 접속사 (c)가 적합하다.

어휘 reportedly 전하는 바에 의하면 encounter 부닥치다, 직면하다 manufacture 제작하다, 생산하다

09 준동사 문제

난이도 ★★
정답 (a)

해석 카카오톡은 10분간 이들의 시스템을 멈추게 만든 점증하는 날씨로 인해 지역에 정전이 발생했으나 회사에서 예비 전력을 사용할 수 있었다고 전했다.

해설 'cause A to V(A가 ~하게 만들다)'라는 구문에 적합한 형태는 to부정사이며, 이때 to부정사엔 특정 시제 개념이 내포될 필요가 없으므로 정답은 (a)이다.

어휘 power outage 정전 incremental 증가하는, 증대하는 shut down 멈추다, 정지하다 backup power 예비 전력

10 준동사 문제

난이도 ★
정답 (b)

해석 에드가타운의 250주년 소풍은 라이브 음악과 노천 맥줏집을 비롯해 수개월간 준비되어 왔다. 하지만, Covid-19의 증가세로 인해 시에선 소풍을 내년에 여는 걸 고려하게 될 것이다.

해설 consider 뒤엔 (동)명사 목적어가 와야 하며, 여기서 동명사 목적어엔 특정 시제 개념이 내포될 필요가 없으므로 (c)는 오답, 따라서 정답은 (b)이다.

어휘 anniversary 기념일, 주년 beer garden 노천 맥줏집 rise 증가, 상승

11 관계사 문제

난이도 ★
정답 (c)

해석 재향 군인 협회(VA)는 군대에서 전향한 재향 군인들을 도울 수 있는 방안들을 갖고 있다. 이는 (재향 군인들이) 이용 가능한 혜택들을 알려주는 검증된 담당자들을 재향 군인들과 연결해 준다.

해설 선행사가 '사람'이고 콤마(,) 뒤엔 that 관계사절이 나올 수 없기 때문에 정답은 (c)이다.

어휘 veteran 재향[퇴역] 군인 representative 대리인, 담당자 walk through ~을 보여주다[알려주다]

12 시제 문제

난이도 ★★
정답 (d)

해석 세계에서 가장 큰 규모의 마라톤인 뉴욕시 마라톤이 2021년 11월 7일에 예정되어 있다. 올림픽에서 네 차례 우승한 사라밀이 이 역사적인 행사에서 달리게 될 것이다.

해설 '미래(2021년 11월 7일)'에 열리기로 예정돼 있는 마라톤 대회에서 '달리게 될 것'이라고 말해야 자연스러우므로 빈칸엔 미래시제 동사 (d)가 적합하다.

어휘 four-time winner 네 차례 우승한 사람

13 가정법 문제

난이도 ★
정답 (d)

해석 제시는 유명한 기자이기 때문에 새 프로젝트를 맡아 매우 바빴고, 따라서 우린 그녀가 신경 쓰이지 않도록 초대하지 않았다. 나중에, 그녀는 그날이 자신의 휴가였기 때문에 만약 우리가 그녀에게 부탁했더라면 우리와 함께 저녁을 먹으러 나갔을 것이라고 말했다.

해설 종속절의 동사가 'had+p.p.'이기 때문에 주절의 동사는 '조동사의 과거형+have+p.p.' 형태가 되어야 하므로 정답은 (d)이다.

어휘 journalist 기자 day off 쉬는 날, 휴가

14 조동사 문제

난이도 ★★
정답 (b)

해석 로버트 P. 맥컬록은 런던교를 사들여 이를 애리조나로 가져왔다. 건축업자들이 이를 해체하여 치우기 전, 각 벽돌엔 번호가 매겨졌고 따라서 이들은 (벽돌을) 정확히 어디에 놓을지 알게 되었다.

해설 빈칸 앞쪽의 동사(was numbered)가 '과거시제'이므로 빈칸엔 과거시제 조동사 (b)가 적합하다.

어휘 take down (구조물을 해체하여) 치우다 brick 벽돌 number 세다, 번호를 매기다

15 should 생략 문제

난이도 ★
정답 (a)

해석 메인 치과 협회는 주에서 실내 의무 마스크 착용 정책을 개정해야 한다고 촉구했으며, 의학적인 이유가 있을 경우 이 정책이 면제되어야 한다고 주장했다.

해설 당위의 동사(urge) 뒤 that절의 동사는 should가 생략된 동사원형이 되어야 하므로 정답은 (a)이다.

어휘 revise 변경[수정]하다, 개정하다 mandatory 의무적인, 강제적인, 직권이 정한

16 시제 문제

난이도 ★
정답 (a)

해석 나는 가상 화폐에 투자를 시작한 이후 종일 시장을 들여다보고 오고 있다. 난 몇 차례 잘못된 투자 결정을 내렸고 이를 만회하고 싶다.

해설 'ever since+과거 시점(~ 이후로)'라는 표현이 나왔으므로 빈칸엔 과거부터 현재까지 쭉 진행 중인 행위를 나타내는 현재완료진행시제 동사 (a)가 적합하다.

어휘 invest in ~에 투자하다 cryptocurrency 가상 화폐 make up for ~을 보상하다[벌충/만회하다]

17 가정법 문제

난이도 ★
정답 (a)

해석 가끔, 사람들은 너무 장시간 동안 냉장고에 남은 음식을 보관한다. 만약 내가 그러면, 일주일도 더 넘게 냉장고에 들어 있는 팔라펠은 먹지 않을 것이다.

해설 종속절의 동사가 '과거형(were)'일 경우 주절의 동사는 '조동사의 과거형+동사원형'이 되어야 하기 때문에 정답은 (a)이다.

어휘 leftover 남은 음식 fridge 냉장고

18 접속부사 문제

난이도 ★
정답 (d)

해석 에어비앤비는 영국에서 25세 이하 손님들의 예약에 대한 규제 정책 관련 소식을 발표했다. 뿐만 아니라, 영국 정부는 주인 등록 시스템을 손보고 있는 중이다.

해설 빈칸 앞뒤 두 문장이 '설명(A라는 정책을 발표했다)-부연 설명(B라는 정책도 진행 중이다)'와 같이 이어져 있기 때문에 빈칸엔 접속부사 (d)가 적합하다.

어휘 publish 출판[발행]하다; 발표[공개]하다 restriction 제한, 규제 registration 등록, 접수

19 준동사 문제

난이도 ★★
정답 (c)

해석 빅데이터는 대규모 지역 사회 사람들을 돕기 위해 주민 건강 문제를 다루는 데 있어 자주 사용된다. 하지만, 빅데이터를 수집하기 전에, 관련 위험 요소에 대한 이해가 있어야 한다.

해설 빈칸 이하는 '~하기 위해'라는 뜻의 목적의 부사구가 되어야 하므로 빈칸엔 to부정사가 들어가야 한다. 따라서 정답은 (c)이다.

어휘 population 인구, 주민 risk 위험 요소[요인]

20 가정법 문제

난이도 ★
정답 (c)

해석 난 스트레스를 다루는 데 문제가 있어 도움을 받고 있었다. 예를 들어, 내가 실직을 하게 되면 난 무엇을 해야 할지 모를 것이다. 나는 치료사와 함께 인지 운동을 하며 스트레스를 받는 매일의 상황을 어떻게 다뤄야 할지 배우고 있다.

해설 종속절의 동사가 '과거형(lost)'일 경우 주절의 동사는 '조동사의 과거형+동사원형'이 되어야 하기 때문에 정답은 (c)이다.

어휘 cognitive 인식[인지]의 therapist 치료사

21 should 생략 문제

난이도 ★
정답 (d)

해설 대통령이 또 다른 공격이 임박했다고 말한 지 단 몇 시간 후 구체적으로 확실한 공격이 발생하여 미국 대사관은 토요일경 모든 이들에게 즉시 카불 공항을 떠나라고 명령했다.

해설 당위의 동사(order) 뒤 that절의 동사는 should가 생략된 동사원형이 되어야 하므로 정답은 (d)이다.

어휘 embassy 대사관 credible 믿을 수 있는, 확실한 imminent 절박[긴박]한 일촉즉발의

22 시제 문제

난이도 ★★
정답 (c)

해설 샘은 배우 생활 동안 멋진 몸매로 유명했지만, 은퇴 후 과식을 해 왔던 것으로 인해 체중이 많이 늘었다. 우리는 그가 우울증에 시달렸던 게 아닐까 생각한다.

해설 빈칸 앞쪽 동사(gained)가 '과거시제'이고 빈칸 뒤쪽에 'since+과거 시점(~ 이후)'라는 시간 표현이 나와 있으므로 빈칸엔 과거완료진행시제 동사 (c)가 적합하다.

어휘 overeat 과식하다 retire 은퇴하다 depression 우울(증)

23 가정법 문제

난이도 ★
정답 (d)

해설 만약 구급차가 통상적으로 허용되는 출동 시간에 맞춰 도착했더라면, 아버지는 살았을 것이다. 생명을 위협하는 질병에 맞는 평균 출동 시간은 보통 7분이다.

해설 종속절의 동사가 'had+p.p.'이기 때문에 주절의 동사는 '조동사의 과거형+have+p.p.' 형태가 되어야 하므로 정답은 (d)이다.

어휘 ambulance 구급차 acceptable 받아들일 만한; 허용할 수 있는 response time 반응 시간, 출동 소요 시간

24 관계사 문제

난이도 ★
정답 (a)

해설 심장병의 위험을 증가시킬 수 있는 나쁜 콜레스테롤의 수치는 식용유를 재사용하는 것으로 인해 증가될 수 있다.

해설 선행사가 '사물'이고 콤마(,) 뒤엔 that 관계사절이 나올 수 없기 때문에 정답은 (a)이다.

어휘 hear disease 심장병 reuse 다시 사용하다, 재사용하다 cooking oil 조리용 기름, 식용유

25 준동사 문제

난이도 ★
정답 (b)

해설 은퇴한 해군 관계자는 기밀 정보를 건네는 것에 대한 대가로서 방위 산업 청부 업체에게 뇌물로 35,000달러를 받은 것을 시인했다.

해설 여기서 본동사 admit은 (동)명사 목적어를 취하는 타동사이기 때문에 정답은 (b)이다.

어휘 bribe 뇌물 defense contractor 방위 산업 청부 업체 in exchange for ~의 교환으로 confidential 비밀[기밀]의

26 시제 문제

난이도 ★
정답 (a)

해설 내 친구 수잔과 나는 우리 도시에서 있을 철인 3종 경기에 참가하기로 결정했다. 우리는 이번 달 말까지 훈련을 하고 있게 될 것이다. 우린 스스로에게 도전하게 되어 매우 신이 난다.

해설 'by+미래 시점(~일 때까지)'라는 시간 표현이 나와 있으므로 빈칸엔 미래의 특정 시점까지 쭉 진행 중일 행위를 나타내는 미래진행시제동사 (a)가 적합하다.

어휘 participate in ~에 참가[참여]하다 triathlon 철인 3종 경기 challenge oneself 스스로에게 도전하다

Grammar Section
Actual Test 04

▶▶ 정답 & 나의 점수 확인

테스트 날짜: _____월 _____일 / 테스트 점수: _____

01 (d) 02 (d) 03 (d) 04 (d) 05 (c) 06 (a) 07 (b) 08 (b) 09 (c) 10 (d) 11 (c) 12 (a) 13 (a)
14 (b) 15 (a) 16 (b) 17 (b) 18 (d) 19 (c) 20 (a) 21 (a) 22 (a) 23 (c) 24 (c) 25 (d) 26 (b)

▶▶ 틀린 문제 체크해 보기

하단에 자신이 틀린 문항의 번호를 적고 해설을 보며 자신이 오답을 고른 이유를 정확히 파악하고,
같은 유형의 문제를 다시는 틀리지 않도록 재차 복습하도록 하세요.

▶▶ 문제별 정답 및 해설

01 시제 문제

난이도 ★★
정답 (d)

해석 저는 저희 측 해외 고객들과의 회의를 준비하기 위해 바쁠 예정입니다. 귀하께선 9월 첫 주 동안 절 방문하실 수 있습니다. 그때 저는 일하지 않고 있을 것입니다.

해설 '9월 첫 주(the first week of September)'라는 미래의 '그 시점(then)'에 '일하고 있지 않는 중일 것'이라고 해야 적합하므로 정답은 미래진행시제 동사 (d)이다.

어휘 organize 준비[조직]하다 meeting 회의 international client 국제[해외] 고객

02 조동사 문제

난이도 ★★
정답 (d)

해석 회사에서 통상적으로 제품을 출시하는 시기인 9월경, 즉 2021년 가을에 애플의 2021 아이폰 라인업이 발표될 예정이다.

해설 '2021년 가을'이라는 미래의 특정 시점에 제품 라인업이 '발표될 것이다(예정이다)'라고 해야 적합하므로 정답은 미래의 조동사 (d)이다.

어휘 unveil 덮개를 벗기다; 발표하다 launch (상품 등의) 개시, 출시 timeline 시각표, 행사 일정표

03 접속사 문제

난이도 ★★
정답 (d)

해석 종합적인 평가를 검토한 후, 브린이 시스템을 가장 잘 알고 있었기 때문에 4명의 후보자들을 제치고 승진하게 되었다.

해설 두 문장이 '결과(승진하게 되었다)-원인(시스템을 가장 잘 알고 있기 때문에)'라는 인과 관계로 연결되어 있으므로 빈칸엔 인과의 접속사 (a)가 적합하다.

어휘 comprehensive 종합적인, 포괄적인 evaluation 평가 promotion 승진

04 준동사 문제

난이도 ★★
정답 (d)

해석 명사구는 사람, 장소, 물건, 혹은 개념을 명명하기 위해 상호 활동하는 단어들의 집합이다. 모든 명사들과 마찬가지로, 명사구는 주어, 목적어, 혹은 보어가 될 수 있다.

해설 빈칸 이하는 '~하기 위해'라는 목적의 뜻을 가진 부사구가 되어야 하므로 빈칸엔 이 같은 용법으로 쓰일 수 있는 to부정사 (d)가 적합하다.

어휘 noun phrase 명사구 name 이름을 지어주다, 명명하다 complement 보어

05 가정법 문제

난이도 ★
정답 (c)

해석 대니는 승진에서 제외되었다. 만약 그가 자신의 상사를 모욕하지 않았더라면, 그는 오랫동안 자신이 바라 왔던 직책을 얻었을 것이다.

해설 종속절의 동사가 'had+p.p.'이기 때문에 주절의 동사는 '조동사의 과거형+have+p.p.' 형태가 되어야 하므로 정답은 (c)이다.

어휘 leave out of ~에서 제외하다 insult 모욕하다 position 위치, 자리; 직위, 직책

06 준동사 문제

난이도 ★
정답 (a)

해석 나의 누이는 사람들을 집에 초대하는 걸 좋아하는데 손목에 통증을 느껴 오고 있다. 현재, 그녀는 푸짐한 만찬을 요리하는 걸 피하고 있다.

해설 avoid 뒤엔 (동)명사 목적어가 와야 하며, 여기서 동명사 목적어엔 특정 시제 개념이 내포될 필요가 없으므로 (c)는 오답. 따라서 정답은 (a)이다.

어휘 have ~ over ~을 손님으로 맞이하다, ~을 (집에) 초대하다 wrist 손목, 팔목

07 준동사 문제

난이도 ★★
정답 (b)

해석 더 높은 교육 수준은 다양한 범위의 긍정적인 결과와 관련되어 있다. 교육의 긍정적 측면 중 하나는 이것이 개인의 정체성을 확고히 하는 데 기여한다는 것이다.

해설 'contribute to V-ing(~하는 것에 기여하다/도움이 되다)'라는 구문에 적합한 형태의 동사는 (b)이다.

어휘 be associated with ~와 관련되다 a wide range of 광범위한, 다양한 outcome 결과 identity 정체(성), 독자성

08 should 생략 문제

난이도 ★
정답 (b)

해석 로젠버그 씨가 출산 휴가를 떠났기 때문에 우리는 노스 씨를 대리인으로 삼고 있다. 노스 씨는 매우 엄격하다. 수업 초반에, 그녀는 모두에게 손을 들라고 요구했다.

해설 당위의 동사(request) 뒤 that절의 동사는 should가 생략된 동사원형이 되어야 하므로 정답은 (b)이다.

어휘 maternity leave 출산 휴가 substitute 대리(인) in the beginning of ~의 초반에

09 관계사 문제

난이도 ★
정답 (c)

해석 내가 거액의 돈을 물려받은 독일에 계신 나의 삼촌은 은둔자였다. 그는 혼자만의 삶을 살았고 다른 사람들을 피했다. 그는 가족 모임에 한 번도 모습을 나타내지 않았다.

해설 선행사가 '사람'이고 콤마(,) 뒤엔 that 관계사절이 나올 수 없기 때문에 정답은 (c)이다.

어휘 inherit 물려받다, 상속하다 recluse 은둔자, 세상을 등진 사람 solitary 혼자서 잘 지내는 show up 나타나다

10 가정법 문제

난이도 ★
정답 (d)

해석 우리 동네에 있는 많은 집들이 최근 강도를 당했다. 나는 좀 더 대대적인 보안 시스템을 갖출 필요를 느꼈다. 만약 절도범들이 내 집에 침입한다면, 이들은 건물 곳곳에 설치된 다수의 보안 시스템을 마주치게 될 것이다.

해설 종속절의 동사가 '과거형(broke)'일 경우 주절의 동사는 '조동사의 과거형+동사원형'이 되어야 하기 때문에 정답은 (d)이다.

어휘 burglarize (집 등을) 털다 burglar 절도범 break into 침입하다 multiple 많은, 다수의 property 부동산; 건물

11 시제 문제

난이도 ★
정답 (c)

해석 학교 아이들은 사라가 끝내 집에서 나와 "나 좀 내버려 둬"라고 소리칠 때까지 5분 동안 그녀의 창문에 돌을 던지고 있다.

해설 'for+기간(~ 동안)'과 'before+현재시제 문장(~이기 전까지)'라는 시간 표현이 나와 있으므로 빈칸엔 현재완료진행시제 동사 (c)가 적합하다.

어휘 come out of ~에서 나오다 yell 소리치다, 고함치다 leave alone 혼자 두다

12 접속부사 문제

난이도 ★★
정답 (a)

해석 적지 않은 시간 동안 화면을 들여다본 후 잠자리에 늦게 드는 행동은 우리의 수면 주기를 망친다. 하지만, 우리 대다수는 메시지를 확인하려고 아침에 제일 먼저 휴대폰부터 집는 실수를 한다.

해설 두 문장이 서로 '대비되는 내용(휴대폰이 수면 주기를 망친다 / 아침 일찍 휴대폰부터 집는다)'을 말하고 있으므로 빈칸엔 역접의 접속부사 (a)가 적합하다.

어휘 hit the bed 잠자리에 들다 considerable 상당한, 적지 않은 sleep cycle 수면 주기

13 가정법 문제

난이도 ★
정답 (a)

해석 사라는 동료들과 의사소통을 하는 데 문제가 있어 왔다. 만약 사라가 자신의 동료들이 너무 힘들어하는 걸 알았더라면, 그녀는 그 일을 하지 않았을 것이다.

해설 종속절의 동사가 'had+p.p.'이기 때문에 주절의 동사는 '조동사의 과거형+have+p.p.' 형태가 되어야 하므로 정답은 (a)이다.

어휘 communication 의사소통 coworker 동료 colleague 동료 take a job 취직하다, 일을 맡다

14 준동사 문제

난이도 ★
정답 (b)

해석 많은 학생들이 일을 미루고 최후의 순간에 이를 끝내려는 노력을 한다. 전문가들은 꾸물거리며 미루는 버릇은 위험을 감수하길 피하려는 것의 또 다른 형태라고 지적한다.

해설 avoid 뒤엔 (동)명사 목적어가 와야 하며, 여기서 동명사 목적어엔 특정 시제 개념이 내포될 필요가 없으므로 (c)는 오답, 따라서 정답은 (b)이다.

어휘 put off 미루다, 연기하다 last minute 최후의 순간, 막판 procrastination 미루는 버릇, 꾸물거림

15 시제 문제

난이도 ★
정답 (a)

해석 대면 소통을 포함한 전통적인 형태의 의사소통 방식은 자취를 감췄다. 요즘에 대부분의 사람들은 편지를 쓰는 대신 이메일을 사용하고 있다.

해설 'these days(요즘에는, 근래에)'이라는 시간 표현이 나왔으므로 빈칸엔 현재진행시제 동사 (a)가 적합하다.

어휘 die out 멸종되다, 자취를 감추다 face-to-face 마주 보는, 대면하는 these days 요즘에는, 근래에

16 조동사 문제

난이도 ★★
정답 (b)

해석 제인과 그의 남편은 그녀가 좋아하는 장소를 찾았다. 그녀는 다른 누군가가 이곳을 사기 전 집에 대해 결정을 내려야 하는데, 조금 부담이 느껴지고 있다.

해설 문맥상 다른 누군가가 집을 사기 전에 이를 뺏기지 않도록 '결정을 내려야 한다'는 당위의 뉘앙스로 말하는 것이 적합하므로 정답은 (b)이다.

어휘 make a decision 결정을 내리다 someone else 다른 누군가 feel pressured 압박감을 느끼다

17 가정법 문제

난이도 ★
정답 (b)

해석 제임스가 이빨을 좀 더 자주 닦았더라면, 그는 치아에 봉을 박을 필요가 없었을 것이다. 그는 이빨을 치료받는 데 상당히 많은 돈이 든다는 사실을 깨달았다.

해설 종속절의 동사가 'had+p.p.'이기 때문에 주절의 동사는 '조동사의 과거형+have+p.p.' 형태가 되어야 하므로 정답은 (b)이다.

어휘 filling (치아에 생긴 구멍에 박는) 봉, 충전재 significant 중요한; 상당한 get treated 치료를 받다

18 should 생략 문제

난이도 ★
정답 (d)

해석 학교는 역사상 최초로 대규모의 스포츠 경기를 연다. 교장은 모든 교사들에게 발생할 수 있는 모든 비상 사태에 대응 가능해야 한다고 요청했다.

해설 당위의 동사(ask) 뒤 that절의 동사는 should가 생략된 동사원형이 되어야 하므로 정답은 (b)이다.

어휘 large-scale 대규모의, 광범한 sporting event 스포츠 경기 principal 학장, 교장 arise 생기다, 발생하다

19 시제 문제

난이도 ★★
정답 (c)

해석 피터는 대학에서 아주 유명한 전임 강사이다. 피터가 안식 기간을 보낼 일본으로 떠나게 될 때쯤이면 1년 이상 대학에서 학생들을 가르치는 셈이 된다.

해설 'for+기간(~ 동안)'과 'by the time+미래 시점(~일 때쯤)'이라는 시간 표현이 나왔으므로 빈칸엔 미래완료진행시제 동사 (c)가 적합하다.

어휘 instructor 교사, (대학의) 전임 강사 leave for ~로 떠나다 sabbatical 안식 기간

20 관계사 문제

난이도 ★
정답 (a)

해석 부모가 모두 학교에서 근무하고 있는 그 소년은 교실에 화재를 일으켜 다른 아이들을 위험에 빠뜨렸다. 교육 위원회는 모두 그의 부모를 알고 있고 그들이 얼마나 큰 충격을 받았는지 알고 있기 때문에 고발하길 주저하고 있다.

해설 빈칸은 '사람' 선행사를 수식하는 관계사절 자리이므로 관계사절이 아닌 (b), 사물 선행사를 받는 (c), 선행사를 취하지 않는 (d)는 탈락, 따라서 정답은 (a)이다.

어휘 endanger 위험에 빠뜨리다 school board 교육 위원회 press charge 고발[기소]하다 devastated 엄청난 충격을 받은

21 시제 문제

난이도 ★★
정답 (a)

해석 스콧 삼촌은 크리스틴이 자신의 새 가죽 코트를 찾는 동안 차를 예열하고 있다. 이들은 오늘 스콧 삼촌이 가장 좋아하는 식당인 Sunny's Pancake Diner에서 식사를 한다.

해설 'while+현재시제 문장(현재 ~하는 동안)'이라는 시점에 어떠한 행위가 발생 중이라고 말하는 것이 적합하므로 정답은 현재진행시제 동사 (a)이다.

어휘 warm up 데우다, 예열하다 leather coat 가죽 코트

22 가정법 문제

난이도 ★
정답 (a)

해석 우리는 눈의 도움으로 다른 사물들을 보며 관찰할 수 있다. 만약 사람에게 눈이 하나만 있었다면, 이미지가 입체적으로 보이지 않았을 것이다.

해설 종속절의 동사가 'had+p.p.'이기 때문에 주절의 동사는 '조동사의 과거형+have+p.p.' 형태가 되어야 하므로 정답은 (a)이다.

어휘 observe 관찰하다 appear 나타나다, 보이기 시작하다 three dimensional 3차원의, 입체적인

23 시제 문제

난이도 ★★
정답 (c)

해석 데이빗과 그의 팀은 Sneek이라 불리는 디지털 감시 플랫폼을 소개받았다. 이들이 일하는 있는 동안, 이 프로그램은 회사 노트북 웹캠을 통해 데이빗과 그의 동료들의 사진을 실시간으로 포착하게 된다.

해설 문맥상 종속절(while ~)의 행위가 '발생하는 동안' 주절의 행위가 일어나게 될 것이라고 이어지는 게 적합하므로 정답은 현재진행시제 동사 (c)이다.

어휘 surveillance 감시 capture 포착하다, 담아내다 live 생중계의, 실황인 workmate (직장) 동료

24 should 생략 문제

난이도 ★
정답 (c)

해석 라틴 아메리카와 캐리비안에 있는 젊은이들의 3분의 1가량이 가난한 삶을 살고 있다. UN과 ECLAC가 종합적인 사회 보호를 요구하는 것은 필수 불가결하다.

해설 당위의 형용사(imperative) 뒤 that절의 동사는 should가 생략된 동사원형이 되어야 하므로 정답은 (c)이다.

어휘 live in poverty 가난한 삶을 살다 imperative 반드시 해야 하는 call for ~을 요구하다[필요로 하다]

25 가정법 문제

난이도 ★
정답 (d)

해석 인도주의적인 구조선이 위태롭게 붐비는 목선에서 396명의 이주자들을 건져 올렸다. 구조선이 아니었다면, 이들은 지중해의 수많은 난민들처럼 익사했을 것이다.

해설 종속절의 동사가 'had+p.p.'이기 때문에 주절의 동사는 '조동사의 과거형+have+p.p.' 형태가 되어야 하므로 정답은 (d)이다.

어휘 humanitarian 인도주의의 migrant 이주자 drown 익사하다 refugee 난민 Mediterranean Sea 지중해

26 준동사 문제

난이도 ★
정답 (b)

해석 34세인 에이미 글렌은 자신의 5살 난 아이에게 헌신적이다. 하지만, 모성에 대해 논할 때, 그녀는 아이를 가진 것을 후회한다고 고백했다.

해설 regret 뒤엔 (동)명사 목적어가 와야 하며, 여기서 동명사 목적어엔 특정 시제 개념이 내포될 필요가 없으므로 (c)는 오답. 따라서 정답은 (b)이다.

어휘 devoted 헌신적인 motherhood 어머니인 상태, 모성 confess 자백하다, 고백하다

Grammar Section
Actual Test 05

▶▶ 정답 & 나의 점수 확인

테스트 날짜: _____ 월 _____ 일 / 테스트 점수: _____

01 (c) 02 (c) 03 (b) 04 (a) 05 (d) 06 (a) 07 (d) 08 (a) 09 (d) 10 (b) 11 (d) 12 (d) 13 (a)
14 (c) 15 (c) 16 (b) 17 (a) 18 (d) 19 (c) 20 (b) 21 (a) 22 (a) 23 (b) 24 (a) 25 (b) 26 (b)

▶▶ 틀린 문제 체크해 보기

하단에 자신이 틀린 문항의 번호를 적고 해설을 보며 자신이 오답을 고른 이유를 정확히 파악하고, 같은 유형의 문제를 다시는 틀리지 않도록 재차 복습하도록 하세요.

▶▶ 문제별 정답 및 해설

01 시제 문제

난이도 ★
정답 (c)

해설 한 운전자는 버밍엄에서 차를 몬 적이 없음에도 차를 끌고 이곳을 지나갔다는 이유로 인해 20달러의 벌금을 받았다. 벤 코스텔로는 6월 이후 120달러의 범칙금 고지서를 받아왔었다고 말했다.

해설 '본동사(said)'가 과거시제이고 문장 뒤쪽에 'since June(6월 이후)'라는 시간 표현이 나왔으므로 빈칸엔 과거완료 진행시제 동사 (c)가 적합하다.

어휘 fine 벌금 penalty charge notice 범칙금 통치서

02 가정법 문제

난이도 ★
정답 (c)

해설 지역 동물원은 수년에 걸쳐 상당한 부진을 겪고 있다. 따라서 도시에선 개조를 위한 아이디어를 모색 중이다. 만약 내가 동물원을 소유했다면, 사람들이 동물들과 좀 더 교감할 수 있게 할 것이다.

해설 종속절의 동사가 '과거형(owned)'일 경우 주절의 동사는 '조동사의 과거형+동사원형'이 되어야 하기 때문에 정답은 (c) 이다.

어휘 run-down 황폐한; 부진한, 쇠퇴한 renovation 개조 own 소유하다 interact with ~와 교감[상호 작용]하다

03 should 생략 문제

난이도 ★
정답 (b)

해설 미주리주 캔자스시티 이사회는 COVID-19 건강 지침을 따르지 않았다는 이유로 술집의 주류 판매 허가증이 폐지되는 것을 명했다. 술집 주인인 존 버크는 시장의 긴급 명령을 따르지 않으며 강력히 저항했다.

해설 당위의 동사(order) 뒤 that절의 동사는 should가 생략된 동사원형이 되어야 하므로 정답은 (b)이다.

어휘 liquor license 주류 판매 허가 revoke 폐지하다 comply with ~을 지키다 defiant 저항하는 stance 입장, 태도

04 준동사 문제

난이도 ★
정답 (a)

해설 이민부 장관인 마르코 멘디치노가 금요일에 한 말에 따르면, 캐나다는 요청이 있을 경우 미국이나 다른 동맹국들을 대표해 아프가니스탄 난민들을 추가적으로 받아들이는 걸 고려할 것이라고 했다.

해설 consider 뒤엔 (동)명사 목적어가 와야 하며, 여기서 동명사 목적어엔 특정 시제 개념이 내포될 필요가 없으므로 (d)는 오답, 따라서 정답은 (a)이다.

어휘 take in ~을 받아들이다 refugee 난민 ally 동맹국, 협력자 minister 장관, 각료

05 접속부사 문제

난이도 ★★
정답 (d)

해설 천연가스는 원유처럼 갱정을 통해 뽑아 올리거나 지구 표면 아래 석유 매장층 인근에서 발견된다. 반면에, 석탄은 고체 화석 연료이다.

해설 두 문장이 서로 '상반되는 주제(천연가스/석탄)'에 대해 이야기하고 있으므로 빈칸엔 역접의 접속부사 (d)가 적합하다.

어휘 natural gas 천연가스 well 갱정 crude oil 원유 oil deposits 석유 매장층 coal 석탄 fossil oil 화석 연료

06 관계사 문제

난이도 ★★
정답 (a)

해설 대학에선 대학원생들을 위한 다양한 수업을 제공할 계획을 세우고 있다. 대부분 영어로 진행되는 총 10개의 수업들이 다음 학기에 제공될 예정이다.

해설 선행사가 '사물'이므로 '사람' 선행사를 받는 관계사 'whose, whom'이 들어간 (a), (b)는 탈락, 그리고 전치사 뒤엔 that 관계사절이 올 수 없으므로 (d) 또한 탈락, 따라서 정답은 (a)이다.

어휘 a variety of 여러 가지의, 다양한 graduate student 대학원생 semester 학기

07 준동사 문제

난이도 ★
정답 (d)

해설 경찰과 의료인들은 범죄 생존자들의 이야기에 대한 의혹을 절대 노골적으로 드러내선 안 된다. 그들은 존엄하게 대접을 받아야 마땅하다.

해설 'deserve to V(~할 가치가 있다, ~해야 마땅하다)'라는 구문에 적합한 형태의 동사는 (d)이다.

어휘 healthcare provider 의료인 explicitly 명백하게, 노골적으로 doubt 의심, 의혹 dignity 위엄, 품위, 존엄성

08 should 생략 문제

난이도 ★
정답 (a)

해설 지난주 한 젊은 남성이 모르는 사람을 각기 다른 부위에 걸쳐 칼로 스무 차례 찔렀다. 검찰관들은 피의자에게 최고형이 주어져야 한다고 요청했다.

해설 당위의 동사(request) 뒤 that절의 동사는 should가 생략된 동사원형이 되어야 하므로 정답은 (a)이다.

어휘 stab 찌르다 prosecutor 검찰관, 검사 maximum sentence 최고형 accused 피고인, 피의자

09 조동사 문제

난이도 ★★
정답 (d)

해설 여러 종류의 원추 세포를 상실한 사람들은 빛에 매우 민감한 경향이 있다. 또한 이들은 특히 밝은 빛에서 선명하게 보는 데 어려움이 있을 수 있다.

해설 문맥상 '사람들에게 어떠한 경향이 있고(tend to V), 그런 경향이 있는 사람들은 어떠한 어려움이 있을 수 있다'고 하는 것이 적합하므로 정답은 (d)이다.

어휘 cone cell 원추 세포 sensitive 예민한, 민감한 have difficulty V-ing ~하는 데 어려움이 있다

10 가정법 문제

난이도 ★
정답 (b)

해설 내 친구 제스는 긴 시간 동안 해외에서 영어를 가르쳤다. 미국으로 돌아온 후, 제스는 좋은 직장을 얻었다. 만약 그녀가 해외 경험이 없었더라면, 회사는 그녀를 고용하지 않았을 것이다.

해설 종속절의 동사가 'had+p.p.'이기 때문에 주절의 동사는 '조동사의 과거형+have+p.p.' 형태가 되어야 하므로 정답은 (b)이다.

어휘 come back to ~로 돌아오다 land on a great job 좋은 직장을 얻다 abroad 해외에(서), 해외로

11 시제 문제

난이도 ★
정답 (d)

해설 지구의 생물 다양성이 너무 다채로워서 많은 종들이 발견되어야 하는 것에 반해, 지금 현재 인간 활동으로 인해 많은 종들이 멸종의 위협을 받고 있다.

해설 'right now(지금 현재)'라는 시간 표현이 나왔으므로 빈칸엔 현재진행시제 동사 (d)가 적합하다.

어휘 biodiversity 생물의 다양성 threaten 협박하다, 위협하다 extinction 멸종, 소멸

12 시제 문제

난이도 ★★
정답 (d)

해설 마르타는 역사에 남을 만한 보스턴 마라톤에서 뛸 계획을 세우고 있었다. 마르타는 다리가 부러지기 전까지 매일 하루에 거의 40마일을 달리고 있었다. 지금 현재 그녀는 몹시 큰 충격에 빠진 상태다.

해설 'before+과거 시점(~ 전까지)' 쭉 어떠한 행위가 있어 왔다고 해야 문맥상 자연스러우므로 빈칸엔 과거완료진행시제 동사 (d)가 적합하다.

어휘 historic 역사적인, 역사에 남을 만한 devasted 엄청난 충격을 받은

13 준동사 문제

난이도 ★
정답 (a)

해설 매리언 존스는 2000년 여름 올림픽에서 5개의 메달을 딴 미국 출신의 위대한 육상 스타였다. 그녀가 더 빨리 달리기 위해 약물을 사용했다는 것을 인정했을 때 그녀는 모든 메달을 반납해야만 했다.

해설 여기서 본동사 admit은 (동)명사 목적어를 취하는 타동사이므로 정답은 (a)이다.

어휘 track star 육상 스타 win a medal 메달을 획득하다 drug (불법적인) 약물, 마약

14 가정법 문제

난이도 ★
정답 (c)

해설 우리는 아직까지 자격 시험을 위한 접수를 받고 있다. 만약 시험을 보기로 결정했다면, 3월 31일까지 접수해야만 한다.

해설 종속절의 동사가 '과거형(decided)'일 경우 주절의 동사는 '조동사의 과거형+동사원형'이 되어야 하기 때문에 정답은 (c)이다.

어휘 registration 등록, 접수 qualification exam 자격 시험 register 등록하다, 접수하다

15 관계사 문제

난이도 ★★
정답 (c)

[해석] 많은 스타들의 사진을 찍어 온 셀럽 사진작가인 앤디 그로츠는 영화 우상의 사진을 보정하길 거부한다. 고인이 된 토니 커티스를 찍은 그의 사진은 그의 경력에 있어 가장 의미 있게 돋보이는 작업물이다.

[해설] 선행사가 '사람'이고 콤마(,) 뒤엔 that 관계사절이 올 수 없으므로 (a), (d)는 탈락, 그리고 선행사를 필요로 하지 않는 (b) 또한 탈락되어 (c)가 정답이다.

[어휘] celebrity 유명 인사 snap 사진을 찍다 numerous 많은 stand out 돋보이다, 빼어나다

16 should 생략 문제

난이도 ★
정답 (b)

[해석] 내 아내와 나는 여전히 새로운 아파트에 적응 중이다. 우리는 아직도 소파를 어디에 둘지 결정하지 못했고 우리 인테리어 디자이너는 소파가 창문 앞으로 가야 한다고 권유했다.

[해설] 당위의 동사(recommend) 뒤 that절의 동사는 should가 생략된 동사원형이 되어야 하므로 정답은 (a)이다.

[어휘] settle in (자리를 잡고) 적응하다 place 놓다, 두다, 배치하다 in front of ~의 앞에

17 시제 문제

난이도 ★★
정답 (a)

[해석] 조나단이 잠들어 있는 동안 누군가 그의 차고에서 회색 크라이슬러 300을 훔쳤다. 카운티 보안관 사무소는 도둑이 그의 집에서 전기톱을 비롯한 다른 물건들을 차 안에 실었다고 말했다.

[해설] 문맥상 '과거의 특정 시점 동안(while+과거 시점)' 어떠한 일이 '진행 중이었다'고 해야 자연스러우므로 빈칸엔 과거진행시제 동사 (a)가 적합하다.

[어휘] garage 차고, 주차장 County Sheriff's Office 카운티 보안관 사무소 load up ~에 짐을 싣다 chainsaw 전기톱

18 가정법 문제

난이도 ★
정답 (d)

[해석] 나는 좀 더 어렸을 때 일본어를 배우고 싶었지만, 기회가 없었다. 수년 후, 나는 도쿄에 있는 대학에서 장학금 제의를 받았다. 내가 만약 이를 수락했다면, 나는 (일본어가) 유창해졌을 것이다.

[해설] 종속절의 동사가 'had+p.p.'이기 때문에 주절의 동사는 '조동사의 과거형+have+p.p.' 형태가 되어야 하므로 정답은 (d)이다.

[어휘] scholarship 장학금 fluent 유창한

19 준동사 문제

난이도 ★★
정답 (c)

[해석] 원추 세포엔 세 가지 종류가 있다. 하나는 파란색을 흡수하고, 하나는 초록색을 흡수하며, 하나는 빨간색을 흡수한다. 이 세 가지 주요 색상의 결합은 우리가 수천 가지 색을 볼 수 있게 한다.

[해설] 'allow A to V(A가 ~하게 하다)'라는 구문에 적합한 형태는 to부정사이며, 여기서 to부정사엔 특정 시제 개념이 내포될 필요가 없으므로 정답은 (c)이다.

[어휘] cone cell 원추 세포 absorb 흡수하다, 빨아들이다 combine 결합하다

20 접속부사 문제

난이도 ★★
정답 (b)

[해석] 귀찮게 해서 미안하지만, 시내 교통이 이렇게 나쁠 거라고는 예상하지 못했어. 내가 집에 가기 전에 내 친구가 도착할 수도 있어. 그렇게 되면, 그녀에게 내게 전화 좀 하라고 부탁해 줘.

[해설] 문맥상 '어떠한 상황이 발생할 경우' 상대방에게 그와 관련된 부탁을 하는 것이 자연스러우므로 빈칸엔 '그런 경우에는'이라는 뜻의 (b)가 적합하다.

[어휘] in that case 그런 경우에는, 그렇다면

21 가정법 문제

난이도 ★
정답 (a)

해설 나는 나의 이전 회계사인 앤써니에게 전화해야 한다. 난 최근 회계 법인 한 곳과 계약을 파기했다. 그들이 수수료를 너무 많이 올리지 않았더라면, 난 그들과 일하는 걸 <u>계속 유지했을 것이다</u>.

해설 종속절의 동사가 'had+p.p.'이기 때문에 주절의 동사는 '조동사의 과거형+have+p.p.' 형태가 되어야 하므로 정답은 (a)이다.

어휘 accountant 회계사 eliminate 없애다, 제거하다 accounting firm 회계 법인

22 시제 문제

난이도 ★
정답 (a)

해설 켈리는 자신이 중간고사 준비를 위해 오늘 밤 도서관에서 <u>공부를 하고 있을 것이며</u>, 따라서 엘리가 도착했을 때 그녀를 못 볼 것이라 얘기했다. 나는 이것 때문에 그들이 다투게 될 것이 걱정된다.

해설 'tonight(오늘 밤)'이라는 시간 표현과 뒤쪽에 나온 '미래시제 동사(will not see)'에 시제를 맞추려면 빈칸엔 미래진행시제 동사 (a)가 적합하다.

어휘 midterms 중간고사 argue 언쟁을 하다, 다투다

23 가정법 문제

난이도 ★
정답 (b)

해설 시내 교통은 정말 끔찍하다. 시내에서 집까지 가는 데 3시간이 걸렸다. 만약 내가 통근에 시간을 낭비할 필요가 없었다면, 직장에서 더 많은 일을 했을 것이다.

해설 종속절의 동사가 '과거형(didn't have to)'일 경우 주절의 동사는 '조동사의 과거형+동사원형'이 되어야 하기 때문에 정답은 (b)이다.

어휘 nightmare 악몽, 아주 끔찍한 일 downtown 시내, 번화가 commute 통근하다 accomplish 성취하다, 해내다

24 조동사 문제

난이도 ★★
정답 (a)

해설 세 블록을 직진해서 가신 후 왼쪽으로 꺾고, 거기서 두 블록을 더 가면 Quickie Mart에서 길 바로 맞은편에 있습니다. 그곳을 절대 지나칠 <u>수 없을 겁니다</u>.

해설 빈칸이 있는 문장 앞에서 '길 안내'를 하고 있고, 이 같은 안내에 따라 가면 '그곳을(찾아가려는 곳) 절대 지나칠 <u>수 없다</u>'고 하는 것이 적합하므로 정답은 (a)이다.

어휘 go straight 곧장 가다, 직진하다 you can't miss it 그것을 절대 지나칠 수 없다 → 찾기 쉽다

25 준동사 문제

난이도 ★
정답 (b)

해설 저희와 함께 온라인에서 영어 말하기를 연습하실 수 있습니다. 이것은 유창해지는 데 있어 가장 빠른 방법입니다. 검증된 영어 개인 교사와 함께 배우시고 맞춤형 수업 및 각 개인에게 최적화된 수업료를 경험하십시오. 지금 예약하세요.

해설 practice 뒤엔 (동)명사 목적어가 와야 하며, 여기서 동명사 목적어엔 특정 시제 개념이 내포될 필요가 없으므로 (d)는 오답, 따라서 정답은 (b)이다.

어휘 fluency 유창성, 능숙도 tailored (특정한 개인·목적을 위한) 맞춤의 personalized 개인 맞춤형의 tuition 수업료

26 시제 문제

난이도 ★
정답 (b)

해설 NASA는 아르테미스 프로그램의 일환으로서 달을 좀 더 탐사하기 위해 우주 비행사들을 보낼 준비 중이다. 2025년이 되면 우주 비행사들은 달에 착륙하게 된다.

해설 문맥상 'by+미래시점(~이 되면)' 어떠한 행위가 완료되어 있을 것이라고 해야 자연스러우므로 빈칸엔 미래완료시제 동사 (b)가 적합하다.

어휘 astronaut 우주 비행사 explore 탐사하다, 탐험하다

어차피 제시카

G-TELP 모의고사

G-TELP | Level 2

Reading and Vocabulary
독해 정답&해설

Actual Test 01 / 정답 & 해설
Actual Test 02 / 정답 & 해설
Actual Test 03 / 정답 & 해설
Actual Test 04 / 정답 & 해설
Actual Test 05 / 정답 & 해설

Reading and Vocabulary Section
Actual Test 01

▶▶ 정답 & 나의 점수 확인

테스트 날짜: _____ 월 _____ 일 / 테스트 점수: _____

53 (c) 54 (d) 55 (a) 56 (c) 57 (c) 58 (a) 59 (b) 60 (b) 61 (c) 62 (a) 63 (d) 64 (b) 65 (b) 66 (d)
67 (a) 68 (c) 69 (b) 70 (c) 71 (a) 72 (b) 73 (a) 74 (a) 75 (c) 76 (d) 77 (b) 78 (b) 79 (a) 80 (d)

▶▶ 출제 경향 & 흐름 파악

지피지기면 백전백승! 출제 경향과 흐름을 한눈에 파악해 봅시다. 출제된 지문이 어떤 종류의 글이었는지, 각 지문과 관련해 어떤 종류의 문제가 출제되었는지 아래의 표를 보며 정리해 보세요.

(인물) 유명 조종사에 대한 소개글	53	학교를 자퇴한 이유	(환경) 폭풍 추격에 대한 설명글	67	태풍 추격의 구체적인 내용
	54	장래 희망을 갖게 된 계기		68	태풍을 추격하는 이유
	55	다른 학교에 가야 했던 이유		69	태풍 발생 장소를 예측하는 방법
	56	사고를 당하기 이전에 했던 일		70	토네이도가 발생하는 원인
	57	인물의 삶에서 얻을 수 있는 교훈		71	특수 차량을 사용하는 이유
	58	어휘 문제: obstacle		72	어휘 문제: collide
	59	어휘 문제: segregated		73	어휘 문제: armored
(건강) 전자기기의 부작용에 대한 기사	60	아이들이 세상을 배우는 방법	(항의) 서비스 불량에 대한 항의 서신	74	서신을 쓴 목적
	61	전자기기 사용이 미치는 영향		75	글쓴이가 말하는 우려 사항
	62	과도한 전자기기 사용의 결과		76	글쓴이가 원했던 요구 사항
	63	전자기기 사용을 줄이는 방법 (1)		77	글쓴이가 겪었던 문제 상황
	64	전자기기 사용을 줄이는 방법 (2)		78	여행 가이드의 문제점
	65	어휘 문제: inhibit		79	어휘 문제: private
	66	어휘 문제: engage		80	어휘 문제: substitute

BESSIE COLEMAN

Bessie Coleman was the first female African American and Native American pilot ever to hold an international pilot license. Known for performing flying tricks, Coleman's nicknames were; "Brave Bessie," and "Queen Bess." She fought discrimination to follow her dream of becoming a pilot. As a Black woman in the 1920s, she faced many 58 obstacles because of her race and gender.

Bessie was born in Atlanta, Texas, in 1892. Her parents were Black and her father was of Native American descent as well. Bessie grew up helping her mother pick cotton and wash laundry to earn extra money. She attended 59 segregated schools, but 53 had to drop out of university because she couldn't afford to continue her study.

She eventually moved to Chicago, Illinois in 1915 and worked in a barber shop painting fingernails. When her brother John returned from fighting in France during World War I, he told Coleman stories about war. 54 Hearing stories about the brave pilots sparked Bessie's new dream: to be a pilot.

55 She applied to U.S. flight schools, but every school rejected her because she was Black and a woman. Famous African American newspaper publisher Robert Abbott told her to move to France where she could learn how to fly. In 1920, Coleman traveled on a ship to France. She found a school run by the Cauron brothers. She earned her international pilot's license on June 15, 1921, within a year of enrolling.

When she returned to the United States in 1922 as an aerial acrobat, Coleman amazed Black and White audiences with her daredevil feats. She would do loops, barrel rolls, and figure eights in her plane. She'd even walk on the wings and parachute out.

In 1923, Coleman survived a bad accident that left her with a broken leg and ribs, but she recovered and started doing stunts at air shows again. 56 Her goal was to open a school for Black pilots, but she never completed that dream. She died a few years later in another plane accident, but her courageous feats of flight have inspired a fleet of Black women pilots who came after her.

어휘 discrimination 차별 descent 혈통, 가문, 가계 segregated 분리된 (인종) 차별적인; 특정 인종용의 drop out of ~에서 중도하차하다 spark 촉발시키다, 유발하다 publisher 발행[출판]자 enroll 입학하다, 등록하다 aerial acrobat 공중 곡예사 daredevil 무모한[저돌적인] 사람 feat (뛰어난) 솜씨[재주] amaze 놀라게 하다 loop 고리 barrel roll 연속 횡전(橫轉) figure eight 8자형 비행 parachute 낙하산; 낙하산을 타고 낙하하다 stunt 스턴트[고난이도 연기], 곡예 courageous 용감한 fleet 함대; 비행기 집단 come after ~의 뒤를 잇다 scholarship 장학금 determination 투지 perseverance 인내(심) fairness 공정성 compassion 연민, 동정심 asset 자산 dispute 분쟁[논란]; 분쟁[논란]을 벌이다

53. 베씨 콜먼은 왜 대학에서 자퇴해야 했는가?
(a) 프랑스에 있는 비행 학교에 가기 위해
(b) 제1차 세계대전 때문에
(c) 돈이 충분치 않았기 때문에
(d) 차별에 직면했기 때문에

> 두 번째 단락에서 그녀가 공부를 계속할 'couldn't afford (형편이 안 돼서)' 대학을 자퇴했다고 했고, 이는 결국 금전적 능력이 받쳐주지 않아 대학을 자퇴한 것으로 해석 가능하기 때문에 정답은 (c)이다.

54. 무엇이 베씨가 조종사가 되는 데 영감을 주었는가?
(a) 일리노이주 시카고로 이사 간 것
(b) 이발소에서 손톱을 칠하며 일한 것
(c) 특정 인종 전용 학교에 가야만 한 것
(d) 그녀의 형제 존에게서 조종사 이야기를 들은 것

> 세 번째 단락에서 그녀의 형제 존에게서 들은 'stories about the brave pilots(용감한 조종사들의 이야기)'가 조종사가 되고자 하는 그녀의 꿈에 불을 지폈다고 했으므로 정답은 (d)이다.

55. 베씨는 왜 미국 대신 프랑스에 있는 비행 학교에 가야 했는가?
(a) 미국 학교에서 그녀의 지원을 받아주지 않았기 때문에
(b) 프랑스 학교에서 그녀에게 장학금을 제공했기 때문에
(c) 그녀의 모든 친구들이 프랑스에 있는 학교에 갔기 때문에
(d) 그녀의 형제 존이 유학을 가라고 권유했기 때문에

> 네 번째 단락에서 그녀가 미국 비행 학교에 지원했으나 이를 'every school rejected(모든 학교가 거부했고)', 그 후 비행술을 배울 수 있는 프랑스에 가라는 권유를 받았다고 했기 때문에 정답은 (a)이다.

56. 베씨는 사고를 당하기 전 무엇을 하길 원했는가?
(a) 프랑스로 돌아가길 원했다.
(b) 전쟁에서 싸우기를 원했다.
(c) 흑인 조종사들을 위한 비행 학교를 시작하고자 했다
(d) 에어쇼에서 활동하기를 원했다.

> 마지막 단락에서 그녀의 목표가 'open a school for Black pilots(흑인 조종사들을 위한 학교를 여는 것)'이었으나 이를 이루지 못했고, 그 후 사고를 당해 사망했다고 했으므로 정답은 (c)이다.

57. 독자들은 베씨의 삶에서 어떤 자질을 배울 수 있는가?
(a) 개방성과 정직함
(b) 충절과 겸손함
(c) 투지와 인내심
(d) 공명정대와 동정심

> 이 글은 인종 및 성별 차별에도 굴하지 않고 조종사가 되려는 자신의 꿈을 좇아 이를 성취해낸 인물의 '투지와 인내심'에 대한 내용을 다루고 있는 걸로 볼 수 있으므로 정답은 (c)이다.

58. 글의 문맥에서, obstacles는 _____을 의미한다.
(a) hurdles (장애)
(b) assets (자산)
(c) properties (재산)
(d) academies (학교)

> 밑줄 친 'obstacles'는 '장애(물), 방해(물)'이라는 뜻을 갖고 있는 명사로서 보기 중 이와 일맥상통하는 유사어는 '(a) hurdle(장애(물))'이다.

59. 글의 문맥에서, segregated는 _____을 의미한다.
(a) banned (금지된)
(b) divided (분열된)
(c) connected (관련된)
(d) disputed (논란이 된)

> 밑줄 친 'segregate'는 '분리된, (인종) 차별적인, 특정 인종용의'라는 뜻을 갖고 있는 형용사로서 이와 일맥상통하는 유사어는 '(b) divided(분열된)'이다.

WHAT DOES TOO MUCH SCREEN TIME DO TO CHILDREN'S BRAINS?

과도한 스크린 사용 시간이 아이들의 뇌에 무슨 일을 일으키는가?

Nearly half of all children 8 and under have their own tablet device and spend an average of about 3 hours a day on screen. What is all this screen time doing to kids' brains?

For young children, especially those under the age of 5, development is happening rapidly. 60 Young children learn by exploring their environment and watching the adults in their lives and then imitating them.

However, excessive screen time may 65 inhibit a child's ability to observe and experience the typical everyday activities they need to engage with in order to learn about the world, leading to a kind of tunnel vision, which can be harmful to overall development.

Children who are often playing on smartphones or tablets don't pay attention to anything else around them. They will not learn about the world around them if all they're doing is looking at a smartphone. 61 This will not just affect their ability to learn new things, but also how they interact with others and how language develops.

Language development expands rapidly between 1 to 3 years of age, and studies have shown that children learn language best when engaging and interacting with adults who are talking and playing with them. There is also some evidence that children who watch a lot of television during the early elementary school years perform less well on reading tests and may show deficits in attention.

According to the recent National Institutes of Health (NIH) study, children who spent more than two hours a day on screen-time activities score lower on language and thinking tests, and some children with more than seven hours a day of screen time experience weakening of cortex, the area of the brain related to critical thinking and reasoning.

Dr. Joseph Cross, an assistant professor at Cornell University, says, "62 if young children spend most of their time engaging with an iPad, smartphone, or the television, all of which are highly entertaining, it can be hard to get them 66 engaged in non-electronic activities, such as playing with toys to foster imagination and creativity, exploring outdoors, and playing with other children to develop appropriate social skills."

63 Dr. Cross recommends that parents keep bedtime, mealtime, and family time screen-free. 64 She also says that parents consider setting a curfew or an agreed-upon time because balancing online and offline time is extremely important.

어휘 imitate 모방하다, 흉내 내다 excessive 지나친, 과도한 inhibit 억제[저해]하다, 못하게 하다 engage (~에) 종사[관여/참여]시키다 tunnel vision 좁은 시야[사고] affect 영향을 미치다 interact with ~와 상호 작용을 하다 expand 확대하다, 늘리다; 발전시키다 deficit 적자; 부족액; (심신의) 결함 National weakening 약화 cortex 피질 critical thinking 비판적 사고 reasoning 추리, 추론 entertaining 재미있는, 즐거움을 주는 foster 조성하다, 발전시키다 explore 답사[탐사/탐험]하다 appropriate 적절한 curfew 통금 시간 agreed-upon 합의된 balance 균형; 균형을 유지하다 nursery 보육원, 탁아소 violent 폭력적인, 난폭한 impulsive 충동적인 stunt 성장[발달]을 방해[저해]하다 participate in ~에 참가[참여]하다 regulate 규제[통제/단속]하다 consent 동의, 합의 dismiss 묵살[일축]하다; 떨쳐 버리다

60. 글에 따르면, 어린아이들은 어떻게 세상에 대해 배우는가?
(a) '세사미 스트리트'와 같은 교육용 TV 프로그램을 봄으로써
(b) 생활 속 성인들을 관찰하고 흉내 냄으로써
(c) 탁아소에서 다른 아이들과 소통함으로써
(d) 교사들이 설계한 활동에 참여함으로써

두 번째 단락에서 아이들이 생활 속에서 'watching adults(어른들을 보고), imitating them(이들을 흉내 내며)' 배운다고 했으므로 정답은 (b)이다.

61. 스크린 사용 시간의 증가는 아이들에게 어떤 영향을 미치는가?
(a) 다른 아이들과 친해질 기회를 더 많이 제공한다.
(b) 아이들을 더 폭력적이고 충동적이게 만든다.
(c) 언어 능력을 영향을 줄 수 있는 적절한 뇌 발달을 억제한다
(d) 학교에서 못 배우는 새로운 정보를 배울 수 있게 한다.

세 번째 단락에서 스크린 사용 증가가 새로운 것을 배우는 것과 다른 이들과 소통하는 방법 및 'how language develops(언어가 발달하는 방식)'에 영향을 끼치게 될 것이라 했으므로 정답은 (c)이다.

62. 디지털 기기에 시간을 많이 쓰는 아이들에게 무슨 일이 생기는가?
(a) 친구들과 노는 것에 흥미를 잃는다
(b) 학교 활동에 기꺼이 참여하고자 한다.
(c) 가족과 더 많은 시간을 보내고 싶어 한다.
(d) 다른 사람들과 소통하는 법을 배운다.

일곱 번째 단락에서 과도한 시간을 전자기기에 쏟는 것은 'playing with other children(다른 아이들과 노는 것)'과 같은 전자기기가 없는 활동에 참여하는 걸 어렵게 만든다고 했으므로 정답은 (a)이다.

63. 크로스 박사에 의하면, 스크린 사용 시간을 줄이려면 가족들이 무엇을 해야 하는가?
(a) 아이들이 결정하게 내버려 둔다
(b) 일기에 스크린 사용 시간을 한다
(c) 스마트폰을 가져간 뒤 똑바로 행동했을 때 준다
(d) 하루 중 특정 시간에 스마트폰과 아이패드를 끈다

마지막 단락에서 취침 시간, 식사 시간, 가족과의 시간 같은 특정 시간대에 'screen-free(스크린이 없게)' 해야 한다고 했고, 이는 결국 전자기기를 끄라는 의미로 해석 가능하기 때문에 정답은 (d)이다.

64. 부모가 아이들의 스크린 사용 시간을 줄이기 위해 할 수 있는 것은?
(a) 스크린 사용 시간을 정한 후 이를 알려준다
(b) 스크린 사용 시간을 단속하되 아이들의 동의를 얻는다
(c) 아이들이 원할 때마다 디지털 기기를 사용하게 한다
(d) 전문가와 상의해 스크린 사용 시간을 결정한다

마지막 단락에서 온라인과 오프라인 시간의 균형을 조절하려면 통금 시간이나 'agreed-upon time(약속=서로가 동의한/합의한) 시간)'을 정하는 걸 고려해야 한다고 했으므로 정답은 (b)이다.

65. 글의 문맥에서, inhibit는 _____을 의미한다.
(a) assist (돕다)
(b) block (막다)
(c) encourage (격려하다)
(d) permit (허락하다)

밑줄 친 'inhibit'는 '억제[저해]하다, 못하게 하다'라는 뜻을 갖고 있는 동사로서 보기 중 이와 일맥상통하는 유사어는 '(b) block(막다, 차단하다)'이다.

66. 글의 문맥에서, engaged는 _____을 의미한다.
(a) entertain (즐겁게 하다)
(b) inform (알리다)
(c) dismissed (떨쳐 버리다)
(d) participated (참여하다)

밑줄 친 'engaged'는 '(~에) 종사[관여/참여]시키다'라는 뜻을 가진 동사로서 보기 중 이와 일맥상통하는 유사어는 '(d) participated(참여하다)'이다.

67-73 (환경) 폭풍 추격에 대한 설명글

STORM CHASERS

폭풍 추격자

Some storm chasers are photographers trying to capture spectacular images of a tornado. But most storm chasers are scientists and meteorologists who study the weather. 67 68 They put themselves in the paths of dangerous storms to collect more information than they could get from far away. How fast is a tornado moving? Will a hurricane hit the coast? Questions like these are hard to answer without getting close to a storm. 67 Storm chasers gather data, take photos, and shoot videos to convince people to prepare for the storm.

Storm chasers have to find a storm before they can chase it. They watch for weather patterns that usually lead to dangerous storms. 69 By looking at all the features of weather such as wind speed, a sudden change in temperature, humidity, storm chasers can predict when and where a storm might form. When the storm chasers have located a forming storm, radar maps guide the team to the storm's location. Storm chasers living in coastal areas often specialize in hurricanes, also called typhoons or cyclones. Hurricanes form over the open ocean near the equator. They are powered by warm, moist air. Hurricanes become most damaging as they move toward a coast.

70 The central United States is nicknamed Tornado Alley. Cold and dry air from the north 72 collides with warm, moist air from the south. Large temperature differences create strong winds. This pattern leads to thunderstorms that may become tornadoes.

They drive in 73 armored trucks filled with weather instruments. They place sensors called turtles on the ground in the path of the storm. The turtles will gather data from inside the storm. 71 The truck is equipped with side armor that blocks the wind from getting under trucks and flipping it over. Strong spikes attach the truck to the ground. Even with safety precautions and special vehicles, storm chasing is very dangerous. Tornadoes can quickly change direction and destroy everything in their path. Hurricanes can cause huge waves that wipe out buildings. Even experienced storm chasers have been hurt or killed by monster storms.

If we are near a storm, we need to get indoors to stay safe. We also should listen to the weather report. Sometimes a battery-powered radio will still work if cell phones go out during a bad storm. Storm chasers urge people to leave the storm chasing to the expert.

폭풍을 쫓는 일부 사람들은 토네이도의 멋진 장면을 포착하려는 사진작가들이다. 하지만 대부분의 태풍 추격자들은 과학자들과 날씨를 공부하는 기상학자들이다. 67 68 이들은 멀리서 얻을 수 있는 것보다 더 많은 정보를 수집하기 위해 위험한 폭풍이 지나가는 길가에 스스로를 내던진다. 토네이도가 얼마나 빨리 이동하는가? 허리케인이 해안을 강타할 것인가? 이 같은 질문들은 태풍을 잘 알지 않으면 답하기 힘들다. 67 태풍 추격자들은 사람들이 태풍에 대비하도록 설득하기 위해 정보를 모으고, 사진을 찍고, 동영상을 찍는다.

태풍 추격자들은 태풍 추격이 가능하기 전에 태풍을 찾아야 한다. 이들은 주로 위험한 태풍에 이르게 되는 날씨 패턴을 지켜본다. 69 태풍 추격자들이 풍속, 갑작스러운 온도 변화, 습도와 같은 날씨의 모든 특징을 살펴보면 언제 어디서 태풍이 생길지 예측할 수 있다. 태풍 추격자들이 형성 중인 태풍의 위치를 찾아내면, 레이더 맵이 이들을 태풍이 있는 곳으로 안내한다. 해안 지역에 사는 태풍 추격자들은 보통 타이푼이나 사이클론이라 불리는 허리케인 전문가이다. 허리케인은 적도 인근 외해에서 형성된다. 이들은 따뜻하고 습한 공기에 의해 맹렬히 움직인다. 허리케인은 해안 쪽으로 가기 때문에 가장 많은 피해를 일으킨다.

70 미국 중부 지역은 'Tornado Alley(토네이도 골목)'이라는 별명이 붙어 있다. 북쪽의 춥고 건조한 공기가 남쪽의 따뜻하고 습한 공기와 72 충돌한다. 큰 온도차가 강한 바람을 만들어낸다. 이 같은 패턴은 토네이도가 될 수 있는 뇌우에 이르게 된다.

이들은 기상 기계로 가득 찬 73 장갑차로 운전한다. 이들은 'turtles(거북이)'라 불리는 센서들을 태풍이 지나가는 길가에 놓는다. '거북이'는 태풍 내부에서 정보를 수집할 것이다. 71 트럭엔 바람이 트럭 밑으로 들어가서 차를 확 뒤집는 걸 방지하기 위한 측면 장갑이 구비되어 있다. 강한 대못이 트럭을 땅에 고정시켜 놓는다. 안전 예방 조치와 특수 차량을 아무리 갖춰도, 태풍 추격은 매우 위험하다. 토네이도는 방향을 재빨리 바꿔 길목에 있는 모든 걸 파괴할 가능성이 있다. 토네이도는 건물들을 완전히 파괴하는 거대한 파도를 일으킬 수 있다. 경험 있는 태풍 추격자들조차 괴물 같은 태풍에 의해 부상을 입거나 사망하기도 했다.

만약 우리가 태풍 가까이에 있다면, 안전하게 있을 수 있도록 실내에 머물러야 한다. 우리는 또한 일기 예보를 들어야 한다. 심각한 태풍이 지나가는 동안 휴대폰이 꺼지면 배터리로 구동되는 라디오는 여전히 작동될 것이다. 태풍 추격자들은 사람들에게 전문가를 쫓아 태풍에서 벗어날 것을 권고한다.

어휘 spectacular 장관을 이루는, 극적인 meteorologist 기상학자 convince 납득시키다, 설득하다 humidity 습도; 습함, 습기 locate ~의 정확한 위치를 찾아내다 specialize in ~을 전문[전공]으로 하다 open ocean 개방된 해안, 외해 equator 적도 power 힘; 작동시키다; 맹렬히 나아가다 moist 촉촉한, 습기가 많은 damaging 손상[피해/훼손/악영향]을 주는 collide 충돌하다, 부딪히다; 상충하다 thunderstorm 뇌우 armored 장갑을 두른 instrument 기구, (측정용) 계기 be equipped with ~을 갖추고 있다 armor 갑옷; 철갑(판); 장갑 flip over 홱 뒤집히다[뒤집다] spike (대)못 precaution 예방 조치[수단] wipe out ~을 완전히 파괴하다[없애 버리다] evacuate 대피시키다; 피난하다 media coverage 매스컴의 보도 broadcast 방송하다 spot 발견하다, 찾다 debris 잔해, 쓰레기 footage (특정한 사건을 담은) 장면

67. 태풍 추격자들은 무엇에 관여하는 것 같은가?
(a) 토네이도 내부에서 풍속을 측정하는 것
(b) 다가올 태풍에 대해 매체에 이야기하는 것
(c) 태풍 근처에서 가능한 많은 사진을 찍으려 노력하는 것
(d) 사람들을 지역에서 대피하게 하도록 노력하는 것

첫 단락에서 태풍 추격자들은 'paths of dangerous storms(태풍이 지나가는 길가)'에 스스로를 내던져 태풍의 사진과 동영상을 찍으며 정보를 수집한다고 했으므로 이로부터 (a)가 답임을 유추할 수 있다.

68. 태풍 추격자들은 왜 위험한 태풍을 뒤쫓는가?
(a) 사람들에게 강력한 태풍의 위험성을 경고하기 위해
(b) 매스컴 보도에 쓰일 멋진 사진을 찍기 위해
(c) 멀리 떨어진 곳에서 얻을 수 없는 정보를 얻기 위해
(d) 이들의 유튜브 채널과 소셜 미디어에 방송하기 위해

첫 단락에서 태풍 추격자들은 'than they could get from far away(멀리 떨어진 곳에서 얻을 수 있는 것보다)' 더 많은 정보를 얻기 위해 기꺼이 태풍에 몸을 던진다고 했으므로 정답은 (c)이다.

69. 태풍 추격자들은 태풍이 어디서 형성될지 어떻게 아는가?
(a) 기상학자들에게서 정보를 얻는다.
(b) 태풍의 신호를 찾아낸다
(c) 태풍을 찾기 위해 차를 타고 돌아다닌다.
(d) 태풍이 발생하길 기다린다.

두 번째 단락에서 태풍 추격자들이 풍속, 온도 변화, 습도와 같은 'all the features of weather((태풍과 관련된) 날씨의 모든 특징)'을 보며 태풍 발생 시기와 장소를 예측한다고 했으므로 정답은 (b)이다.

70. 글에 따르면, 'Tornado Alley'에서의 토네이도 발생 원인은 무엇인가?
(a) 남쪽에서 온 뜨겁고 습한 공기
(b) 북쪽에서 온 차갑고 건조한 공기
(c) 극심한 온도 차이
(d) 지역에서 잦게 발생하는 뇌우

세 번째 단락에서 북쪽의 춥고 건조한 공기와 남쪽의 따뜻하고 습한 공기가 충돌하여 발생하는 'large temperature differences(큰 온도 차이)'가 토네이도 발생 원인이라 설명했으므로 정답은 (c)이다.

71. 글에 따르면, 태풍 추격자들은 왜 장갑차를 사용하는가?
(a) 날아다니는 잔해에서 트럭을 보호하기 위해
(b) 태풍 내에서 빠르게 운전하게 위해
(c) 태풍의 극적인 장면을 얻기 위해
(d) 정보를 수집하는 데 필요한 장비를 나르기 위해

네 번째 단락에서 바람이 트럭을 'flipping it over(홱 뒤집는 걸)' 방지하게 위해 트럭에 장갑 장치가 돼 있다고 설명했으며, 이는 곧 '바람에 의한 피해를 방지'하기 위한 것'을 뜻하므로 정답은 (a)이다.

72. 글의 문맥에서, collides는 _____을 의미한다.
(a) attach (붙이다)
(b) crash (충돌하다)
(c) forecast (예측하다)
(d) train (훈련하다)

밑줄 친 collides는 '충돌하다, 부딪히다; 상충하다'라는 뜻의 동사로서 보기 중 이와 일맥상통하는 것은 '(b) crash(충돌하다, 부딪히다)'이다.

73. 글의 문맥에서, armored는 _____을 의미한다.
(a) protected (보호하는)
(b) predicted (예측하는)
(c) exposed (노출된)
(d) forced (강요된)

밑줄 친 armored는 '장갑을 두른'이라는 뜻의 형용사이며, 장갑을 두르는 것은 무언가를 '보호하기 위한 것'이므로 보기 중 문맥상 이와 일맥상통하는 것은 '(a) protected(보호하는)'이다.

74-80 (항의) 서비스 불량에 대한 항의 서신

Best tours,
711 Vermont Road
Berkeley CA
91471
Dear Sir/Madam,

My wife and I have just returned from one of your "Romantic city tours" in Bangkok (October 20 – 24) and **74** I am writing to complain about the holiday we were given.

First of all, **75** the hotel was not at all what we had been led to expect from your website. You advertised air-conditioned rooms with a mini bar and **79** private bathroom, but what we got was a tiny room with none of the promised appliances. Worst of all, we had to share a bathroom with five other parties on our floor. I don't think having a stool with your room number in a shared bathroom isn't considered private. The temperature was 30 degrees Celsius inside everyday even at night, so you can imagine our discomfort. **76** As for the hotel staff, whenever we called down to the reception, no one was around. There did not even seem to be any cleaning staff since our beds were made only once during the whole of our stay.

Moreover, **77** the tourist guide included in your offer called in sick shortly after we arrived at the hotel and there was nobody in charge to organize a suitable **80** substitute. **78** We were disappointed to find out that the tour guide only spoke broken English and we had difficulties understanding him. The tour guide took us to various shopping malls where we could have gone by ourselves.

As you can see, we are highly dissatisfied with the holiday your company provided. We expect a letter of apology as well as a full refund. We are determined to take this matter a step further, if our demands are not met.

Sincerely,
M.J. Jones

베스트 투어,
버몬트 가 711
버클리 CA
91471

관계자 분께

제 아내와 저는 이제 막 방콕에서의 "로맨틱 도시 투어 (10/20~24)"에서 돌아왔으며, **74** 저희가 보낸 휴가에 대해 항의하고자 이렇게 서신을 씁니다.

우선, **75** 호텔이 귀사의 웹사이트에서 저희가 보고 예상했던 호텔이 전혀 아니었습니다. 귀사에선 미니바와 **79** 전용 화장실이 있는 냉난방 시설이 갖춰진 객실을 광고했는데, 저희가 배정된 곳은 약속된 시설이 전혀 없는 작은 방이었습니다. 무엇보다도 최악은, 저희 층에 있는 다른 다섯 무리의 사람들과 화장실을 같이 써야 했다는 겁니다. 저는 같이 쓰는 화장실에서 객실 번호를 지닌 채 볼일을 보는 것이 '전용'을 의미한다고 생각하지 않습니다. 실내 온도는 매일, 심지어 밤에도 30도였고, 따라서 저희가 겪은 불편함을 상상하실 수 있을 겁니다. **76** 호텔 직원들은, 저희가 리셉션을 향해 부를 때마다 없었습니다. 저희가 머무는 내내 딱 한 번만 침대가 정돈된 걸 봤을 때 청소 직원이 전혀 없었던 것 같아 보입니다.

게다가, **77** 귀사의 제안에 포함돼 있던 여행 가이드는 저희가 호텔에 도착하자마자 병가를 냈고 적합한 **80** 대리인 준비를 담당할 그 누구도 없었습니다. **78** 저희는 여행 가이드가 서툰 영어만 할 줄 안다는 사실에 실망했고 그를 이해하기 어려웠습니다. 여행 가이드는 저희가 스스로 갈 수도 있었던 다양한 쇼핑몰에 우리를 데려갔습니다.

보다시피, 저희는 귀사에서 제공한 휴가가 매우 불만족스럽습니다. 저희는 사과의 편지와 함께 전액 환불을 요구하는 바입니다. 저희는 저희의 요구 사항이 충족되지 않을 경우 이 사안에 있어 추가 조치를 취하기로 결정했습니다.

진심을 담아,
M.J 존스

어휘 complain about ~에 대해 불평하다 air-conditioned 냉난방 장치를 한 private 개인 소유의, 전용의 appliance 기기 have a stool 변소에 가다 discomfort 불편(함) call in sick 전화로 병결을 알리다, 병가를 내다 substitute 대신하는 사람[것], 대리자 full refund 전액 환불 take a step 조치를 취하다 file (소송 등) 제기[제출]하다 gratitude 고마움, 감사 inability 무능, 불능 untidy 단정치 못한, 어수선한 business hours 영업[업무] 시간 make up for 벌충[만회]하다 tardiness 느림, 완만함; 지각 unsanitary 비위생적인, 보건상 나쁜 exclusive 독점적인, 전용의 inclusive 일체의 경비가 포함된, 포괄적인 conclusive 결정적인, 확실한 executive 경영[운영]의 management 경영, 관리 involvement 관련, 관여, 개입 encouragement 격려, 고무 replacement 대체(물); 대신할 사람, 후임자

74. M. J. 존스가 베스트 투어에 보낸 서신의 목적은 무엇인가?
   (a) 공식적인 항의를 제기하기 위해
   (b) 감사함을 표현하기 위해
   (c) 머무는 기간 중 분실한 물건에 대해 알리기 위해
   (d) 사업 운영에 있어 도움을 제공하기 위해

서신의 첫 단락에서 글쓴이가 'to complain about the holiday(휴가에 대해 항의하고자)' 서신을 쓴다고 밝혔으므로 정답은 (a)이다.

75. 서신에 따르면, M.J. 존스가 가장 우려하는 것은 무엇인가?
   (a) 장소를 관리하는 호텔 직원의 무능함
   (b) 어수선한 객실 상태
   (c) 잘못된 광고
   (d) 냉난방 시설이 없는 방에서의 더운 날씨

두 번째 단락에서 글쓴이가 호텔이 웹사이트에서 봤던 그 호텔이 아니었고, 객실에 전용 미니바와 화장실 및 냉난방 시설이 있다고 'you advertised(회사에서 광고했는데)' 없다고 했으므로 정답은 (c)이다.

76. 서신에 따르면, 호텔 리셉션엔 무엇이 요구되는가?
   (a) 통역가와 여행 가이드를 제공하는 것
   (b) 손님들 사이에서 여행을 준비하는 것
   (c) 하루에 한 번씩 객실을 청소하는 것
   (d) 업무 시간에 리셉션에 있는 것

두 번째 단락에서 글쓴이가 리셉션을 향해 부를 때마다 'no one was around(아무도 없었다)'고 말하며 불만을 표하고 있고, 이는 곧 업무 시간에 직원이 리셉션에 없었음을 뜻하므로 정답은 (d)이다.

77. 여행 가이드가 병가를 냈을 때 무슨 일이 일어났는가?
   (a) 여행 가이드가 결근을 벌충했다.
   (b) 그날 여행을 하지 못했다
   (c) 회사가 다른 여행을 준비했다.
   (d) 여행 가이드가 다른 사람을 보냈다.

세 번째 단락에서 여행 가이드가 병가를 냈는데 대리인 준비를 'on one in charge(맡은 사람이 아무도 없었다)'고 했고, 이로부터 안내자가 없어 여행을 못했다는 사실을 유추할 수 있으므로 정답은 (b)이다.

78. 여행 가이드의 주요 문제는 무엇이었는가?
   (a) 지각
   (b) 의사소통 불능
   (c) 무례한 태도
   (d) 비위생적인 행동

세 번째 단락에서 여행 가이드가 'spoke broken English (서툰 영어를 구사했기)' 때문에 그를 이해하기 어려웠다고 했고, 이로부터 가이드가 의사소통에 문제가 있었음을 알 수 있으므로 정답은 (b)이다.

79. 글의 문맥에서, private는 _____을 의미한다.
   (a) exclusive (전용의)
   (b) inclusive (포괄적인)
   (c) conclusive (결정적인)
   (d) executive (경영의)

밑줄 친 private는 '개인 소유의, 전용의'라는 뜻을 가진 형용사로서 보기 중 이와 일맥상통하는 것은 '(a) exclusive (전용의)'이다.

80. 글의 문맥에서, substitute는 _____을 의미한다.
   (a) management (관리)
   (b) involvement (개입)
   (c) encouragement (격려)
   (d) replacement (후임자)

밑줄 친 substitute는 '대신하는 사람[것], 대리자'라는 뜻을 가진 명사로서 보기 중 이와 일맥상통하는 것은 '(d) replacement(대신할 사람, 후임자)'이다.

Actual Test 01 / Vocab 주요 어휘 총정리

Actual Test 01에 등장했던 주요 어휘를 한눈에 훑어보며 정리해 보도록 합시다.
모르는 어휘가 있을 경우 박스(□)에 체크(V) 표시를 한 뒤 재차 암기하도록 하세요.

- ☐ discrimination 차별
- ☐ drop out of ~에서 중도하차하다
- ☐ spark 촉발시키다, 유발하다
- ☐ enroll 입학하다, 등록하다
- ☐ courageous 용감한
- ☐ come after ~의 뒤를 잇다
- ☐ scholarship 장학금
- ☐ determination 투지
- ☐ perseverance 인내(심)
- ☐ fairness 공정성
- ☐ compassion 연민, 동정심
- ☐ asset 자산
- ☐ dispute 분쟁[논란]; 분쟁[논란]을 벌이다
- ☐ imitate 모방하다, 흉내 내다
- ☐ excessive 지나친, 과도한
- ☐ inhibit 억제[저해]하다, 못하게 하다
- ☐ engage (~에) 종사[관여/참여]시키다
- ☐ affect 영향을 미치다
- ☐ interact with ~와 상호 작용을 하다
- ☐ expand 확대하다, 늘리다; 발전시키다
- ☐ National weakening 약화
- ☐ reasoning 추리, 추론
- ☐ foster 조성하다, 발전시키다
- ☐ explore 답사[탐사/탐험]하다
- ☐ appropriate 적절한
- ☐ curfew 통금 시간
- ☐ balance 균형; 균형을 유지하다
- ☐ violent 폭력적인, 난폭한
- ☐ impulsive 충동적인
- ☐ stunt 성장[발달]을 방해[저해]하다
- ☐ participate in ~에 참가[참여]하다
- ☐ regulate 규제[통제/단속]하다
- ☐ consent 동의, 합의
- ☐ dismiss 묵살[일축]하다; 떨쳐 버리다
- ☐ convince 납득시키다, 설득하다

- ☐ humidity 습도; 습함, 습기
- ☐ locate ~의 정확한 위치를 찾아내다
- ☐ specialize in ~을 전문[전공]으로 하다
- ☐ power 힘; 작동시키다; 맹렬히 나아가다
- ☐ moist 촉촉한, 습기가 많은
- ☐ damaging 손상[피해/훼손/악영향]을 주는
- ☐ collide 충돌하다, 부딪히다; 상충히디
- ☐ instrument 기구, (측정용) 계기
- ☐ be equipped with ~을 갖추고 있다
- ☐ flip over 확 뒤집히다[뒤집다]
- ☐ precaution 예방 조치[수단]
- ☐ wipe out ~을 완전히 파괴하다[없애 버리다]
- ☐ evacuate 대피시키다; 피난하다
- ☐ complain about ~에 대해 불평하다
- ☐ private 개인 소유의, 전용의
- ☐ appliance 기기
- ☐ discomfort 불편(함)
- ☐ call in sick 전화로 병결을 알리다, 병가를 내다
- ☐ substitute 대신하는 사람[것], 대리자
- ☐ full refund 전액 환불
- ☐ take a step 조치를 취하다
- ☐ file (소송 등을) 제기[제출]하다
- ☐ gratitude 고마움, 감사
- ☐ inability 무능, 불능
- ☐ untidy 단정치 못한, 어수선한
- ☐ business hours 영업[업무] 시간
- ☐ make up for 벌충[만회]하다
- ☐ exclusive 독점적인, 전용의
- ☐ inclusive 일체의 경비가 포함된, 포괄적인
- ☐ conclusive 결정적인, 확실한
- ☐ executive 경영[운영]의
- ☐ management 경영, 관리
- ☐ involvement 관련, 관여, 개입
- ☐ encouragement 격려, 고무
- ☐ replacement 대체(물); 대신할 사람, 후임자

Reading and Vocabulary Section
Actual Test 02

▶▶ 정답 & 나의 점수 확인

테스트 날짜: _____월 _____일 / 테스트 점수: _____

53 (d) 54 (c) 55 (a) 56 (b) 57 (b) 58 (a) 59 (d) 60 (a) 61 (d) 62 (b) 63 (c) 64 (a) 65 (d) 66 (d)
67 (b) 68 (a) 69 (b) 70 (c) 71 (a) 72 (d) 73 (d) 74 (d) 75 (a) 76 (a) 77 (c) 78 (d) 79 (c) 80 (b)

▶▶ 출제 경향 & 흐름 파악

지피지기면 백전백승! 출제 경향과 흐름을 한눈에 파악해 봅시다. 출제된 지문이 어떤 종류의 글이었는지, 각 지문과 관련해 어떤 종류의 문제가 출제되었는지 아래의 표를 보며 정리해 보세요.

(인물) 환경 운동가에 대한 소개글	53	인물이 사회에 남긴 영향	(자연) 싱크홀에 대한 설명글	67	싱크홀의 정의
	54	어렸을 때 건강이 안 좋았던 이유		68	싱크홀이 형성되는 장소
	55	어렸을 때 일찍 일어났던 이유		69	싱크홀이 형성되는 요인
	56	사회적 업적에 기여한 방식		70	싱크홀이 파괴적인 이유
	57	보호 운동의 창시자로 불린 이유		71	싱크홀을 막는 방법
	58	어휘 문제: strict		72	어휘 문제: dissolve
	59	어휘 문제: conservation		73	어휘 문제: devastating
(사회) 유명 소셜 미디어에 대한 기사	60	단체에서 분석한 조사 내용	(추천서) 대학 장학 프로그램 추천서	74	이메일의 목적
	61	'틱톡'이 가진 주요 특징		75	존이 칭찬을 받는 요인
	62	'틱톡'이 다른 플랫폼에 끼친 영향		76	존이 잘할 거라 생각하는 이유
	63	'틱톡'이 미국에서 직면한 문제점		77	존의 학내 역할을 언급한 이유
	64	세계적 유행병 후 '틱톡'의 행보		78	존을 위한 향후 조치
	65	어휘 문제: unprecedented		79	어휘 문제: rare
	66	어휘 문제: mimic		80	어휘 문제: execute

JOHN MUIR

John Muir was an influential Scottish-born American naturalist, author, writer and the founder of an important organization. 53 His words inspired many people to make an effort to protect wilderness. They also helped bring about the protection of many nature areas, including Yosemite Valley.

John Muir was born on April 21, 1838, in Scotland. When John was eleven, his family moved to Wisconsin, in the United States, so his father could start a farm. 54 John's father was very 58 strict and forced his children to work long hours doing farm labor. He only allowed them one small meal a day. The children's health suffered as a result.

John did not attend school, but he loved to learn. 55 His father allowed him to wake up early to have time to read. He studied many different subjects on his own. If he had any free time during the day, he explored the woods and fields around the family farm. During John's teen years, he spent part of his early morning time working on inventions. In 1860, he displayed his inventions at the Wisconsin State Fair where his talent was recognized and awarded. He studied math and science at the University of Wisconsin, but soon left to travel on foot around parts of Canada and the Midwest. He took odd jobs to pay his way.

56 After traveling to Yosemite in 1889, Muir published two articles about the area's beauty. Other people worked with Muir by asking the government to protect Yosemite. The next year, Yosemite became the third U.S national park. In his later years, Muir spent more time writing about his travels. He also led a twelve-year fight to protect a valley in Yosemite from being flooded by a dam. Even though he couldn't stop the dam from being built, the fight raised awareness about the protection of wild places. John Muir died on December 24, 1914.

57 John Muir was a founding father of the 59 conservation movement. He was one of the first people to call for taking action to protect wild places. His letters, essays and books of his adventures in nature, especially in the Sierra Nevada mountains of California, have been read by millions of people. For his outstanding accomplishments in preserving America's environment, he is known to many as the "Father of the National Parks" and "son of the wilderness."

어휘 influential 영향력이 있는, 영향력이 큰 naturalist 동식물 연구가, 박물학자 inspire (~이 ~할 마음을 먹게끔) 자극하다 wilderness 황야, 미개한 대자연, 드넓은 원시림 bring about 유발하다, 초래하다 Midwest 미국 중서부 pay one's way 빚지지 않고 살아가다, 자활하다 odd jobs 간간히 하는 이런저런 일 awareness (무엇의 중요성에 대한) 의식[관심] founding father 창시자, 설립자 conservation (자연 환경) 보호, (유적 등의) 보존 call for ~을 요구하다, ~을 필요로 하다 take action 조치를 취하다 outstanding 뛰어난, 걸출한 accomplishment 업적, 공적 preserve 지키다, 보존[보호]하다 legacy 유산 advocate 지지하다, 옹호하다 underfeed 충분한 음식을 주지 않다 contribute to ~에 기여하다 protest against ~에 대해서 항의하다 speak up for ~을 강력하게 변호하다 inflexible 융통성 없는, 완강한

53. 뮤어의 유산은 무엇인 것 같은가?
(a) 이민자들의 권리를 옹호하는 집단의 구성한 것
(b) 어린아이들 사이에서 과학과 생물학을 활성화시킨 것
(c) 미국의 아름다움에 관해 글을 쓴 것
(d) 자연 보호 인식을 고취시킨 것

첫 단락에서 뮤어가 남긴 말이 'inspired many people to make an effort to protect wilderness(많은 사람들로 하여금 자연을 지킬 노력을 하게 만들었다)'고 했으므로 정답은 (d)이다.

54. 뮤어와 그의 형제자매들은 왜 건강이 악화됐는가?
(a) 뮤어의 아버지가 돈이 충분히 없었기 때문에
(b) 뮤어에게 형제자매가 너무 많았기 때문에
(c) 일을 너무 많이 하고 잘 먹지 못했기 때문에
(d) 이들의 부모가 새 삶에 적응하느라 너무 바빴기 때문에

두 번째 단락에서 뮤어의 아버지가 자녀들을 'work long hours(장시간 동안 일하게)' 만들었고 'one small meal a day(하루에 단 한끼의 조촐한 식사)'만 허용하여 건강이 악화됐다 했으므로 정답은 (d)이다.

55. 왜 뮤어는 어렸을 때 일찍 일어났는가?
(a) 학업 계획을 진행해 나가기 위해
(b) 농장 일에 대해 더 많이 알기 위해
(c) 주들의 주 박람회에 가기 위해
(d) 지역의 산맥을 여행하기 위해

세 번째 단락에서 뮤어의 아버지가 뮤어가 'to have time to read(독서할 시간을 갖도록)' 그를 일찍 일어나게 허락했다고 했고, 이는 곧 '독서 → 공부(학업) 진행'과 같이 해석 가능하므로 정답은 (a)이다.

56. 뮤어는 요세미티가 국립 공원이 되는 데 어떻게 기여했는가?
(a) 정부 정책에 항의함으로써
(b) 요세미티에 대한 글을 씀으로써
(c) 토지 개발업자들과 싸움으로써
(d) 대통령에게 서신을 보냄으로써

네 번째 단락에서 뮤어가 요세미티에 대해 'published two articles(두 개의 기사를 발표했다)'고 했고, 이를 계기로 다른 사람들과 합심하여 요세미티를 국립 공원으로 만들었다고 했으므로 정답은 (b)이다.

57. 뮤어는 왜 보호 운동의 창시자로 불리는가?
(a) 미국 내에서 보호 운동에 참여했기 때문에
(b) 자연 보호를 강력히 변호한 최초의 인물이기 때문에
(c) 정부 정책에 가장 큰 영향력을 갖고 있었기 때문에
(d) 요세미티를 국립 공원으로 만들었기 때문에

마지막 단락에서 존 뮤어가 운동의 창시자라고 언급하며 그가 자연 지역 보호에 필요한 조치를 요구한 'one of the first people(최초의 사람들 중 한 명)'이라고 했으므로 정답은 (b)이다.

58. 글의 문맥에서, strict는 _____을 의미한다.
(a) inflexible (완강한)
(b) independent (독립적인)
(c) generous (너그러운)
(d) enjoyable (즐거운)

밑줄 친 strict는 '엄격한'이라는 뜻을 가진 형용사로서 보기 중 이와 일맥상통하는 것은 '(a) inflexible(완강한, 융통성이 없는)'이다.

59. 글의 문맥에서, conservation은 _____을 의미한다.
(a) communication (의사소통)
(b) freedom (자유)
(c) tradition (전통)
(d) preservation (보호)

밑줄 친 conservation은 '(자연 환경) 보호, (유적 등의) 보존'이라는 뜻을 가진 명사로서 보기 중 이와 일맥상통하는 것은 '(d) preservation(보호)'이다.

60-66 (사회) 유명 소셜 미디어에 대한 기사

TikTok IS NOW THE WORLD'S MOST DOWNLOADED APP

Originally called A.me and later Douyin, the app was launched by ByteDance in Beijing, China in September 2016. This led to the app's rebranding as TikTok in September 2017 and was later launched outside of China in international markets. By January 2018, it was already number one in several countries including Thailand. TikTok's software allows people to record videos, add favorite songs or audio already posted to the app, apply effects and edit them.

60 According to a global analysis compiled by Nikkei, TikTok has officially overtaken Facebook, Instagram, WhatsApp, and every other messaging platform to become the most downloaded social media app in the world. Until 2019, Facebook had held that title. However, TikTok has grown around the world at an 65 unprecedented rate, so that now it's taken over social media.

The most popular videos on Youtube currently stretch around ten minutes — a lot shorter than traditional TV or video entertainment. 61 TikTok has been paving the way for something completely new: very quick, snappy videos averaging between nine to fifteen seconds. In the beginning, most TikToks were quick, funny clips aimed at making you smile or laugh. However, its style has expanded to include educational clips, life hacks, mini cooking tutorials, and much more.

62 TikTok has even been inspiring other platforms to 66 mimic its style, after seeing its popularity boom — such as instagram Reels, or YouTube Shorts. Both of these have been pushed as additional short-video platforms alongside the main platform.

63 For a while last year, people didn't really think TikTok was going to make it in the US, after Donald Trump, the president of America had threatened to get rid of the app from the United States due to a national security risk. He said that the Chinese government had access to its user data. The company repeatedly denied the allegations. Trump's executive order was later withdrawn by the next president of the US, Joe Biden.

64 The pandemic served to provide a massive boost to TikTok's popularity, as not only were most people stuck at home with limited means of entertainment, but also because many famous artists were forced to cancel shows and tours, and decided to take to this platform instead.

처음에 A.me, 그리고 나중엔 Douyin이라 불렸던 이 앱은 2016년 9월 중국 베이징의 ByteDance에 의해 출시되었다. 이 앱은 2017년 9월 TikTok(틱톡)이라는 브랜드로 재탄생했고 이후 중국 외부 국제 시장에서 출시되었다. 2018년 1월경, 이 앱은 태국을 포함해 이미 많은 국가에서 1위를 차지했다. 틱톡의 소프트웨어는 사람들이 동영상을 촬영하여 앱에 이미 게시된 가장 좋아하는 노래나 오디오를 추가하고 여기에 효과를 더하고 편집하는 걸 가능하게 한다.

60 니케이에 따른 세계 분석에 의하면, 틱톡은 공식적으로 페이스북, 인스타그램, 왓츠앱, 그리고 모든 메시징 플랫폼을 앞질렀으며 세계에서 가장 많이 다운로드된 소셜 미디어 앱이 되었다. 2019년까지, 페이스북이 그 타이틀을 쥐고 있었다. 하지만, 틱톡은 전 세계에 걸쳐 65 전례 없는 속도로 성장했고, 현재 소셜 미디어를 장악하고 있다.

현재 유튜브에서 가장 인기 많은 영상들은 통상적인 TV나 비디오 오락물보다 훨씬 짧은 약 10분 길이이다. 61 틱톡은 평균 9초에서 15초 사이의 아주 빠르고 짧은 영상으로 완전히 새로운 길을 열었다. 처음에, 대부분의 틱톡들은 당신을 미소 짓거나 웃게 만들 목적의 빠르고 재미있는 영상들이었다. 하지만, 이젠 교육 영상, 라이프 핵스, 간단한 요리 튜토리얼 및 그 이상을 포함하는 것으로 확장됐다.

62 심지어 틱톡은 다른 플랫폼들이 이들의 인기 상승을 본 후 이들의 스타일을 66 따라 하게 만들었으며, 인스타그램 릴, 유튜브 쇼츠가 그 예이다. 이들은 모두 메인 플랫폼과 어깨를 나란히 하는 부가적인 짧은 영상 플랫폼이 되었다.

63 지난해 한동안, 미국 대통령인 도널드 트럼프가 국가 안보 위험 때문에 미국에서 앱을 제거하겠다는 엄포를 놓은 이후 사람들은 틱톡이 미국에서 성공하지 못할 것이라고 생각했다. 그는 중국 정부가 사용자들의 정보에 접근할 수 있다고 말했다. 회사는 이 주장을 지속적으로 부인했다. 트럼프의 행정 명령은 이후 다음 미국 대통령인 조 바이든에 의해 철회되었다.

64 세계적 유행병은 대부분의 사람들이 제한된 여가 수단과 함께 집에 갇혀 있게 되고 유명한 예술가들이 어쩔 수 없이 쇼와 투어를 취소하고 그 대신 이 플랫폼(틱톡)으로 옮겨 가기로 결정하게 되면서 틱톡의 인기가 어마어마하게 상승하는 데 기여했다.

어휘 rebrand 브랜드 이미지를 새롭게 하다 comply 따르다, 준수하다 overtake 추월하다, 앞지르다 unprecedented 전례[유례] 없는, 미증유의 take over (~을) 인계 받다; 탈취[장악]하다 pave the way 길을 닦다, 상황을 조성하다 snappy 짧고 분명한; 경쾌한, 재빠른 mimic 흉내 내다, 모방하다 popularity 인기 make it 성공하다 threaten 협박하다, 위협하다 allegation (특히 증거 없는) 주장, 혐의 executive order 행정 명령, 대통령령 withdraw 철회[취소]하다; 철수시키다 pandemic 세계적인 유행병 boost 격려, 힘; 증가 means 수단, 방법 investigate 수사하다, 조사하다 leak 새다, 누설되다 notable 주목할 만한, 유명한 interactive 상호 작용을 하는, 대화식의 pose (위험·문제 등을) 제기하다 unregulated 통제되어 있지 않은 distant 먼, 동떨어진 extraordinary 놀라운, 비범한, 이례적인

60. 니케이는 유명 소셜 미디어 플랫폼에 대해 최근 무엇을 조사했는가?
 (a) 새로운 소셜 미디어 플랫폼의 성장
 (b) 가짜 뉴스의 관리
 (c) 소셜 미디어 사용자들의 나이와 성별
 (d) 개인 정보 누출의 위험성

두 번째 단락에서 니케이가 'the most downloaded social media app in the world(세계에서 가장 많이 다운로드된 소셜 미디어 앱)'인 틱톡에 대해 이야기하고 있으므로 정답은 (a)이다.

61. 틱톡 영상의 주목할 만한 특징은 무엇인가?
 (a) 콘텐츠
 (b) 기술
 (c) 개방성
 (d) 길이

세 번째 단락에서 틱톡이 평균 9초에서 15초 사이의 'very quick, snappy videos(아주 빠르고 짧은 영상들)'을 선보이며 완전히 새로운 길을 열었다고 하고 있으므로 정답은 (d)이다.

62. 틱톡이 유튜브와 인스타그램 같은 다른 소셜 미디어 플랫폼에 어떻게 영향을 끼친 것 같은가?
 (a) 새로운 광고 캠페인의 출시
 (b) 짧은 영상 포맷의 창안
 (c) 플랫폼의 배치 변경
 (d) 좀 더 많은 대화 기능의 추가

네 번째 단락에서 틱톡이 다른 플랫폼들로 하여금 '인스타그램 릴, 유튜브 쇼츠'와 같은 'short-video platforms(짧은 영상 플랫폼)'을 만들게 하는 계기를 제공했다고 하고 있으므로 정답은 (b)이다.

63. 틱톡은 미국에서 어떤 문제점에 직면했는가?
 (a) 불법적인 약물 사용의 조장
 (b) 십대들 사이에서의 폭력 증가
 (c) 국가 안보 위험 문제의 제기
 (d) 통제되지 않은 시각적인 콘텐츠

다섯 번째 단락에서 미국 대통령인 도널드 트럼프가 'national security risk(국가 안보 위험)' 때문에 틱톡을 미국에서 제거하겠다고 엄포를 놓았다고 했으므로 정답은 (c)이다.

64. 세계적 유행병 상황에서 틱톡에게 무슨 일이 일어날 것인가?
 (a) 더더욱 확장될 것으로 예상된다.
 (b) 사람들이 더 긴 영상을 올리게 만들어야만 할 것이다.
 (c) 정부 기관과 함께 일할 걸로 예상된다.
 (d) 현재의 인기를 잃고 사라지게 될 것이다.

마지막 단락에서 유행병이 'massive boost to TikTok's popularity(틱톡의 인기가 어마어마하게 상승)'하는 데 기여했다고 했고, 따라서 이로 인해 틱톡의 영향력이 더 확장될 것이라 볼 수 있으므로 정답은 (a)이다.

65. 글의 문맥에서, unprecedented는 _____을 의미한다.
 (a) distant (동떨어진)
 (b) available (이용 가능한)
 (c) present (현재의)
 (d) extraordinary (이례적인)

밑줄 친 unprecedented는 '전례[유례] 없는'이라는 뜻의 형용사로서 보기 중 이와 일맥상통하는 것은 '(d) extraordinary(이례적인, 놀라운, 비범한)'이다.

66. 글의 문맥에서, mimic은 _____을 의미한다.
 (a) continue (계속하다)
 (b) protect (보호하다)
 (c) allow (허용하다)
 (d) imitate (모방하다)

밑줄 친 mimic은 '흉내 내다, 모방하다'라는 뜻의 동사로서 보기 중 이와 일맥상통하는 것은 '(d) imitates(모방하다, 따라 하다)'이다.

67-73 (자연) 싱크홀에 대한 설명글

SINKHOLES
싱크홀

67 Sinkholes are pits in the ground that form in areas where water gathers without external drainage. A sinkhole forms in the ground when the dirt and rocks wash away and there is nothing underneath the ground anymore to support it. **68** Sinkholes mainly occur as water drains below ground. It can **72** dissolve subterranean caverns, particularly in areas where the bedrock is made of water-soluble evaporate rocks such as salt or limestone.

67 Sinkholes can be natural or man-made. **69** Natural sinkholes occur due to erosion or underground water. They start developing a long time before it actually appears. There is water continually seeping in between the mud, rocks and minerals, as it makes its way down to the ground water reservoirs. As this happens, the water slowly erodes the rocks and minerals. Sometimes the flow of water increases to the point where it washes away the underground structure of the land. And when the structure becomes too weak to support the surface of the earth, it collapses and opens up a hole. This is how sinkholes are formed. Sometimes sinkholes can open suddenly and swallow buildings, cars, and people.

70 In 2010, one of the most **73** devastating sinkholes in recent times hit Guatemala City. It was particularly bad because the sinkhole was formed in the middle of the busy city. It swallowed a three-story factory killing 15 people. The hole was more than 100 meters deep – deep enough to swallow two Statues of Liberty. The sinkhole was caused by a number of factors including an influx of water from storms and leakage from a local sewage pipe.

Underground mines can also cause sinkholes. Near one Russian city, underground water filled an old mine. The bedrock of salt began dissolving. In 1986, a huge sinkhole opened up. It grew to 238 meters deep and covered more than 25 football fields. It is still growing and new sinkholes are opening up. Hundreds of people have had to leave their homes. To be safe, the entire city may need to move. The deepest sinkhole in the world is located in China. It is Xiaozhai Tiankeng, which literally means 'heavenly pit.' This particular example in the Chongqing district is a staggering 662 meters deep and 626 meters wide.

The Sarisarinama sinkholes in Venezuela were discovered in 1961. Scientists have discovered plants and animals inside that are found nowhere else. **71** A sinkhole can be stopped if it is found in time. If someone finds a sinkhole starting, people can put grout into the hole, and it can cause the sinkhole to be stopped. This can help to save areas from a lot of damage.

67 싱크홀은 물이 모여 외부 배출이 안 되는 곳에서 형성되는 땅속 구덩이이다. 싱크홀은 먼지와 암반이 쓸려 내려가 지면 아래에 이를 지탱할 것이 아무것도 없게 됐을 경우 땅속에 형성된다. **68** 싱크홀은 주로 지면 아래로 물이 빠지면서 발생한다. 이것은 특히 소금이나 석회암 같은 수용성 증발암으로 된 기반암이 있는 곳에서 지하 동굴을 **72** 용해시킬 수 있다.

67 싱크홀은 자연적일 수도, 인공적일 수도 있다. **69** 천연 싱크홀은 침식이나 지하수로 인해 발생한다. 이들은 실질적으로 눈에 보이게 되기 전까지 긴 시간 형성을 시작한다. 진흙, 암반, 광물 사이에 끊임없이 물이 스며들어 지하수 저수지로 흘러간다. 이렇게 되면, 물은 서서히 암반과 광물을 침식시킨다. 가끔 물의 흐름이 땅의 지하 구조물이 씻겨 내려갈 정도로 증가한다. 그리고 구조물이 지구 표면을 지탱하기에 너무 약해지게 되면, 이것은 붕괴되어 구멍을 개방하게 된다. 이것이 바로 싱크홀이 형성되는 방법이다. 일부 싱크홀들은 갑작스럽게 개방되어 건물, 차량, 그리고 사람들을 집어삼킬 수 있다.

70 2010년도에, 근래에 있어 가장 **73** 파괴적이었던 싱크홀 중 하나가 과테말라 시티를 강타했다. 이것은 싱크홀이 혼잡한 도시 중앙에 형성됐었기 때문에 특히나 심각했다. 이것은 15명의 사상자를 내며 3층 높이의 공장을 집어삼켰다. 구멍은 깊이가 100미터 이상이었고, 자유의 여신상 두 개를 집어삼키기에 충분했다. 이 싱크홀은 태풍으로 인해 밀어닥친 물과 지역 하수관의 누수를 포함한 몇 가지 요인으로 인해 야기되었다.

지하 광산 또한 싱크홀을 야기할 수 있다. 한 러시아 도시 근처에서, 지하수가 오래된 광산을 메웠다. 소금으로 된 기반암이 용해되기 시작했다. 1986년도에, 거대한 싱크홀이 개방되었다. 이것은 238미터 깊이였고 축구장 25개 이상을 덮는 수준이었다. 이것은 여전히 성장 중이고 새로운 싱크홀들이 개방되고 있다. 수백 명의 사람들이 자신들의 집을 떠나야 했다. 안전을 위해서, 도시 전체가 이사를 가야 할지도 모른다. 세계에서 가장 깊은 싱크홀은 중국에 위치해 있다. 이것은 '샤오자이텐쿵'인데, 문자 그대로 '천국의 구덩이'를 의미한다. 충칭 지구에 있는 이 특별한 사례는 깊이가 662미터이고 너비가 626미터로 믿기 힘든 수준이다.

베네수엘라에 있는 '사리사리나마' 싱크홀은 1961년에 발견되었다. 과학자들은 그 어디에서도 찾을 수 없는 식물과 동물을 내부에서 발견했다. 싱크홀은 제때 발견되면 이를 막을 수 있다. **71** 형성을 시작한 싱크홀을 찾게 되면, 사람들이 구멍 안에 회반죽을 넣어 이것이 싱크홀의 성장을 막을 수 있다. 이것은 수많은 피해로부터 지역들을 구제하는 데 도움이 된다.

어휘 pit (크고 깊은) 구덩이 drainage 배수 (시설), 하수, 오수 wash away ~을 유실되게 하다[쓸어 가다] drain 물을 빼내다[빠지다] dissolve 녹다[녹이다], 용해되다[시키다] subterranean cavern 지하 동굴 bedrock (튼튼한) 기반; 기반암 water-soluble 물에 용해되는, 수용성의 limestone 석회석[암] man-made 사람이 만든, 인공[인조]의 erosion 부식, 침식 underground water 지하수 seep 스미다, 배다 ground water 지하수 reservoir 저수지 erode 침식시키다, 약화시키다 collapse 붕괴되다, 무너지다 devastating 대단히 파괴적인, 엄청난 손상을 가하는 influx 밀어닥침, 밀려듦 leakage 누출, 새어나감 sewage pipe 하수관 underground mine 지하 광산 staggering 충격적인, 믿기 어려운 grout 회반죽 terrain 지형, 지역 topsoil 표토 glacier 빙하 waste disposal 폐기물 처리 distinctive 독특한 destructive 파괴적인

67. 싱크홀은 무엇인가?
  (a) 사람이 만든 관광지
  (b) 자연적이고 인공적인 지세(지형)
  (c) 특정 장소에서의 지리적 암반 형성
  (d) 과테말라 시티의 자연 현상의 명칭

첫 단락에서 싱크홀은 'pits in the grounds(땅속 구덩이)'라고 했고, 두 번째 단락에서 이것이 'natural or man-made(자연적이거나 인공적)'일 수 있다고 했으므로 정답은 (b)이다.

68. 어느 지역에서 싱크홀이 형성될 가능성이 높은가?
  (a) 수용성 기반암이 있는 장소
  (b) 표토가 적은 장소
  (c) 빙하가 있는 장소
  (d) 배수가 잘 안 되는 장소

첫 단락에서 싱크홀은 특히 'water-soluble evaporate rocks(수용성 증발암)'으로 된 기반암이 있는 곳에서 지면 아래로 빠진 물이 지하 동굴을 용해시키며 형성된다고 했으므로 정답은 (a)이다.

69. 싱크홀 형성에 가장 큰 원인이 되는 요소는 무엇인가?
  (a) 도시의 지면에 구멍을 뚫는 것
  (b) 수용성 암반과 함께 있는 지하수
  (c) 규제 받지 않는 폐기물 처리
  (d) 산꼭대기의 녹은 눈

첫 단락에서 '수용성 암반'이 있는 곳이 싱크홀이 형성되는 장소라 했고, 두 번째 단락에선 위와 같은 장소에서 침식이나 'underground water(지하수)'로 인해 싱크홀이 생긴다고 했으므로 정답은 (b)이다.

70. 과테말라 시티에 있는 씽크홀이 왜 대단히 파괴적이었는가?
  (a) 시간이 지나며 서서히 형성됐기 때문에
  (b) 한동안 메꿔지지 않은 채 있었기 때문에
  (c) 도시 중앙에서 발생했기 때문에
  (d) 일꾼들이 덮지 않고 내버려 뒀기 때문에

세 번째 단락에서 과테말라 시티의 씽크홀이 'in the middle of the busy city(혼잡한 도시의 중앙에)' 형성되어 특히나 매우 심각했다고 서술하고 있으므로 정답은 (c)이다.

71. 싱크홀을 찾게 되면 무엇을 할 필요가 있는가?
  (a) 이를 즉시 메꾼다
  (b) 정부 당국에 알린다
  (c) 스스로 조사한다
  (d) 연못을 만들기 위해 물을 넣는다

마지막 단락에서 싱크홀을 찾았을 경우 'put grout into the hole(구멍에 회반죽을 채워 넣으면)' 싱크홀을 막을 수 있다고 했고, 이는 결국 싱크홀을 메꾸라는 말로 해석 가능하므로 정답은 (a)이다.

72. 글의 문맥에서, dissolve는 _____을 의미한다.
  (a) solve (해결하다)
  (b) prove (입증하다)
  (c) depart (떠나다)
  (d) melt (녹이다)

밑줄 친 dissolve는 '녹다[녹이다], 용해하다[용해시키다]'라는 뜻의 동사로서 보기 중 이와 일맥상통하는 것은 '(d) melt(녹다, 녹이다)'이다.

73. 글의 문맥에서, devastating은 _____을 의미한다.
  (a) distinctive (독특한)
  (b) represent (대표하다)
  (c) increasing (증가하는)
  (d) destructive (파괴적인)

밑줄 친 devastating은 '대단히 파괴적인, 엄청난 손상을 가하는'이라는 뜻의 형용사로서 보기 중 이와 일맥상통하는 것은 '(d) destructive(파괴적인)'이다.

74-80 (추천서) 대학 장학 프로그램 추천서

May 15, 2020
College Scholars Program
University of Tennessee
354 Jefferson Rd.
Danville, NC 34098

To Whom It May Concern,

74 It is with much enthusiasm that I recommend John B. Bloomberg for inclusion in the College Scholars Program at the University of Tennessee.

I had the pleasure of teaching John in his 11th grade honors English class at Morristown-Hamblen High school. From the first day of class, John impressed me with his ability to articulate difficult concepts and texts, his sensitivity to the nuances within literature, and his passion for reading, writing, and creative expressions — both in and out of the classroom. John displayed a level of creativity, wit, an analytical thought that is quite **79** rare among high school students.

75 His writing and research skills are excellent. For his major essay project in AP English, he researched and wrote a remarkable study of visual imagery in the work of Ron Padgett, a contemporary American poet. **76** John is ready to assume and excel in upper division classwork, and possesses the self-motivation to successfully create and **80** execute an independent course of honors study.

Throughout the year John was an active participant in our discussions, and he always supported his peers. His caring nature and personality allowed him to work well with others in a team setting, as he always respects others' opinions even when they differ from his own.

77 John also demonstrated leadership skills in a school band and the Student Council. He was our band's drum major for two years and served as Vice President of the Student Council and Editor of our high school yearbook.

I am certain that John is going to continue to do great and creative things in his future. He is talented, caring, intuitive, dedicated, and focused in his pursuits. John is truly a stand-out individual who will impress everyone he meets.

78 Please let me know if I can provide any more information to strengthen John's candidacy for the College Scholars Program.

Sincerely,
Peter Evans

어휘 enthusiasm 열정, 열의 inclusion 포함; 포함된 사람[것] impress 깊은 인상을 주다 articulate 분명히 표현하다[설명하다] sensitivity 세심함; 감성; 예민함 nuance 미묘한 차이, 뉘앙스 analytical 분석적인 rare 드문, 희귀한 visual imagery 시각적 심상 용법 contemporary 동시대의; 현대의, 당대의 assume 추정[상정]하다; 맡다; 띠다[취하다] excel 뛰어나다, 탁월하다 execute 처형[사형]하다; 실행[수행]하다 peer 또래, 동년배 caring 보살피는, 배려하는 demonstrate 실례를 들어가며 보여주다; 보여주다, 발휘하다 drum major 지휘자, 고적대장 yearbook 연감, 연보 intuitive 직관력이 있는 pursuit 추적, 추격; 추구; 직업, 일 candidacy 입후보, 출마 inquire 묻다, 알아보다 persistent 끈질긴; 끊임없이 지속[반복]되는 respectful 존경심을 보이는, 공손한 uncommon 흔치 않은, 드문

74. 이메일의 목적은 무엇인가?
(a) 대학 장학생 프로그램에 대해 문의하기 위해
(b) 테네시 대학의 일자리를 제안하기 위해
(c) 프로그램에 대해 좀 더 많은 정보를 요청하기 위해
(d) 학생을 프로그램에 추천하기 위해

첫 단락에서 'Collage Scholars Program(대학 장학생 프로그램)'에 'recommend John B. Bloomberg(존 B 블룸버그를 추천하기)'를 위해 이 서신을 쓰고 있다는 사실을 알 수 있으므로 정답은 (d)이다.

75. 존은 무엇으로 가장 많은 칭찬을 받는가?
(a) 시에 대한 창의적인 연구 작업
(b) 수업에서의 예의 바른 태도
(c) AP 수업에서의 끊임없는 노력
(d) 교사들에 대한 공손한 태도

세 번째 단락에서 존이 'writing and research skills(글쓰기와 연구 능력)'이 탁월하고 'contemporary American poet(현대 미국 시인)'인 존 파젯에 대한 논문도 잘 썼다고 말하고 있으므로 정답은 (a)이다.

76. 피터 에반스는 왜 존이 프로그램에서 잘할 거라고 생각하는가?
(a) 그가 대학 수준의 공부에 준비되어 있기 때문에
(b) 대학에 갈 학점이 충분하기 때문에
(c) 곧 고등학교를 졸업할 것이기 때문에
(d) 대학교에 갈 나이가 충분히 되었기 때문에

세 번째 단락에서 존이 'upper division classwork(상위 분할 학교 수업)'을 맡아 뛰어난 능력을 발휘할 준비가 돼 있다고 했고, 이는 곧 '상위 수업 → 대학 수업'으로 해석 가능하므로 정답은 (a)이다.

77. 피터는 왜 학교 밴드와 학생회에서 존이 맡은 역할을 언급했는가?
(a) 존이 드럼을 잘 친다는 것을 보여주기 위해
(b) 존이 유명한 학생이었다는 것을 보여주기 위해
(c) 존이 리더십 또한 갖추고 있음을 보여주기 위해
(d) 존이 이력을 위해 정말 노력했음을 보여주기 위해

다섯 번째 단락에서 존이 학교 밴드와 학생회에서 'demonstrated leadership skills(리더십 능력을 발휘했다)'고 하면서 그가 맡았던 역할에 대해 이야기하고 있으므로 정답은 (c)이다.

78. 존을 지지하기 위해 피터는 무엇을 기꺼이 하겠는가?
(a) 동료들에게 추가적인 추천서를 요청할 것이다.
(b) 대학에 연락해 존의 입학을 확실시할 것이다.
(c) 다른 학교들에 좀 더 많은 이메일을 쓸 것이다.
(d) 존의 업적에 대해 더 많은 정보를 제공할 것이다

마지막 단락에서 존이 후보자가 되는 데 'any more information(더 필요한 정보)'를 제공해도 되는지 여부를 묻고 있고, 이는 곧 존에 대해 향후 더 많은 정보를 제공할 의지가 있음을 뜻하므로 정답은 (d)이다.

79. 글의 문맥에서, rare는 _____을 의미한다.
(a) slow (느린)
(b) engaged (관련된)
(c) uncommon (드문)
(d) undercooked (설익은)

밑줄 친 rare는 '드문, 희귀한'이라는 뜻을 가진 형용사로서 보기 중 이와 일맥상통하는 것은 '(c) uncommon(드문, 흔치 않은)'이다.

80. 글의 문맥에서, execute는 _____을 의미한다.
(a) set up (설립하다)
(b) carry out (수행하다)
(c) get rid of (제거하다)
(d) take over (인수하다)

밑줄 친 execute는 '실행하다, 수행하다'라는 뜻을 가진 동사로서 보기 중 이와 일맥상통하는 것은 '(b) carry out(수행하다)'이다.

Actual Test 02 / Vocab 주요 어휘 총정리

Actual Test 02에 등장했던 주요 어휘를 한눈에 훑어보며 정리해 보도록 합시다.
모르는 어휘가 있을 경우 박스(□)에 체크(∨) 표시를 한 뒤 재차 암기하도록 하세요.

- ☐ influential 영향력이 있는, 영향력이 큰
- ☐ inspire (~이 ~할 마음을 먹게끔) 자극하다
- ☐ bring about 유발하다, 초래하다
- ☐ pay one's way 빚지지 않고 살아가다, 자활하다
- ☐ awareness (무엇의 중요성에 대한) 의식[관심]
- ☐ founding father 창시자, 설립자
- ☐ conservation (자연 환경) 보호, (유적 등의) 보존
- ☐ call for ~을 요구하다, ~을 필요로 하다
- ☐ take action 조치를 취하다
- ☐ outstanding 뛰어난, 걸출한
- ☐ accomplishment 업적, 공적
- ☐ preserve 지키다, 보존[보호]하다
- ☐ legacy 유산
- ☐ advocate 지지하다, 옹호하다
- ☐ contribute to ~에 기여하다
- ☐ protest against ~에 대해서 항의하다
- ☐ speak up for ~을 강력하게 변호하다
- ☐ inflexible 융통성 없는, 완강한
- ☐ comply 따르다, 준수하다
- ☐ overtake 추월하다, 앞지르다
- ☐ unprecedented 전례[유례] 없는, 미증유의
- ☐ take over (~을) 인계 받다; 탈취[장악]하다
- ☐ pave the way 길을 닦다, 상황을 조성하다
- ☐ mimic 흉내 내다, 모방하다
- ☐ popularity 인기
- ☐ make it 성공하다
- ☐ threaten 협박하다, 위협하다
- ☐ allegation (특히 증거 없는) 주장, 혐의
- ☐ withdraw 철회[취소]하다; 철수시키다
- ☐ boost 격려, 힘; 증가
- ☐ means 수단, 방법
- ☐ investigate 수사하다, 조사하다
- ☐ leak 새다, 누설되다
- ☐ notable 주목할 만한, 유명한
- ☐ interactive 상호 작용을 하는, 대화식의

- ☐ pose (위협·문제 등을) 제기하다
- ☐ unregulated 통제되어 있지 않은
- ☐ extraordinary 놀라운, 비범한, 이례적인
- ☐ wash away ~을 유실되게 하다[쓸어 가다]
- ☐ drain 물을 빼내다[빠지다]
- ☐ dissolve 녹다[녹이다], 용해되다[시키다]
- ☐ man-made 사람이 만든, 인공[인조]의
- ☐ seep 스미다, 배다
- ☐ erode 침식시키다, 약화시키다
- ☐ collapse 붕괴되다, 무너지다
- ☐ devastating 대단히 파괴적인, 엄청난 손상을 가하는
- ☐ leakage 누출, 새어나감
- ☐ staggering 충격적인, 믿기 어려운
- ☐ distinctive 독특한
- ☐ destructive 파괴적인
- ☐ inclusion 포함; 포함된 사람[것]
- ☐ impress 깊은 인상을 주다
- ☐ articulate 분명히 표현하다[설명하다]
- ☐ sensitivity 세심함; 감성; 예민함
- ☐ analytical 분석적인
- ☐ rare 드문, 희귀한
- ☐ contemporary 동시대의; 현대의, 당대의
- ☐ assume 추정[상정]하다; 맡다; 띠다[취하다]
- ☐ excel 뛰어나다, 탁월하다
- ☐ execute 처형[사형]하다; 실행[수행]하다
- ☐ peer 또래, 동년배
- ☐ caring 보살피는, 배려하는
- ☐ demonstrate 실례를 들어가며 보여주다; 발휘하다
- ☐ intuitive 직관력이 있는
- ☐ pursuit 추적, 추격; 추구; 직업, 일
- ☐ candidacy 입후보, 출마
- ☐ inquire 묻다, 알아보다
- ☐ persistent 끈질긴; 끊임없이 지속[반복]되는
- ☐ respectful 존경심을 보이는, 공손한
- ☐ uncommon 흔치 않은, 드문

Reading and Vocabulary Section
Actual Test 03

▶▶ 정답 & 나의 점수 확인

테스트 날짜: _____월 _____일 / 테스트 점수: _____

53 (a) 54 (a) 55 (a) 56 (d) 57 (d) 58 (b) 59 (a) 60 (c) 61 (d) 62 (c) 63 (a) 64 (b) 65 (c) 66 (b)
67 (a) 68 (c) 69 (d) 70 (b) 71 (a) 72 (c) 73 (a) 74 (d) 75 (c) 76 (c) 77 (d) 78 (c) 79 (a) 80 (b)

▶▶ 출제 경향 & 흐름 파악

지피지기면 백전백승! 출제 경향과 흐름을 한눈에 파악해 봅시다. 출제된 지문이 어떤 종류의 글이었는지, 각 지문과 관련해 어떤 종류의 문제가 출제되었는지 아래의 표를 보며 정리해 보세요.

(인물) 유명한 소설가에 대한 소개글	53	집필한 책의 정보	(과학) 지구의 생물 다양성에 대한 설명글	67	생물 다양성의 정의
	54	집필의 영감이 된 원천		68	생물 다양성이 위험에 처한 이유
	55	다른 곳으로 이사 간 이유		69	hotspot의 정의
	56	다른 직업을 권유 받은 이유		70	생태계가 가진 특성
	57	설립한 단체의 목적		71	생물 다양성의 향후 전망
	58	어휘 문제: precocious		72	어휘 문제: maintain
	59	어휘 문제: solace		73	어휘 문제: jeopardy
(사회) 흑인 인권 운동에 대한 기사	60	BLM 운동의 목적	(안내) 주문 방법에 대한 안내 서신	74	이메일의 목적
	61	BLM 운동가들의 활동 방법		75	가격을 확인할 수 있는 방법
	62	흑인 사망 사건의 문제점		76	영구 계정을 얻게 되는 시기
	63	BLM 운동이 화제가 된 이유		77	계정 활성화에 필요한 조건
	64	BLM 운동의 주된 전략		78	세관에 연락해야 하는 이유
	65	어휘 문제: unjust		79	어휘 문제: temporary
	66	어휘 문제: trigger		80	어휘 문제: quota

53-59 (인물) 유명한 소설가에 대한 소개글

J.K. ROWLING

Joanne Rowling is the well renowned British author of the Harry Potter book series. 53 The Harry Potter series has gained worldwide attention and critical acclaim, and has even been made into a film series by the production house Warner Bros. The books have sold more than 400 million copies.

Joanne was born to Peter James and Anne Rowling in Gloucester, England. From an early age, she was fond of making up stories that she narrated to her sister and grandmother. She wrote her first book at the age of six— a story about a rabbit, called 'Rabbit.' At just eleven, she wrote her first novel— about seven cursed diamonds and the people who owned them.

She attended St. Michael's Primary school whose headmaster at that time, Alfred Dunn, is said to be the basis for the character Albus Dumbledore in her books. 54 Rowling claims that the 58 precocious character Hermione Granger is modeled after herself and her years at Wyedean College and her old school friend Sean Harris, who owned a turquoise Ford Anglia like in the book, is the basis for the character Ron Weasley.

After graduating with a degree in French and Classics from the University of Exeter, Rowling moved to London to work as a bilingual research assistant for Amnesty International. Although she began work on the Harry Potter series in 1990 the first book wasn't published. She married the father of her child. 55 After her marriage ended, Rowling moved to Scotland where she decided to spend all her energy writing the first Harry Potter book.

Rowling did not have an easy time becoming successful. She struggled with rejection at 12 different publishing houses. She found the time to write in between being a single parent to her young daughter and found 59 solace in her writing. 56 She was even dissuaded by her editor to find a full-time job other than writing to earn money. She proved everyone wrong with the success of her first book.

The book was first published in 1997, under the name J.K. Rowling in England and was published in the US under a different title, Harry Potter and the Sorcerer's Stone. Six further titles followed in the Harry Potter Series, each achieving record-breaking success.

57 J.K Rowling started a non-profit organization known as 'Lumos,' to aid orphaned children and children in trouble to find a loving home. Lumos is committed to making family care for all children a global reality by 2050.

어휘 well renowned 유명한, 잘 알려진 critical acclaim 비평가의 절찬[호평] be fond of ~을 좋아하다 narrate 이야기를 하다[들려주다] cursed 저주받은 primary school 초등학교 headmaster 교장 precocious 조숙한, 아이 같지 않은 model after ~을 본떠서 만들다 turquoise 터키석[옥]; 청록색 Classics 서양 고전학 bilingual 이중 언어 사용자 Amnesty International 국제 사면 위원회 struggle with ~로 고심하다[씨름하다] rejection 거절; 배제, 폐기 publishing house 출판사 find the time 시간을 내다 in between 중간에, 틈에 solace 위안, 위로 dissuade ~을 설득[만류]하다 record-breaking 기록을 깨는 be committed to ~에 헌신[전념]하다 adapt 맞추다[조정하다]; 개작하다[각색하다] flop 실패작 indifferent 냉담한, 무관심한 comfort 위로, 편안함 isolation 소외, 고립 solidarity 단결, 결속, 연대

53. 해리 포터 시리즈는 무엇인가?
 (a) 흥행작이자 영화 시리즈로 각색되었다
 (b) 실패작이자 큰 재정적 손실을 야기했다
 (c) 학교에서 가르치는 걸작
 (d) 재정적인 성공을 거두었으나 문학적 가치는 없다

첫 단락에서 해리 포터가 'worldwide attention(세계적인 관심)'과 비평가들의 호평을 받고 'made into a film series(영화 시리즈로 만들어지기)'까지 했다고 설명돼 있으므로 정답은 (a)이다.

54. 글에 따르면, 롤링은 어디에서 이야기에 대한 영감을 얻었는가?
 (a) 그녀 자신과 주변 사람들로부터
 (b) 그녀가 어릴 때 읽었던 책으로부터
 (c) 그녀가 봤던 영화로부터
 (d) 그녀의 상상력으로부터

세 번째 단락에서 롤링이 한 여성 캐릭터를 'modeled after herself(자신을 본떠 만들었으며)' 한 남성 캐릭터의 시초가 'her old friend(그녀의 오래된 친구)'라고 했으므로 (a)가 답임을 유추할 수 있다.

55. 롤링은 왜 스코틀랜드로 이사를 갔는가?
 (a) 자신의 책 시리즈에 집중하기 위해
 (b) 자신과 자신의 아이를 책임질 수 있도록 일하기 위해
 (c) 지역 신문을 위한 글을 쓰기 위해
 (d) 다음에 무엇을 할지 생각하기 위해

네 번째 단락에서 롤링이 스코틀랜드로 이사를 가서 'writing the first Harry Potter book(첫 번째 해리 포터 책을 쓰는 것)'에 모든 에너지를 쏟기로 결심했다고 했으므로 정답은 (a)이다.

56. 편집자는 왜 그녀에게 다른 직업을 구하라고 말했는가?
 (a) 그녀의 글을 전혀 좋아하지 않았기 때문에
 (b) 그녀가 글을 잘 쓰지 못했기 때문에
 (c) 그가 일에 있어 다른 사람을 고용했기 때문에
 (d) 그녀가 글쓰기로 돈을 벌지 못했기 때문에

다섯 번째 단락에서 편집자가 'other than writing to earn money(돈을 벌기 위해 글을 쓰는 것 외에)' 다른 직업을 찾아보라고 권했고, 이는 곧 롤링이 글쓰기로 돈을 벌지 못했음을 시사하므로 정답은 (d)이다.

57. Lumos의 목적은 무엇이었는가?
 (a) 어린 마술사들을 교육시키는 것
 (b) 아이들이 책을 읽도록 격려하는 것
 (c) 그녀의 책을 위한 특별한 혜택을 제공하는 것
 (d) 부모가 없는 아이들을 돕는 것

마지막 단락에서 Lumos가 'orphaned children(고아인 아이들)' 및 화목한 가정을 찾는 데 어려움이 있는 아이들을 돕는 비영리 단체라고 설명돼 있으므로 정답은 (d)이다.

58. 글의 문맥에서, precocious는 _____을 의미한다.
 (a) focused (집중적인)
 (b) intelligent (총명한)
 (c) indifferent (냉담한)
 (d) stunt (멍청한 행동)

밑줄 친 precocious는 '조숙한, 아이 같지 않은'이라는 뜻의 형용사이며, 이는 곧 '어른스럽게 총명한'이라는 의미로 볼 수 있기 때문에 정답은 (b)이다.

59. 글의 문맥에서, solace는 _____을 의미한다.
 (a) comfort (위로)
 (b) isolation (고립)
 (c) loneliness (외로움)
 (d) solidarity (결속)

밑줄 친 solace는 '위안, 위로'라는 뜻의 명사로서 보기 중 이와 일맥상통하는 것은 '(a) comfort (위로, 편안함)'이다.

BLACK LIVES MATTER

흑인의 목숨도 소중하다

60 Black lives matter, international social movement, formed in the United States in 2013, dedicated to fighting racism and anti-Black violence, especially in the form of police brutality. The name Black Lives Matter signals condemnation of the 65 unjust killings of Black people by police. Supporters point to the fact that black people are much more likely to be shot by police in the US. They say that in the US and many other countries, they also suffer many other forms of discrimination. They want action to address unequal treatment and oppression that goes all the way back to the era of slavery, but which continues today.

BLM activists have held large and influential protests in cities across the United States as well as internationally. 61 BLM was co-founded as an online movement using the hashtag BlackLivesMatter on social media by three Black community organizers – Patrisse Khan-Cullors, Alicia Garza, and Opal Tometi. 62 They formed BML after Trayvon Martin, an unarmed Black teenager, in Sanford, Florida, was shot and killed by a Neighborhood-watch volunteer in February 2012.

63 The BLM movement expanded in 2014 after the police killings of an unarmed Black man, Eric Garner. Garner died after a white police officer held him in a prolonged illegal choke hold, which was captured in a video taken by a bystander. Large protests captured national and international attention.

In 2020, George Floyd, an unarmed Black man, was killed by a white police officer who knelt on his neck for several minutes. Following the death of Mr. Floyd, the term "defund the police" made headlines. Cities including Minneapolis, Portland, Philadelphia and Seattle have started shifting budgets away from police and into areas like schools and housing. It 66 triggered massive demonstrations in cities throughout the United States and across the globe. In the UK, demonstrations drew attention to the UK's colonial past and saw statues of people linked to the slave trade removed.

The Black Live Matter movement seeks to draw attention to the many ways in which Black people are treated unfairly in society and the ways in which institutions, laws, and policies help to perpetuate that unfairness. 64 The movement has fought racism through nonviolent protests.

60 '흑인의 목숨도 소중하다'는 인종 차별 행위 및 흑인을 적대시하는 폭력, 특히 경찰의 잔혹한 행위에 대해 싸우는 데 전념하는 2013년 미국에서 형성된 국제적인 사회적 움직임이다. '흑인의 목숨도 소중하다'라는 문구는 경찰에 의한 흑인들의 65 부당한 죽음에 대한 비난을 시사한다. 지지자들은 미국에서 흑인들이 경찰에게 총살당할 확률이 더 크다는 사실을 지적한다. 이들은 미국 및 다른 많은 나라에서 수많은 형태의 다른 차별들로 고통당한다고 말한다. 이들은 오늘날에도 지속 중인 노예 제도 시절로 거슬러 올라가는 불공평한 대우 및 억압을 심각히 다루길 원한다.

BLM 운동가들은 미국 전역의 도시에서, 그리고 국제적으로 영향력 있는 대규모 시위를 벌였다. 61 BLM 운동은 파트리스 칸 쿨러스, 알리샤 가르자, 오팔 토메티라는 세 명의 흑인 지역 조직자들이 BlackLivesMatter라는 해시태그를 소셜 미디어에 사용하는 온라인 움직임과 함께 생겨났다. 62 이들은 2012년 2월 비무장 상태였던 흑인 십대인 트레이번 마틴이 플로리다 샌포드에서 지역 경비 자원자에게 총을 맞고 사망한 이후 BLM을 조직했다.

63 BLM 운동은 비무장 상태의 흑인 에릭 가머가 경찰에게 살해당한 이후 2014년에 확장되었다. 가머는 백인 경찰관이 오랜 시간 그의 목을 불법적으로 조르며 잡고 있었던 것으로 인해 사망했고, 이는 지나가던 행인에 의해 동영상으로 촬영되었다. 대규모 시위가 국가적, 그리고 국제적인 관심을 이끌어냈다.

2020년, 비무장 상태였던 조지 플로이드는 백인 경찰관이 수분 동안 그의 목에 무릎을 꿇고 앉아 있던 것으로 인해 사망했다. 플로이드가 사망한 이후, "경찰의 예산을 삭감하라"는 문구가 대대적으로 보도되었다. 미니애폴리스, 포틀랜드, 필라델피아 및 시애틀을 포함한 도시에선 경찰의 예산을 학교와 주택으로 옮기기 시작했다. 이것은 미국 및 세계 각지에 있는 도시에서 광범위한 시위를 66 촉발했다. 영국에선, 시위가 과거 영국 식민 통치 시대에 대한 관심을 불러일으켰고 노예 무역과 관련이 있던 사람들의 동상이 철거되는 장면을 목도하게 했다.

'흑인의 목숨도 소중하다'라는 운동이 추구하는 것은 흑인들이 사회에서 불공평한 대우를 받는 수많은 상황들, 그리고 기관, 법망, 정책이 불평등을 지속시키는 상황에 관심을 가져오는 것이다. 64 이 운동은 비폭력 주의 시위자들을 통해 인종 차별에 맞서 싸워 왔다.

어휘 dedicated to ~에 전념[헌신]하는 racism 인종 차별 (주의/행위) brutality 잔인성, 야만성, 무자비; 잔인한 행위, 만행 condemnation 비난 unjust 부당한, 불공평한 oppression 압박, 압제, 억압, 탄압 protest 항의 (운동), 시위 unarmed 무기를 가지고 있지 않은, 비무장의 prolonged 오래 계속되는, 장기적인 choke hold 목 조르기 bystander 구경꾼, 행인 defund 재원을 철회하다 trigger 촉발시키다, 작동시키다 demonstration 시위, 데모 colonial 식민(지)의, 식민지 시대의 perpetuate 영구화하다, 영속시키다 unfairness 불공평(함) nonviolent 비폭력의 oppose 반대하다 outrageous 너무나 충격적인, 터무니없는 defenseless 무방비의, 방어할 수 없는 break out of ~에서 탈피[탈출]하다 testimony 증거; 증언 provoke 유발하다, 도발하다 rig 조작하다

---

60. 글에 따르면, BLM 운동의 주된 목적은 무엇인가?
(a) 폭력적이고 억압적인 정부에 맞서 싸우는 것
(b) 소수 집단에 대한 현 정책을 반대하는 것
(c) 흑인에 대한 불공정한 대우를 지적하는 것
(d) 소셜 미디어에서 더 많은 지지자들을 얻는 것

> 첫 단락에서 BLM은 'anti-Black violence(흑인을 적대시하는 폭력)', 그리고 흑인에 대한 'police brutality(경찰의 잔혹한 행위)'에 맞서 싸우는 움직임이라고 설명돼 있으므로 정답은 (c)이다.

61. BLM 운동가들은 어떻게 온라인 캠페인을 이끌었는가?
(a) 사람들이 이들의 인스타그램을 따르도록 만듦으로써
(b) 이들의 소셜 미디어에 경찰 동영상을 올림으로써
(c) 충격적인 경찰 동영상을 공유함으로써
(d) 사람들에게 BlackLivesMatter라는 태그를 달라고 요청함으로써

> 두 번째 단락에서 BLM 운동가들의 'using the hashtag BlackLivesMatter(BlackLivesMatter라는 해시태그를 사용하는)' 움직임을 통해 BLM 운동이 창안되었다고 설명돼 있으므로 정답은 (d)이다.

62. 글에 따르면, 트레이번 마틴의 사건에서 무엇이 문제였는가?
(a) 그가 후드티로 얼굴을 가렸다.
(b) 그가 무장해서 위험한 상태였다.
(c) 그는 무방비 상태였다
(d) 그는 감옥에서 탈출했다.

> 두 번째 단락에서 트레이버 마틴이 'unarmed Black teenager(비무장 상태였던 흑인 십대)'였음에도 지역 경비 자원자의 총에 맞아 사망했다고 설명돼 있으므로 정답은 (c)이다.

63. 2014년에 BLM 운동이 왜 국가 및 국제적 관심을 많이 이끌어냈는가?
(a) 동영상 증거가 있었기 때문에
(b) 목격자의 증언이 있었기 때문에
(c) 경관이 사망했기 때문에
(d) 대규모 시위가 있었기 때문에

> 세 번째 단락에서 비무장 상태였던 흑인 에릭 가머가 경찰에게 살해당하는 장면이 'captured in a video(동영상으로 촬영되었고)', 그 이후 BLM 운동이 확장되었다고 설명돼 있으므로 정답은 (a)이다.

64. BLM 운동의 주된 전략은 무엇인가?
(a) 공공장소에서의 플래시몹
(b) 평화적인 시위
(c) 소셜 미디어에서의 게시물 공유
(d) 정부 건물을 점거하는 행위

> 마지막 단락에서 BLM 운동이 'nonviolent protests(비폭력 주의 시위자들)'의 주도하에 인종 차별에 맞서 싸웠다고 설명돼 있고, 이는 곧 BLM이 '평화 시위'임을 시사하므로 정답은 (b)이다.

65. 글의 문맥에서, unjust는 _____을 의미한다.
(a) gentle (온화한)
(b) cruel (잔인한)
(c) unfair (부당한)
(d) violent (폭력적인)

> 밑줄 친 unjust는 '부당한, 불공평한'이라는 뜻의 형용사로서 보기 중 이와 일맥상통하는 것은 '(c) unfair(부당한, 불공평한)'이다.

66. 글의 문맥에서, triggered는 _____을 의미한다.
(a) composed (구성했다)
(b) provoked (유발했다)
(c) rigged (조작했다)
(d) unprecedented (전례 없는)

> 밑줄 친 triggered는 '촉발시키다, 작동시키다'라는 뜻의 동사로서 보기 중 이와 일맥상통하는 것은 '(b) provoked(유발했다)'이다.

BIODIVERSITY

67 Biodiversity, the diversity of life on Earth, is essential to the healthy functioning of ecosystems. Healthy ecosystems, interdependent webs of living organisms and their physical environment, are vital to all life on Earth. Our ecosystems provide us with clean air, fresh water, food, resources and medicine. Biodiversity, the variation of life on Earth, is a major factor in nature's strength.

68 While Earth's biodiversity is so rich that many species have yet to be discovered, many species are being threatened with extinction due to human activities, putting the Earth's magnificent biodiversity at risk. According to the Landmark United Nations-backed report, agricultural activities have had the largest impact on ecosystems that people depend on for food, clean water and a stable climate. The loss of species and habitats poses as much a danger to life on Earth as climate change does.

Some areas in the world, such as areas of Mexico, South Africa, Brazil, the southwestern United States, and Madagascar, have more biodiversity than others. **69** Areas with extremely high levels of biodiversity are called hotspots. **70** All of the Earth's species work together to survive and **72** maintain their ecosystems. For example, the grassland feeds cattle. Cattle then produce manure that returns nutrients to the soil, which helps to grow more grass. This manure can also be used to fertilize cropland. Many species provide important benefits to humans, including food, clothing, and medicine.

Much of the Earth's biodiversity, however, is in **73** jeopardy due to human consumption and other activities that disturb and even destroy ecosystems. Pollution, climate change, and population growth are all threats to biodiversity. These threats have caused an unprecedented rise in the rate of species extinction. **71** Some scientists estimate that half of all species on Earth will be wiped out within the next century.

Helping people to understand what biodiversity loss means for them and their children, can be a very effective incentive for the positive change required to ensure more sustainable lifestyles and choices in energy, food and water consumption, which will in turn ease threats to biodiversity. In many ways, conservation is also good for business. According to the OECD, restoring 46 percent of the world's degraded forests could provide up to US $30 in benefits for every dollar spent, boosting employment and increasing community awareness of biodiversity's importance.

어휘 biodiversity 생물의 다양성 functioning 기능, 작용 ecosystem 생태계 interdependent 상호 의존적인 living organism 생물, 생명체 variation 변화, 변형 extinction 멸종, 소멸 put at risk ~을 위험에 처하게 하다 agricultural 농업[농사]의 habitat 서식지 manure 거름, 천연 비료 nutrient 영양소, 영양분 fertilize 비료를 주다 cropland (농)경지 jeopardy 위험 consumption 소비[소모](량) estimate 추산하다, 추정하다 wipe out ~을 완전히 파괴하다[없애 버리다] incentive 장려[우대]책 sustainable 지속[유지] 가능한 ease 덜해지다[덜어주다], 편해지다[편하게 하다] restore 회복시키다 degraded 타락한, 퇴화한, 저하된 employment 고용, 채용 diverse 다양한 plantation 농장, 조림지 keystone 핵심 predator 포식자, 포식 동물 beyond one's grasp 손이 미치지 않는 곳에 sustain 살아가게 하다; 계속[지속]시키다

67. 글에 따르면, '생물의 다양성'은 무엇인가?
 (a) 다양하고 복잡한 생태계
 (b) 대규모 농장 시스템
 (c) 생태계에서의 인간 활동
 (d) 대학에서의 연구 분야

첫 단락에서 생물의 다양성이 'diversity of life on Earth (지구상 생명체의 다양성)'이며 'healthy functioning ecosystems(생태계가 건강하게 기능하는 것)'에 필수적이라고 설명돼 있으므로 정답은 (a)이다.

68. 왜 생물 다양성이 위험에 처해 있는가?
 (a) 핵심 종들이 없어진 것으로 인해
 (b) 생물의 타고난 주기(순환)로 인해
 (c) 사람들이 행하는 일들로 인해
 (d) 많은 포식자들로 인해

두 번째 단락에서 지구의 다양성을 위험에 처하게 만드는 'human activities(인간 활동)'으로 인해 많은 종들이 멸종의 위협을 받고 있다고 설명돼 있으므로 정답은 (c)이다.

69. 글에 따르면, hotspots는 무엇인가?
 (a) 인간 활동이 많은 지역
 (b) 아름다운 풍경이 있는 지역
 (c) 법으로 보호받고 있는 지역
 (d) 뛰어난 생물 다양성을 보유한 지역

세 번째 단락에서 'areas with extremely high levels of biodiversity(생물 다양성 수준이 아주 높은 지역들)'이 hotspots로 불린다고 설명돼 있으므로 정답은 (d)이다.

70. 초원의 예시를 봤을 때, 생태계에 대해 무엇을 말할 수 있는가?
 (a) 생태계는 우리의 손이 미치지 않는 곳에 있다.
 (b) 생태계는 상호 의존적이다
 (c) 생태계는 연구될 필요가 있다.
 (d) 생태계는 충분히 보호받고 있지 못하다.

세 번째 단락에서 지구상의 모든 종들이 생태계를 유지하기 위해 'work together(함께 일한다(협업한다)'고 하면서 초원이 소를 먹이고, 소가 다시 초원을 키우는 예시를 들고 있으므로 정답은 (b)이다.

71. 글에 따르면, 다음 세기에 지구의 생물 다양성에 무슨 일이 일어날 걸로 예상되는가?
 (a) 지구상에 있는 종의 50퍼센트가 멸종할 것이다
 (b) 지구상에 있는 종의 25퍼센트가 멸종할 것이다.
 (c) 종의 10퍼센트만이 살아남을 것이다.
 (d) 모든 것이 절멸할 것이다.

네 번째 단락에서 일부 과학자들이 다음 세기 내에 'half of all species on Earth(지구상에 있는 모든 종들의 절반)'이 완전히 사라지게 될 것으로 추정한다고 설명돼 있으므로 정답은 (a)이다.

72. 글의 문맥에서, maintain은 _____을 의미한다.
 (a) manage (관리하다)
 (b) survive (살아남다)
 (c) sustain (지속하다)
 (d) overcome (극복하다)

밑줄 친 maintain은 '유지하다, 계속하다'라는 뜻의 동사로서 보기 중 이와 일맥상통하는 것은 '(c) sustain(지속하다, 계속하다)'이다.

73. 글의 문맥에서, jeopardy는 _____을 의미한다.
 (a) danger (위험)
 (b) beauty (아름다움)
 (c) complexity (복잡성)
 (d) flexibility (융통성)

밑줄 친 jeopardy는 '위험'이라는 뜻의 명사로서 보기 중 이와 일맥상통하는 것은 '(a) danger(위험)'이다.

74-80 (안내) 주문 방법에 대한 안내 서신

Dear Dahyun Oh,

Thank you so much for all the information provided, it truly helps me understand your company a little further.

74 To get started, I have provided a link below to our image release as well as our policies so you can review them. I have also attached our first order form; this is simply to enter your first order and send it back to me when ready.

We only require that the first order is placed this way.

https://www.treasureusa.com/Indexasp?page

75 Below you will see a **79** temporary online access to our site where you will be able to log on and view pricing and availability. **76** Once your first order ships from our warehouse in the US, you will be provided with your own permanent log in where you will be able to place orders, view inventory and pricing, view your invoices, and obtain tracking numbers for your order.

We require a first time order of $500 (USD) and **77** we require all accounts to maintain a yearly **80** quota of $3,000 (USD) to keep the account in active status with us.

All pricing is in USD. **78** Customs or import duties may apply. Please contact your local customs office for further information. We do offer a conversion chart which can be located on the website at the time of log in.

For the shipping to Korea, we use mainly UPS or FedEx, we do not have flat shipping rates as we are a wholesale company and we go with dimensional weight to determine the shipping cost, but we were able to negotiate excellent rates with our carriers on behalf of our customers given the volume that we do on a daily basis.

Online Temp User ID: EA #2

Temp User Name: POTENTIAL INTL CUS DEMO

Password has been changed to 12345

Effective: 3/12/2020 to 3/19/2020

https://www.treasureusa.com/Indexasp?pag

In the meantime please do not hesitate to contact me should you have any questions.

Kindest regards,

Karim Haggard
International Account Manager
105 S. Puente Street, Brea
CA 92821 USA

Sincerely,
Peter Evans

오다현 님께
알려주신 모든 정보에 대단히 감사드리며, 이것이 귀사를 좀 더 잘 이해하는 데 실로 도움이 되었습니다.

74 우선, 저희 측 이미지와 방침을 보실 수 있는 링크를 아래에 명시했으니 이를 살펴보시면 됩니다. 또한 첫 주문 양식도 첨부했으며, 첫 주문 입력 후 준비됐을 때 다시 보내기만 하면 되는 간단한 양식입니다.

첫 주문만 이 같은 방식으로 이뤄지면 됩니다.

https://www.treasureusa.com/Indexasp?page

75 아래를 보시면 저희 사이트에 접속해 가격 및 물건 입수 가능 여부를 확인할 수 있는 **79** 임시 온라인 접속 정보가 나와 있습니다. **76** 첫 주문품이 미국에 있는 저희 창고에서 발송되기 시작하면, 주문을 넣은 뒤 재고품, 가격, 송장을 확인하고 주문 추적 번호를 받을 수 있는 영구적인 접속 권한이 부여될 것입니다.

첫 주문은 미화 500달러가 돼야 하며 **77** 저희 측 계정을 계속해서 유효한 상태로 유지하고자 하실 경우 모든 계정들은 연간 미화 3,000달러 **80** 한도를 유지해야 합니다.

모든 가격은 미화로 책정됩니다. **78** 관세 및 수입 관세가 적용될 수 있습니다. 더 많은 정보를 얻고자 하시면 귀사의 지역 세관에 연락하시기 바랍니다. 저희 측에서 환전 차트를 제공하며, 이는 웹사이트에 접속 시 찾아보실 수 있습니다.

한국으로 수송하는 경우 저희는 주로 UPS나 FedEx를 사용하며, 저희가 도매 회사이고 치수 무게로 발송비를 책정하기 때문에 균일한 운송료를 적용하진 않지만 매일 다루는 수량을 고려해 고객을 대신하여 저희 측 운송 회사와 협상하여 만족스러운 운송료를 책정할 수 있었습니다.

온라인 임시 사용자 ID: EA #2

비밀번호가 12345로 변경됨

시행일: 2020년 3월 12일부터 2020년 3월 19일까지

https://www.treasureusa.com/Indexasp?pag

그 사이 질문 사항이 있으실 경우 주저 없이 저에게 연락주시기 바랍니다.

안녕히 계십시오.

카림 해가드
국제 경리 부장
브레아 푸엔테 가 105 S.
CA 92821 USA

진심을 담아,
피터 에반스

어휘 temporary 일시적인, 임시의 pricing 가격 책정 availability 유효성, 유용성, 효용; (입수) 가능성 ship 수송[운송]하다 warehouse 창고 permanent 영구적인 inventory 물품 목록; 재고(품) account 계좌, 예금(액); 신용 거래 yearly 연간의 quota 한도[할당](량); 몫 customs 세관; 관세 import duty 수입 관세 conversion 전환, 변환; 환전 shipping rate 운송료 wholesale 도매의; 대량의 dimensional 치수의, 차원의 on a daily basis 매일 shipping cost 발송비 carrier 항공사, 수송[운송] 회사 in the meantime 그동안, 그 사이에 distant 먼, (멀리) 떨어져 있는 indication 지시, 표시 allocation 할당(량); 배당(량) quotation 인용; 시가, 시세 collaboration 협력, 합작

74. 이메일의 목적은 무엇인가?
    (a) 다현에게 신상품을 소개하는 것
    (b) 다현의 주문이 지연됨을 알리는 것
    (c) 다현에게 특가 상품을 제안하는 것
    (d) **다현이 첫 주문을 넣는 걸 돕는 것**

> 두 번째 단락에서 글쓴이가 다현에게 'first order form(첫 주문 양식)'을 첨부했다고 하면서 이에 대해 소개하고 있고, 따라서 이것이 첫 주문 절차에 대한 안내임을 알 수 있으므로 정답은 (d)이다.

75. 다현이 상품 가격을 확인하고 싶을 경우, 무엇을 해야 하는가?
    (a) ID를 얻기 위해 이메일에 답변한다.
    (b) 웹사이트에서 ID를 생성해야 한다.
    (c) **웹사이트에 접속할 수 있는 일회용 ID를 쓰게 될 것이다**
    (d) 전화해서 영구적인 ID를 얻어야 한다.

> 세 번째 단락에서 'temporary online access(임시 온라인 접속 정보)'를 통해 사이트에 접속하여 가격 및 물건 입수 가능 여부를 확인할 수 있다고 설명돼 있으므로 정답은 (c)이다.

76. 카림은 언제 다현의 임시 계정을 영구 계정으로 바꿀 것인가?
    (a) 다현의 신용을 확인하고 난 후
    (b) 다현이 웹사이트에 접속하고 난 후
    (c) **그녀에게 첫 주문품을 보내고 난 후**
    (d) 다현이 첫 주문을 넣고 난 후

> 세 번째 단락에서 'once your first order ships from our warehouse(첫 주문품이 창고에서 발송되기 시작하면)' 영구적인 접속 권한이 부여될 것이라고 설명돼 있으므로 정답은 (c)이다.

77. 카림은 다현의 계정을 유효한 상태로 유지하기 위해 그녀가 무엇을 하길 원하는가?
    (a) 다현은 하루에 한 번 웹사이트에 접속해야 한다.
    (b) 다현은 지역 세관에 문의해야 한다.
    (c) 다현은 카림에게 이메일 답장을 해야 한다.
    (d) **다현은 일정 가격의 주문을 해야 한다**

> 네 번째 단락에서 계정을 계속해서 유효한 상태로 유지하려면 'a yearly quota of $3,000(연간 3,000달러 한도)'를 유지해야 한다고 했고, 이는 곧 일정 금액의 물건을 주문해야 함을 뜻하므로 정답은 (d)이다.

78. 카림은 왜 다현이 지역 세관에 연락하길 원하는가?
    (a) 회사에서 이것이 필요하기 때문에
    (b) 문제가 있기 때문에
    (c) **세금이 있을 수 있기 때문에**
    (d) 규제가 있을 수 있기 때문에

> 다섯 번째 단락에서, 글쓴이는 'customs or import duties(관세 및 수입 관세)'가 있을 수 있다고 하면서 더 많은 정보를 얻고 싶을 경우 지역 세관에 연락하라고 설명돼 있으므로 정답은 (c)이다.

79. 글의 문맥에서, temporary는 _____을 의미한다.
    (a) **short-term (단기의)**
    (b) long-term (장기의)
    (c) distant (멀리 떨어진)
    (d) permanent (영구적인)

> 밑줄 친 temporary는 '임시의, 일시적인'이라는 뜻의 형용사이고, 이는 곧 '단발성의, 단기적인'이라는 의미라고 생각할 수 있으므로 정답은 (a)이다.

80. 글의 문맥에서, quota는 _____을 의미한다.
    (a) indication (지시)
    (b) **allocation (할당량)**
    (c) quotation (시세)
    (d) collaboration (협력)

> 밑줄 친 quota는 '한도, 할당(량)'을 뜻하는 명사로서 보기 중 이와 일맥상통하는 것은 '(b) allocation(할당량), 배당(량)'이다.

Actual Test 03 / Vocab 주요 어휘 총정리

Actual Test 03에 등장했던 주요 어휘를 한눈에 훑어보며 정리해 보도록 합시다.
모르는 어휘가 있을 경우 박스(☐)에 체크(V) 표시를 한 뒤 재차 암기하도록 하세요.

- ☐ well renowned 유명한, 잘 알려진
- ☐ narrate 이야기를 하다[들려주다]
- ☐ bilingual 이중 언어 사용자의
- ☐ struggle with ~로 고심하다[씨름하다]
- ☐ rejection 거절; 배제, 폐기
- ☐ solace 위안, 위로
- ☐ dissuade ~을 설득[만류]하다
- ☐ be committed to ~에 헌신[전념]하다
- ☐ adapt 맞추다[조정하다]; 개작하다[각색하다]
- ☐ indifferent 냉담한, 무관심한
- ☐ comfort 위로, 편안함
- ☐ isolation 소외, 고립
- ☐ solidarity 단결, 결속, 연대
- ☐ dedicated to ~에 전념[헌신]하는
- ☐ racism 인종 차별 (주의/행위)
- ☐ brutality 잔인성, 야만성, 무자비
- ☐ condemnation 비난
- ☐ unjust 부당한, 불공평한
- ☐ oppression 압박, 압제, 억압, 탄압
- ☐ protest 항의 (운동), 시위
- ☐ unarmed 무기를 가지고 있지 않은, 비무장의
- ☐ prolonged 오래 계속되는, 장기적인
- ☐ defund 재원을 고갈시키다, 재정 원조를 철회하다
- ☐ trigger 촉발시키다, 작동시키다
- ☐ demonstration 시위, 데모
- ☐ colonial 식민(지)의, 식민지 시대의
- ☐ perpetuate 영구화하다, 영속시키다
- ☐ unfairness 불공평(함)
- ☐ oppose 반대하다
- ☐ outrageous 너무나 충격적인, 터무니없는
- ☐ defenseless 무방비의, 방어할 수 없는
- ☐ break out of ~에서 탈피[탈출]하다
- ☐ testimony 증거; 증언
- ☐ provoke 유발하다, 도발하다
- ☐ interdependent 상호 의존적인

- ☐ variation 변화, 변형
- ☐ extinction 멸종, 소멸
- ☐ put at risk ~을 위험에 처하게 하다
- ☐ agricultural 농업[농사]의
- ☐ habitat 서식지
- ☐ nutrient 영양소, 영양분
- ☐ fertilize 비료를 주다
- ☐ jeopardy 위험
- ☐ consumption 소비[소모](량)
- ☐ estimate 추산하다, 추정하다
- ☐ wipe out ~을 완전히 파괴하다[없애 버리다]
- ☐ incentive 장려[우대]책
- ☐ sustainable 지속[유지] 가능한
- ☐ ease 덜해지다[덜어주다], 편해지다[편하게 하다]
- ☐ restore 회복시키다
- ☐ employment 고용, 채용
- ☐ predator 포식자, 포식 동물
- ☐ sustain 살아가게 하다; 계속[지속]시키다
- ☐ temporary 일시적인, 임시의
- ☐ availability 유효성, 유용성, 효용; (입수) 가능성
- ☐ ship 수송[운송]하다
- ☐ permanent 영구적인
- ☐ inventory 물품 목록; 재고(품)
- ☐ account 계좌; 예금(액); 신용 거래
- ☐ quota 한도[할당](량); 몫
- ☐ customs 세관; 관세
- ☐ conversion 전환, 변환; 환전
- ☐ wholesale 도매의; 대량의
- ☐ dimensional 치수의, 차원의
- ☐ carrier 항공사, 수송[운송] 회사
- ☐ distant 먼, (멀리) 떨어져 있는
- ☐ indication 지시, 표시
- ☐ allocation 할당(량), 배당(량)
- ☐ quotation 인용; 시가, 시세
- ☐ collaboration 협력, 합작

Reading and Vocabulary Section
Actual Test 04

▶▶ 정답 & 나의 점수 확인

테스트 날짜: _____월 _____일 / 테스트 점수: _____

53 (a) 54 (b) 55 (c) 56 (d) 57 (a) 58 (d) 59 (c) 60 (a) 61 (d) 62 (c) 63 (d) 64 (b) 65 (b) 66 (d)
67 (a) 68 (b) 69 (b) 70 (b) 71 (a) 72 (d) 73 (c) 74 (a) 75 (b) 76 (b) 77 (d) 78 (d) 79 (c) 80 (a)

▶▶ 출제 경향 & 흐름 파악

지피지기면 백전백승! 출제 경향과 흐름을 한눈에 파악해 봅시다. 출제된 지문이 어떤 종류의 글이었는지, 각 지문과 관련해 어떤 종류의 문제가 출제되었는지 아래의 표를 보며 정리해 보세요.

(인물) 유명한 건축가에 대한 소개글	53	유명하게 된 원인	(문화) 식충성 (곤충 섭취)에 대한 설명글	67	식충성의 정의
	54	미국으로 이사를 간 이유		68	식충성이 혐오스러운 이유
	55	대학에서 공부한 학업 내용		69	꿀개미에 대한 북미의 인식
	56	현재도 사용되고 있는 건축 양식		70	식충성의 이점
	57	건축물이 논란이 된 이유		71	식충성에 대한 인식 변화
	58	어휘 문제: distinctive		72	어휘 문제: prevalent
	59	어휘 문제: controversial		73	어휘 문제: negligible
(사회) 가상 현실 '메타머스'에 대한 설명글	60	메타버스의 정의	(안내) 멤버십 취소 관련 안내 이메일	74	이메일의 목적
	61	메타버스가 삶에 미친 영향		75	돈이 환불되는 방식
	62	메타버스가 관심을 받는 이유		76	향후 받게 될 이메일의 내용
	63	D2A의 정의		77	멤버십 취소 후 변경 사항
	64	메타버스에서 돈을 쓰는 이유		78	서비스 이용에 필요한 사항
	65	어휘 문제: populate		79	어휘 문제: confirmed
	66	어휘 문제: advent		80	어휘 문제: compulsory

I.M. PEI

53 Chinese-born American architect I.M. Pei was known for his strikingly contemporary, elegant, and functional buildings. They can be found throughout the United States and in other countries, including Canada, France, and Japan.

Leoh Ming Pei was born in Guangzhou, China, on April 26, 1917. He spent his summers in the countryside. He had an interest in rocks, nature, and history. **54** He came to the United States in 1935, during a period of considerable political turbulence in China. He initially enrolled at the University of Pennsylvania in Philadelphia but then **55** transferred to the Massachusetts Institute of Technology in Cambridge. He graduated from there in 1940 with a degree in architectural engineering.

In 1955, Pei formed his own firm, I.M. Pei and Associates, based in New York City. Pei's style of architecture is called modern or modernist. This style of architecture makes use of newer construction materials, such as concrete, glass, and steel. Modernist buildings are often designed with straight and simple lines, without a lot of decorations. **56** One **58** distinctive design that came out of his form is seen in many parts of the country— the five-sided control towers at many major American airports.

The Louvre Pyramid in Paris, the Bank of China Tower in Hong Kong and the East Building of the National Gallery of Art in Washington, D.C. are probably the most well-known projects in Pei's portfolio. However, Pei's projects, including arts facilities, university buildings, libraries and civic centers, are more diverse than the most well-known projects.

One of his most **59** controversial projects was the design for a 71-foot (22-meter) steel-and-glass pyramid (1989) that was built in the courtyard of the world-famous Louvre Museum in Paris, France. **57** It was heavily criticized because it is tempering with the Louvre's majestic old French Renaissance architecture. Glass and steel pyramid looked like an unlikely contemporary addition.

Not all of Pei's buildings were successes. The Hancock Tower in Boston is one example. The huge glass-covered skyscraper was nearly finished when disaster struck. Panes of glass began falling out of the building. They had to be replaced with plywood until a solution could be found. More than 10,000 panes of glass had to be replaced. Later on, though, the building wound up winning awards.

Pei received numerous honors during his career including the Pritzker Architecture Prize. He wanted his building to "stand the test of time." Pei died on May 16, 2019, at 102 years old.

어휘 architect 건축가 strikingly 두드러지게, 눈에 띄게 contemporary 동시대의; 현대의, 당대의 elegant 우아한 functional 기능 위주의, 실용적인 considerable 상당한, 많은; 중요한 turbulence 격동, 격변; 난류, 난기류 initially 처음에 architectural engineering 건축 공학 architecture 건축학[술]; 건축 양식 modernist 현대풍[식]의 사람, 근대주의자 make use of ~을 이용[활용]하다 construction 건설, 공사 distinctive 독특한 control tower (항공) 관제탑 civic center 공관 지구; 공공 시설[건물]; 시민 회관 controversial 논란이 많은 courtyard 뜰 criticize 비판하다, 비난하다 temper 완화시키다; 지배하다, 억제하다 majestic 장엄한, 위풍당당한 plywood 합판, 베니어판 stand the test of time 세월의 시험을 견디다 exile 추방하다, 유배하다 unrest (사회·정치적인) 불안[불만] shatter 산산이 부서지다

53. I.M. 페이는 무엇으로 가장 유명한가?
 (a) 전 세계에 걸쳐 있는 독특한 건물들을 설계한 것
 (b) 성공한 중국계 미국인이 된 것
 (c) 당시 많은 나라들을 여행한 것
 (d) 미국에 있는 유명 대학에 간 것

첫 단락에서 페이가 'contemporary, elegant and functional buildings(현대적이고, 우아하며, 실용적인 건물들)'로 잘 알려져 있고 다양한 나라 곳곳에서 그의 건물을 볼 수 있다고 했으므로 정답은 (a)이다.

54. 페이는 왜 미국으로 이사 갔는가?
 (a) 중국 정부가 그를 추방했기 때문에
 (b) 중국 내에 정치적 불안이 있었기 때문에
 (c) 미국에서 더 많은 기회를 봤기 때문에
 (d) 미국에서 영어를 공부하고 싶었기 때문에

두 번째 단락에서 페이가 'a period of considerable political turbulence in China(중국에서 중요한 정치적 격변의 시기)'가 진행되던 때에 미국으로 건너갔다고 설명돼 있으므로 정답은 (b)이다.

55. 페이는 매사추세츠 공과 대학에서 무엇을 공부했는가?
 (a) 중국의 역사와 정치
 (b) 항공 관제
 (c) 건물을 설계하고 시공하는 것
 (d) 프랑스 미술과 미술사

두 번째 단락에서 페이가 매사추세츠 공과 대학에서 'degree in architectural engineering(건축 공학 학위)'를 따고 졸업했다고 했고, 이는 곧 건물 설계 및 시공 관련 공부를 했음을 의미하므로 정답은 (c)이다.

56. 여전히 사용되고 있는 페이의 디자인은 무엇이었는가?
 (a) 루브르 박물관의 피라미드
 (b) 대학 건물과 도서관
 (c) 예술 시설
 (d) 공항 관제탑

세 번째 단락에서 현재까지도 나라 곳곳에서 볼 수 있는 페이의 디자인 중 하나가 다섯 개의 면으로 된 미국 주요 공항에 있는 'control towers(관제탑)'라 했으므로 정답은 (d)이다.

57. 루브르 박물관에 있는 피라미드가 왜 논란이 많았는가?
 (a) 너무 현대적으로 보였기 때문에
 (b) 유리가 부서질 것 같기 때문에
 (c) 피라미드처럼 생겼기 때문에
 (d) 시공하기에 위험했기 때문에

다섯 번째 단락에서 페이가 만든 피라미드가 루브르의 오래된 건축 양식을 억제한다는 이유로 비난을 받았고 이것이 'contemporary addition(현대적 증축물)'처럼 보인다고 설명돼 있으므로 정답은 (a)이다.

58. 글의 문맥에서, distinctive는 _____을 의미한다.
 (a) common (흔한)
 (b) ordinary (평범한)
 (c) familiar (친숙한)
 (d) unique (독특한)

밑줄 친 distinctive는 '독특한'이라는 뜻을 가진 형용사로서 보기 중 이와 일맥상통하는 것은 '(d) unique(유일무이한, 독특한)'이다.

59. 글의 문맥에서, controversial은 _____을 의미한다.
 (a) viral (바이러스성의)
 (b) universal (보편적인)
 (c) disputed (반박을 받은)
 (d) faded (쇠퇴한)

밑줄 친 controversial은 '논란이 많은'이라는 뜻을 가진 형용사이며, 이는 곧 '반박을 받아 논란이 많은'이라는 의미로 생각할 수 있으므로 정답은 (c)이다.

METAVERSE

The term metaverse is made up of the prefix "meta," which means beyond and the stem "verse," which means universe. The term is typically used to describe three-dimensional virtual spaces. It was coined by American writer Neal Stephenson in his 1993 sci-fi hit Snow Crash.

60 What is the metaverse? It's best explained as a collection of 3D worlds you explore as an avatar. Metaverse describes a non-physical world in which individuals can interact through different kinds of virtual technology. For example, 61 a metaverse could permit people living on different sides of the world to meet up through technology and virtually go on a vacation, play sports or work together on projects. People linked to the metaverse would be connected at all times and physical distance would not limit their ability to interact. The main technologies that would drive such a world would be virtual reality, or VR and augmented reality, AR. Other, yet-to-be invented technologies would likely also be used to improve experiences within the metaverse. Today virtual worlds are formed, 65 populated, and already generating serious money.

62 63 Because the metaverse brings a new dimension to the internet, brands and businesses will need to consider their current and future role within it. Some brands are already forging the way and establishing a new genre of marketing in the process: direct to avatar (D2A). Gucci sold a virtual bag for more than the real thing in Roblox; Nike dropped virtual Jordans in Fortnite; Coca-Cola launched avatar wearables in Decentraland, and Sotherby's has an art gallery that your avatar can wander in your spare time.

D2A is being supercharged by blockchain technology and the 66 advent of digital ownership via NFTs, or tokens. More than $191 million was transacted on the "play to earn" blockchain game Axie Infinity in its first 30 days this year.

The companies are investing huge sums because they see the younger generations doing the same: 87% of Generation Z and 83% of millennials are playing video games and engaging with digital spaces on smartphones and computers at least weekly if not daily. 64 Moreover, more than 65% of Gen Zers have spent money on in-game items.

어휘 prefix 접두사 universe 우주; 세계 stem 줄기, 대; 어간 three-dimensional 3차원의 virtual 가상의 coin (새로운 낱말을) 만들다; 주조하다 sci-fi 공상 과학 소설 virtually 가상으로 augmented reality 증강 현실 populate 살다, 거주하다 serious money 거액의 돈 dimension 크기, 치수; 규모; 차원, 관점 forge 구축하다; 위조하다 establish 설립[설정]하다; 수립하다 wearable 입을 수 있는; 의복, 옷 wander 거닐다, 돌아다니다 supercharge ~에 (에너지·감정·긴장 등을) 지나치게 주다 advent 도래, 출현 ownership 소유(권) transact 거래하다 invest 투자하다 process 가공하다, 처리하다 currency 통화; 통용 recklessly 무모하게, 개의치 않고 inhabit 살다, 거주[서식]하다 situate (어떤 위치에) 두다; 고려하다 irregular 고르지 못한; 불규칙적인 passive 수동적인, 소극적인 emergence 출현, 발생

60. 메타버스는 무엇인가?
(a) 아바타가 탐험할 수 있는 가상 공간
(b) 미국 작가가 쓴 공상 과학 소설
(c) 휴대폰에 제공되는 온라인 게임 서비스
(d) 온라인 쇼핑 플랫폼

두 번째 단락에서 메타버스가 'a collection of 3D worlds you explore as an avatar(아바타로 탐험하는 3차원 세상의 집합체)'라고 설명하고 있으므로 정답은 (a)이다.

61. 메타버스는 사람들의 삶을 어떻게 바꿀 것인가?
(a) 다른 이들과 일하는 것이 더 수월해질 것이다
(b) 정보를 좀 더 효율적으로 처리한다
(c) 쇼핑이 더 쉽고 빨라질 것이다
(d) 물리적 거리가 별로 문제되지 않을 것이다

두 번째 단락에서 사람들이 메타버스를 통해 다양한 가상 활동을 한다고 설명하면서 메타버스가 'would not limit their ability to interact(소통 능력을 제한하지 못한다)'고 하고 있으므로 정답은 (d)이다.

62. 글에 따르면, 브랜드들과 사업체들은 메타버스에 왜 관심이 있는가?
(a) 사람들이 가상 공간에서 집과 박물관을 지을 수 있다.
(b) 사람들이 아바타로 가상 세계를 탐험할 수 있다.
(c) 사람들이 가상 화폐로 물건과 서비스를 구매할 수 있다
(d) 사람들이 메타버스에서 친구들과 게임을 할 수 있다.

세 번째 단락에서 일부 기업들이 메타버스를 대상으로 길을 개척 중이며, 그 예로서 특정 기업들이 가상 공간에서 물건을 발표하고 판매하는 행위를 하고 있다고 설명하고 있으므로 정답은 (c)이다.

63. D2A는 무엇인가?
(a) 가상 상점
(b) 아바타
(c) 가상 세계
(d) 디지털 통화(화폐)

세 번째와 네 번째 단락에서 D2A로 가상 공간에서 물건이 거래되고, 이것이 NFTs나 토큰을 통한 'digital ownership(디지털 소유권)'으로 공급되고 있다고 했으므로 이것이 '(d) 디지털 통화'임을 알 수 있다.

64. Z 세대가 왜 메타버스에서 돈을 쓸 것으로 예상되는가?
(a) 메타버스에서 이미 게임을 많이 하고 있다.
(b) 온라인에서 구매하는 것에 이미 익숙하다
(c) 막강한 구매력을 보였다.
(d) 무모하게 돈을 쓰는 경향이 있다.

마지막 단락에서 65퍼센트 이상의 Z 세대들이 'spent money on in-game items(인 게임 아이템에 돈을 쓰고 있다)'고 설명했고, 이는 곧 Z 세대가 이미 온라인 소비에 익숙함을 뜻하므로 정답은 (b)이다.

65. 글의 문맥에서, populated는 _____을 의미한다.
(a) indifferent (냉담한)
(b) inhabited (거주하는)
(c) interested (관심이 있는)
(d) situated (고려하는)

밑줄 친 populated는 '(사람들이) 거주하는'이라는 뜻의 동사로서 보기 중 이와 일맥상통하는 것은 '(b) inhibited(거주하는)'이다.

66. 글의 문맥에서, advent는 _____을 의미한다.
(a) irregular (불규칙적인)
(b) disappear (사라지다)
(c) passive (소극적인)
(d) emergence (출현)

밑줄 친 advent는 '도래, 출현'을 뜻하는 명사로서 보기 중 이와 일맥상통하는 것은 '(d) emergence(출현, 발생)'이다.

ENTOMOPHAGY

67 Entomophagy, the consumption of insects as a source of nutrition by humans. Entomophagy is practiced in most parts of the world, though it is especially 72 prevalent in the tropics, where more than 2,000 different species of insects are known to be consumed.

68 Eating insects is considered as disgusting or primitive in Western societies. Even though there was a substantial aversion to including insects in food, The Food and Agriculture Organization (FAO) of the United Nations (UN) has been making continuous efforts to popularize entomophagy as a healthy, sustainable, and environment-friendly practice.

There are more than 2,000 different kinds of edible insects in the world. Beetles are the most commonly eaten insect. For example, the larvae of the palm weevil that are enjoyed in parts of Africa and Asia. The number and type of insect species people eat varies in different parts of the world. Insects are surprisingly delicious. Stink bugs taste like apples, and termites taste like carrots. Many insects such as grasshoppers, crickets, and beetle larvae taste a bit nutty, especially if they've been roasted. This most likely because of their high fat content and crunchy mineral-rich outer skeletons. Insects often taste like what they eat. 69 Honeypot ants select certain worker ants and feed them nectar until their bellies expand. They have a sweet flavor and are considered a delicacy in North America and Australia. 70 Not only are insects tasty, but they're nutritious. Many insects, especially crickets and termites, are high in protein, an essential nutrient.

70 In comparison with livestock, insects have minimal resource requirements in terms of feed, land resources, and water. Apart from this, the carbon footprint of insects is 73 negligible. Insect meat is rich in iron, calcium, and fat. Insects release minimal greenhouse gasses.

Even though there are many benefits of including insects into our diet, the aversion towards them still exists. Humans are taught to think about food beyond the nutritional quality it possesses. Accordingly, some food items are considered modern and are well accepted and some are considered primitive and face a general rejection. As a result, until recently, entomophagy was not a very common practice in the modern world. 71 Yet, in many countries, there is now a growing appreciation of insects as food and feed.

어휘 entomophagy 식충성 consumption 소비[소모](량) nutrition 영양 prevalent 일반적인, 널리 퍼져 있는 consume 소모하다; 먹다, 마시다 primitive 원시 사회의; 미개의 substantial 상당한, 크고 튼튼한 aversion 아주 싫어함, 혐오감 popularize 대중화하다, 많은 사람들에게 알리다 edible 먹을 수 있는, 식용의 beetle 딱정벌레 larvae 유충 palm weevil 야자나무 바구미 stink bug 악취를 풍기는 벌레, 노린재 termite 흰개미 grasshopper 메뚜기 cricket 귀뚜라미 nutty 견과 맛이 나는 crunch 아작아작 씹다 honeypot ant 꿀개미 nectar (꽃의) 꿀; (진한) 과일즙 delicacy 섬세함; 별미, 진미 livestock 가축 carbon footprint 탄소 발자국 negligible 무시해도 될 정도의 calcium 칼슘 greenhouse gas 온실가스 ethnic 민족[종족]의; 민족 전통적인 immune system 면역 체계 insignificant 대수롭지 않은, 하찮은

67. 식충성은 무엇인가?
(a) 곤충을 음식으로 소비하는 것
(b) 곤충을 별미로 요리하는 것
(c) 프로젝트를 위해 곤충을 수집하는 것
(d) 식용 가능한 곤충을 발견하는 것

첫 단락에서 식충성이 'consumption of insects as a source of nutrition(영양의 원천으로서 곤충을 소비하는 것)'이라고 했고, 이는 곧 곤충을 음식으로 먹는다는 사실을 뜻하므로 정답은 (a)이다.

68. 서방에선 왜 곤충 섭취에 대한 상당한 혐오감이 있는가?
(a) 아무도 이걸 음식으로 먹지 않기 때문에
(b) 역겹고 안전하지 않다고 생각되기 때문에
(c) 이것을 제대로 요리하는 법을 모르기 때문에
(d) 이것이 매우 드물고 비싸기 때문에

두 번째 단락에서 서방 사회에선 곤충을 먹는 것을 'disgusting and primitive(역겹거나 미개하게)' 생각한다고 했고, 이것이 바로 곤충 섭취에 대한 혐오감으로 이어진 것이기 때문에 정답은 (b)이다.

69. 북미에선 꿀개미를 무엇이라고 생각하는가?
(a) 흔한 음식
(b) 희귀한 음식
(c) 지역 음식
(d) 전통 음식

세 번째 단락에서 꿀개미들은 단맛이 나고 북미와 호주에서 이 같은 꿀개미들을 'delicacy(별미)'로 여긴다고 했고, 별미라는 것은 항상 먹는 일반식이 아닌 특별한 진미를 뜻하기 때문에 정답은 (b)이다.

70. 곤충을 먹는 것의 이점은 무엇인가?
(a) 면역 체계를 강화한다.
(b) 영양가가 높고 오래 간다.
(c) 약효가 있는 가치를 지니고 있다.
(d) 맛이 뛰어나고 많은 사람들을 먹인다.

세 번째와 네 번째 단락에서 곤충은 'nutritious(영양가가 높고) minimal resource requirements(자원 소요량이 매우 적다고)' 설명돼 있으며, 자원 소요량이 적으면 오래도록 이용 가능하기 때문에 정답은 (b)이다.

71. 식충성에 대한 태도는 어떻게 변화하고 있는가?
(a) 긍정적
(b) 부정적
(c) 결정되지 않은
(d) 냉담한

마지막 단락에서 현재 많은 나라에서 곤충을 'food and feed(음식과 식사로서)' 가치를 지닌 것으로 'appreciation(인정/인식)'하는 경향이 늘어나고 있다고 했으므로 정답은 (a)이다.

72. 글의 문맥에서, prevalent는 _____을 의미한다.
(a) unique (독특한)
(b) moist (촉촉한)
(c) dim (어둑한)
(d) common (흔한)

밑줄 친 prevalent는 '일반적인, 널리 퍼져 있는'이라는 뜻을 가진 형용사로서 보기 중 이와 일맥상통하는 것은 '(d) common(흔한)'이다.

73. 글의 문맥에서, negligible은 _____을 의미한다.
(a) substantial (상당한)
(b) neutral (중립적인)
(c) insignificant (대수롭지 않은)
(d) unusual (흔히 있는)

밑줄 친 negligible은 '무시해도 될 정도의'라는 뜻을 가진 형용사로서 보기 중 이와 일맥상통하는 것은 '(c) insignificant(대수롭지 않은)'이다.

74-80 (안내) 멤버십 취소 관련 안내 이메일

Hello Mr. Yang

Hope this email finds you well.

We hope you are doing well along with your family. We sincerely hope that everyone remains safe and stays healthy.

To make things right, **74** we've cancelled the Audible membership under the email yangtsu@gmail.com address and **75** issued a refund in the amount of $16.44 back to your Visa credit card. Depending on your bank, a refund will typically take about 7–10 business days to appear in your account. **76** An automated email with the subject "**79** confirmed: Changes to your Audible Membership Plan" would also have been sent on that day confirming your cancellation as well. Note that we are not able to receive messages sent to this address.

However, **77** you can still listen to any of your titles in your library even after your membership is cancelled.

There is a short survey below the email directly regarding the level of support provided by me and your feedback will be greatly appreciated.

78 Have you checked our new offering of free podcasts in which membership is not **80** compulsory. I suggest you look into it by going through this link.

http://wwwaudible.com/search/keywords=free+podcast

Thank you again for contacting Audible. If you would like more help, contact us. We are here for you 24 hours a day, 7 days a week. Give us a call at 1–888–283–5051 and we'll do everything we can to ensure your next listen is a great one.

As a valued customer, your experience is important to us. Please answer the question below regarding your customer service experience. Your feedback will help us better serve your future needs.

To contact us about unrelated issue, please visit us at

www.audible.com

Sincerely,
Mohammead S.
Customer Service
Audible.com

어휘 audible (목소리 · 음이) 들리는 issue a refund 환불금을 지급하다, 환불해 주다 automated 자동화된, 자동의 confirm 확인해 주다; 확정하다, 공식화하다 cancellation 취소, 무효화 compulsory 강제적인, 의무적인, 필수의 look into ~을 조사하다[주의 깊게 살피다] valued 귀중한, 소중한 unrelated 관련[관계] 없는 terminate 끝나다, 종료되다 store credit 반환하는 물건 값이 적힌 표 deposit 착수금, 보증금; 예금[예치]하다 penalty 처벌, 형벌; 벌금, 위약금 subscription 구독(료) finalize 마무리 짓다, 결정하다 restrict 제한[한정]하다; 방해하다 mandatory 법에 정해진, 의무적인 optional 선택적인 voluntary 자발적인, 자진한

74. 이메일의 목적은 무엇인가?
(a) 멤버십을 종료하고 돈을 환불하는 것
(b) 주문 상태 변화를 알리는 것
(c) 멤버십 요금이 청구되지 않았다고 알리는 것
(d) 새로운 제목의 팟캐스트 서비스를 제공하는 것

두 번째 단락에서 글쓴이가 'cancelled the Audible membership(오더블 멤버십을 취소했으며)' 상대방의 신용 카드로 'issued a refund(환불금을 지급했다)'고 했으므로 본 이메일의 목적은 (a)이다.

75. 돈은 어떻게 환불될 예정인가?
(a) 스토어 크레딧으로 환불한다
(b) 양 씨의 신용 카드로 돈을 입금한다
(c) 다른 오디오북과 교환한다
(d) 서비스 조기 종료 위약금의 50%를 깎아준다

두 번째 단락에서 'your Visa credit card(귀하의 비자 신용 카드)'로 환불금을 지급했다고 했고, 이는 곧 양 씨의 신용 카드로 환불금을 입금했다는 의미이므로 정답은 (b)이다.

76. 양 씨는 이후 어떤 이메일을 받게 되는가?
(a) 환불 확정
(b) 취소 확정
(c) 완전히 새로운 제안
(d) 새로운 오디오북 제목의 목록

두 번째 단락에서 'confirming your cancellation(귀하의 취소를 확정하는)' 자동 이메일이 발송될 것이라 말했으므로 정답은 (b)이다.

77. 멤버십 취소 후 오디오북엔 무슨 일이 일어나는가?
(a) 책들이 영구 삭제될 것이다.
(b) 다시 돌아오면 책에 접근할 수 있다.
(c) 그들에게 책에 대한 이메일을 다시 보낼 수 있다.
(d) 여전히 구매한 책에 접근할 수 있다

세 번째 단락에서 멤버십이 취소된 후에도 'listen to any of your titles in your library(귀하의 서재에 있는 책들을 청취할 수 있다)'고 했고, 이는 곧 예전에 구매한 책에 접근 가능하다는 의미이므로 정답은 (d)이다.

78. 새롭게 제공되는 팟캐스트에 접근하려면 무엇이 필요한가?
(a) 멤버십
(b) 스토어 크레딧
(c) 구독
(d) 없음

네 번째 단락에서 'membership is not compulsory(멤버십이 필수가 아닌) free podcasts(무료 팟캐스트)'가 새롭게 제공되는 걸 아는지 묻고 있고, 이걸 듣는 데엔 아무런 조건이 붙지 않았으므로 정답은 (d)이다.

79. 글의 문맥에서, confirmed는 _____을 의미한다.
(a) unknown (알려지지 않은)
(b) hidden (감춰진)
(c) finalized (완료된)
(d) restricted (제한된)

밑줄 친 confirmed는 'confirm(확정[확인]하다)'라는 동사에서 파생된 표현으로서 보기 중 이와 일맥상통하는 것은 '(c) finalized(완료된)'이다.

80. 글의 문맥에서, compulsory는 _____을 의미한다.
(a) mandatory (의무적인)
(b) optional (선택적인)
(c) voluntary (자발적인)
(d) open (개방된)

밑줄 친 compulsory는 '강제적인, 의무적인, 필수의'라는 뜻을 가진 형용사로서 보기 중 이와 일맥상통하는 것은 '(a) mandatory(의무적인)'이다.

Actual Test 04 / Vocab 주요 어휘 총정리

Actual Test 04에 등장했던 주요 어휘를 한눈에 훑어보며 정리해 보도록 합시다.
모르는 어휘가 있을 경우 박스(☐)에 체크(V) 표시를 한 뒤 재차 암기하도록 하세요.

- ☐ architect 건축가
- ☐ contemporary 동시대의; 현대의, 당대의
- ☐ functional 기능 위주의, 실용적인
- ☐ considerable 상당한, 많은; 중요한
- ☐ turbulence 격동, 격변; 난류, 난기류
- ☐ initially 처음에
- ☐ architecture 건축학[술]; 건축 양식
- ☐ make use of ~을 이용[활용]하다
- ☐ construction 건설, 공사
- ☐ distinctive 독특한
- ☐ controversial 논란이 많은
- ☐ criticize 비판하다, 비난하다
- ☐ temper 완화시키다; 지배하다, 억제하다
- ☐ majestic 장엄한, 위풍당당한
- ☐ exile 추방하다, 유배하다
- ☐ unrest (사회·정치적인) 불안[불만]
- ☐ shatter 산산이 부서지다
- ☐ three-dimensional 3차원의
- ☐ virtual 가상의
- ☐ coin (새로운 낱말을) 만들다; 주조하다
- ☐ populate 살다, 거주하다
- ☐ serious money 거액의 돈
- ☐ dimension 크기, 치수; 규모; 차원, 관점
- ☐ forge 구축하다; 위조하다
- ☐ establish 설립[설정]하다; 수립하다
- ☐ wearable 입을 수 있는; 의복, 옷
- ☐ wander 거닐다, 돌아다니다
- ☐ advent 도래, 출현
- ☐ ownership 소유(권)
- ☐ transact 거래하다
- ☐ invest 투자하다
- ☐ process 가공하다, 처리하다
- ☐ currency 통화; 통용
- ☐ inhabit 살다, 거주[서식]하다
- ☐ situate (어떤 위치에) 두다; 고려하다

- ☐ irregular 고르지 못한; 불규칙적인
- ☐ passive 수동적인, 소극적인
- ☐ emergence 출현, 발생
- ☐ consumption 소비[소모](량)
- ☐ nutrition 영양
- ☐ prevalent 일반적인, 널리 퍼져 있는
- ☐ consume 소모하다; 먹다, 마시다
- ☐ primitive 원시 사회의; 미개의
- ☐ substantial 상당한; 크고 튼튼한
- ☐ aversion 아주 싫어함, 혐오감
- ☐ popularize 대중화하다, 많은 사람들에게 알리다
- ☐ delicacy 섬세함; 별미, 진미
- ☐ livestock 가축
- ☐ negligible 무시해도 될 정도의
- ☐ ethnic 민족[종족]의; 민족 전통적인
- ☐ immune system 면역 체계
- ☐ insignificant 대수롭지 않은, 하찮은
- ☐ issue a refund 환불금을 지급하다, 환불해 주다
- ☐ automated 자동화된, 자동의
- ☐ confirm 확인해 주다; 확정하다, 공식화하다
- ☐ cancellation 취소, 무효화
- ☐ compulsory 강제적인, 의무적인, 필수의
- ☐ look into ~을 조사하다[주의 깊게 살피다]
- ☐ valued 귀중한, 소중한
- ☐ unrelated 관련[관계] 없는
- ☐ terminate 끝나다, 종료되다
- ☐ store credit 반환하는 물건 값이 적힌 표
- ☐ deposit 착수금, 보증금; 예금[예치]하다
- ☐ penalty 처벌, 형벌; 벌금, 위약금
- ☐ subscription 구독(료)
- ☐ finalize 마무리 짓다, 완결하다
- ☐ restrict 제한[한정]하다; 방해하다
- ☐ mandatory 법에 정해진, 의무적인
- ☐ optional 선택적인
- ☐ voluntary 자발적인, 자진한

Reading and Vocabulary Section
Actual Test 05

▶▶ 정답 & 나의 점수 확인

테스트 날짜: _____ 월 _____ 일 / 테스트 점수: _____

53 (b) 54 (c) 55 (d) 56 (d) 57 (a) 58 (b) 59 (c) 60 (d) 61 (d) 62 (a) 63 (c) 64 (a) 65 (d) 66 (b)
67 (c) 68 (a) 69 (a) 70 (c) 71 (b) 72 (b) 73 (a) 74 (c) 75 (c) 76 (b) 77 (a) 78 (d) 79 (a) 80 (d)

▶▶ 출제 경향 & 흐름 파악

지피지기면 백전백승! 출제 경향과 흐름을 한눈에 파악해 봅시다. 출제된 지문이 어떤 종류의 글이었는지, 각 지문과 관련해 어떤 종류의 문제가 출제되었는지 아래의 표를 보며 정리해 보세요.

(인물) 유명 컴퓨터 기술자에 대한 소개글	53	인물이 유명한 이유	(의학) 색맹의 원인 및 유형에 대한 설명글	67	색맹의 정의
	54	인물이 뛰어났던 분야		68	색상을 식별하게 하는 요소
	55	개발하고 싶어 했던 제품		69	원추 세포가 없는 경우의 결과
	56	제품으로 하고자 했던 일		70	색맹에 영향을 받는 대상
	57	회사를 떠난 이유		71	색맹을 관리할 수 있는 방법
	58	어휘 문제: affordable		72	어휘 문제: severe
	59	어휘 문제: conceive		73	어휘 문제: dim
(문화) 고대 그리스 이상주의에 대한 설명글	60	그리스 이상주의의 정의	(안내) 학교 폐쇄 조치에 대한 안내 서신	74	서신의 목적
	61	협력과 나눔에 가치를 둔 이유		75	학교가 폐쇄를 결정한 이유
	62	그리스 정부의 특징		76	수업이 진행되는 방식
	63	운동 경기를 장려한 이유		77	민박 가정에 연락하는 이유
	64	파르테논이 중요한 이유		78	비상 시 권고되는 행동
	65	어휘 문제: devoted		79	어휘 문제: ensure
	66	어휘 문제: feat		80	어휘 문제: available

STEVE WOZNIAK

스티브 위즈니악

53 Steve Wozniak invented the Apple computer and helped found the Apple Computer Company. He is one of the wealthiest and most famous inventors in the U.S. Wozniak left the world of business to spend his time teaching children about computers.

Stephen Gary Wozniak was born on August 11, 1950 in San Jose, California, to Margaret Wozniak, a homemaker, and Jerry Wozniak, an electrical engineer. **54** Although he was never a star student in the traditional sense, Wozniak had an aptitude for building working electronics from scratch. Wozniak built his own radio transmitter and receiver from a kit. At 11, he built a machine he called a "ticktacktoe" computer.

Wozniak went to the University of California, at Berkeley. There, with the help of a high school friend named Steve Jobs, who was later to be his business partner at Apple Computer, **55** Wozniak wanted to design an inexpensive personal computer, which was easy to program, **58** affordable, and fun. **56** When he completed his computer design, Jobs thought it could be a commercial success and wanted to market it. Jobs came up with the name "Apple." They sold personal possessions to raise money and worked in Jobs's family garage. Not long after Apple was founded, Wozniak created the Apple I. **56** With Wozniak's knowledge of electronics and Jobs' marketing skills, the two were well-suited to do business together. Wozniak went on to **59** conceive the Apple II. Priced at only $1,298, the computer was a great success.

By the end of its first year, the company had made almost three quarters of a million dollars in sales. The company grew and went public just four years after it started in 1980. The next two personal computers from Apple, the Apple III and the Lisa, were not very successful. Jobs put all his efforts into the development of the Macintosh. The Macintosh was introduced with much fanfare during the Super Bowl. It was a huge success. However, Apple was coming under increasing pressure from the PC designed by IBM. The PC was much cheaper than the Macintosh and Apple sales began to decline. Jobs took the blame and resigned from Apple in 1985.

57 Frustrated with Apple management, Wozniak also left the company and founded numerous ventures, including CL9, the company responsible for the first programmable universal remote control.

Wozniak was awarded, along with Jobs, a National Medal of Technology by the U.S. President Ronald W. Reagan and published his autobiography.

어휘 invent 발명하다 homemaker (전업)주부 electrical engineer 전기 기술자, 전기 기사 star student 최우수 학생 aptitude 소질, 적성 from scratch 아무런 사전 준비[지식] 없이 kit 조립 용품 세트 inexpensive 비싸지 않은 program 프로그램; 프로그램을 짜다[설정하다] affordable (가격이) 알맞은 commercial success 상업적인 성공 market (상품을) 내놓다[광고하다] possession 소유(물), 소지(품) garage 차고, 주차장 well-suited 적합한, 편리한; 궁합이 좋은 conceive (생각·계획 등을) 마음속으로 하다[품다] go public 주식을 공개[상장]하다 fanfare 팡파르; 과시; 선전, 광고 decline 줄어들다, 감소하다 resign 사직[사임]하다, 물러나다 programmable 프로그램 작동이 가능한 autobiography 자서전 funding 자금 (제공) incapable ~을 할 수 없는, ~하지 못하는 durable 내구성이 있는, 오래가는

---

53. 스티브 워즈니악은 무엇으로 가장 유명한가?
  (a) 범용 리모콘을 만든 것으로
  (b) 유명한 회사 설립에 도움을 준 것으로
  (c) 스티브 잡스와 친구인 것으로
  (d) 학교에서 아이들을 가르치는 것으로

> 첫 단락에서 워즈니악이 애플 컴퓨터를 개발했으며 'helped found the Apple Computer Company(애플 컴퓨터 회사를 창립하는 데 도움을 주었다)'고 설명돼 있으므로 정답은 (b)이다.

54. 워즈니악은 무엇을 잘했는가?
  (a) 시험에서 좋은 점수를 얻는 것
  (b) 컴퓨터로 tic tac toe를 하는 것
  (c) 실용적인 기기를 고안하는 것
  (d) 어린아이들을 가르치고 돕는 것

> 두 번째 단락에서 워즈니악이 전형적으로 우수한 학생은 아니었지만 'building working electronics(실용적인 전자 기기를 만드는 데)' 소질이 있었다고 설명돼 있으므로 정답은 (c)이다.

55. 워즈니악은 어떤 컴퓨터를 만들길 원했는가?
  (a) 상업적으로 성공적인
  (b) 복잡하고 전문적인
  (c) 비싸고 멋진
  (d) 저렴하고 작동이 용이한

> 세 번째 단락에서 'easy to program, affordable, and fun(프로그램을 짜기 쉽고, 가격이 알맞고, 재미있는)' 퍼스널 컴퓨터를 설계하고 싶어 했다고 설명돼 있으므로 정답은 (d)이다.

56. 스티브 잡스는 워즈니악의 컴퓨터로 무엇을 하길 원했는가?
  (a) 이들을 만들고 싶어 했다.
  (b) 자금을 얻고 싶어 했다.
  (c) 이들을 변경하고 싶어 했다.
  (d) 이들을 팔고 싶어 했다

> 세 번째 단락에서 잡스가 워즈니악이 만든 컴퓨터를 'wanted to market it(시장에 내놓아 팔고 싶어 했으며)' 그가 'marketing skills(마케팅 능력)' 또한 갖추고 있다고 서술되어 있으므로 정답은 (d)이다.

57. 워즈니악은 왜 애플 회사를 떠났는가?
  (a) 경영에 불만족스러움을 느꼈다
  (b) 새로운 컴퓨터를 만들 수 없다고 느꼈다.
  (c) 만족감을 느끼고 회사에서 은퇴했다.
  (d) 일을 하기에 너무 늙었다고 느꼈다.

> 다섯 번째 단락에서 워즈니악이 'frustrated with Apple management(애플 경영에 좌절을 느껴서)' 회사를 떠났다고 서술되어 있으므로 정답은 (a)이다.

58. 글의 문맥에서, affordable은 _____을 의미한다.
  (a) afraid (두려운)
  (b) economical (경제적인)
  (c) fancy (화려한)
  (d) durable (내구성이 있는)

> 밑줄 친 affordable은 '가격이 알맞은'이라는 뜻의 형용사이며, 가격이 알맞다는 건 결국 '경제적'이라는 의미로 해석 가능하기 때문에 정답은 (b)이다.

59. 글의 문맥에서, conceive는 _____을 의미한다.
  (a) miss (놓치다)
  (b) avoid (피하다)
  (c) design (설계하다)
  (d) destroy (파괴하다)

> 밑줄 친 conceive는 '(생각·계획 등을) 마음속으로 하다, 고안하다'라는 뜻을 가진 동사로서 보기 중 이와 일맥상통하는 것은 '(c) desgn(설계하다)'이다.

GREEK IDEALISM

그리스 이상주의

Ancient Greek civilization emerged around 1200 BC in a privileged place between the Mediterranean Sea and the Aegean Sea. This territory was made up of a peninsula and a group of islands. Ancient Greeks were settlers. They didn't just conform to staying in their territory. They wanted to look for and colonize new lands to expand their civilization. They reached many parts of the Mediterranean Sea extending their commercial activity and craftsmanship trade. 60 Ancient Greek society was 65 devoted to finding the highest standards of perfection. Some of these Greek ideas still have an influence on modern life and are the basis of what is referred to as the classical ideal.

Values

61 The ancient Greeks valued cooperation and sharing, personal achievement, hospitality, friendship, and hard work. These were the foundation for ancient Greek society. Men and women were expected to live up to these high ideals for a harmonious and orderly society.

Government

Ancient Greeks called their cities poleis and each one of them had its own government. The earliest form of democracy began in ancient Athens. The city was divided into ten tribes. 62 Each tribe would send fifty men to a council of five hundred. They served for a month after which another fifty representatives were appointed. Only male citizens could serve. It was the first representative government, and it served as a model for many countries' systems of government around the world.

Athletics

63 In ancient Greece, physical beauty was seen as a direct link to mental beauty. The people of this time celebrated the body and had high standards for both men and women. An ideal male would be athletic and muscular as sports were highly important in that era. The classic athletic activities were boxing, wrestling, and track and field. Ancient Greeks held athletic games between city-states. These became the first Olympic Games.

Architecture and Art

The Greek ideal for art and architecture was order and harmony. States were idealized and created to show perfect human forms. 64 The Parthenon is the ultimate example of order and harmony and a 66 feat of engineering genius. The massive columns tilt inward slightly to hold up the heavy roof. It is also used to proclaim to the world the success of Athens in defeating the invading Persians and symbolizing the wealth and power the city possessed. Greek-inspired architecture is seen today throughout the world.

어휘 civilization 문명 (사회) emerge 나오다; 생겨나다, 부상하다 privileged 특권[특전]을 가진; 영광스러운 territory 지역, 영토 settler 정착민 conform (관습 등에) 따르다[순응하다]; ~에 일치하다 colonize 식민지로 만들다 craftsmanship 손재주; (장인의) 기능; 숙련 devoted to ~에 헌신하는[전념하는] cooperation 협력, 협동, 협동 hospitality 환대, 후대 live up to ~의 기대에 부응하다 harmonious 조화로운 orderly 정돈된, 정연한 tribe 부족, 종족 appoint 임명[지명]하다 athletic (몸이) 탄탄한 muscular 근육의, 근육질의 track and field 육상 경기 city–state 도시 국가 ultimate 궁극[최종]적인; 최고[최상]의 feat 위업, 개가 tilt 기울다, (뒤로) 젖혀지다 proclaim 선언[선포]하다 invade 침입[침략]하다 strive 노력하다, 분투하다 disloyal 불충실한, 불충한 unfaithful 부정직한, 부정한 dedicated 전념하는, 헌신적인

60. 그리스 이상주의는 무엇인가?
    (a) 여성과 남성의 이상적인 모습
    (b) 성취하고자 노력하는 기준(규범)
    (c) 이상적인 정부 시스템
    (d) 예술과 건축에 대한 개념

첫 단락에서 고대 그리스가 'devoted to finding the highest standards of perfection(최고 수준의 완벽함을 찾는 것에 전념했다)'고 했고, 이는 곧 최고를 추구하기 위해 노력했음을 뜻하므로 정답은 (b)이다.

61. 그리스 사람들은 왜 협력과 나눔에 가치를 두었는가?
    (a) 아테네 주변의 다른 도시 국가들을 장악하기 위해
    (b) 도시 국가들을 위한 올림픽 대회를 열기 위해
    (c) 그리스인들의 부와 힘을 퍼뜨리기 위해
    (d) 정연하고 조화로운 사회를 유지하기 위해

두 번째 단락에서 고대 그리스인들은 협력과 나눔 등을 가치로 삼아 이에 맞춰 살며 'harmonious and orderly society(조화롭고 질서 정연한 사회)'를 만들고자 노력했다고 했으므로 정답은 (d)이다.

62. 그리스 정부에 있어 특별한 점은 무엇인가?
    (a) 대표자(대리인)가 있다
    (b) 왕과 왕비가 있다.
    (c) 귀족과 기사가 있다.
    (d) 제 명의 선출된 왕이 있다.

세 번째 단락에서 고대 그리스의 각 종족이 50명의 남성을 의회에 보내 복무하게 하고, 그다음 또 다른 'fifty representatives(50명의 대표자들)'을 뽑아 복무하게 했다고 했으므로 정답은 (a)이다.

63. 그리스인들은 왜 운동 경기를 장려했는가?
    (a) 전쟁에 대비하고 싶어 했기 때문에
    (b) 올림픽에서 우승하고 싶었기 때문에
    (c) 완벽한 신체가 완벽한 정신을 보여주기 때문에
    (d) 스파르타와 경쟁하고 있었기 때문에

네 번째 단락에서 고대 그리스에선 'physical beauty was seen as a direct link to mental beauty(신체적 아름다움은 정신적 아름다움에 직결된다)'고 생각하여 운동이 중요했다고 했으므로 정답은 (c)이다.

64. 파르테논은 왜 중요한가?
    (a) 그리스 이상주의를 상징하기 때문에
    (b) 거대한 기둥을 갖고 있기 때문에
    (c) 지붕이 지탱하기에 굉장히 무겁기 때문에
    (d) 많은 사람들이 이것을 보러 오기 때문에

마지막 단락에서 파르테논이 고대 그리스의 핵심 가치인 'order and harmony(질서와 조화)'를 보여주는 최고의 예시라 했고, 이는 곧 그리스의 이상주의를 상징하는 것이라 볼 수 있으므로 정답은 (a)이다.

65. 글의 문맥에서, devoted는 _____을 의미한다.
    (a) disloyal (불충한)
    (b) unfaithful (부정한)
    (c) different (다른)
    (d) dedicated (헌신적인)

밑줄 친 devoted는 '헌신하는, 전념하는'이라는 뜻을 가진 형용사로서 보기 중 이와 일맥상통하는 것은 '(d) dedicated(헌신적인, 전념하는)'이다.

66. 글의 문맥에서, feat는 _____을 의미한다.
    (a) courage (용기)
    (b) achievement (위업)
    (c) practice (관행)
    (d) adventure (모험)

밑줄 친 feat는 '위업, 개가'라는 뜻을 가진 명사로서 보기 중 이와 일맥상통하는 것은 '(b) achievement(위업, 성취, 업적)'이다.

67-73 (의학) 색맹의 원인 및 유형에 대한 설명글

COLOR BLINDNESS

색맹

White light has every color of the rainbow hidden inside it. Each color is a different wavelength. Things appear to be different colors because they absorb and reflect different wavelengths of light. A strawberry looks red because it reflects red wavelengths while absorbing most others.

People see colors because our eyes respond differently to different wavelengths of light. When light enters one of the eyes, it gets focused on the retina. The retina is a thin layer of tissue at the back of the eyeball. The light triggers rod cells and cone cells. These cells send signals to the brain, which uses the signals to make images. Rods detect only light and dark and are very sensitive to low light levels. 68 Cone cells detect color and are concentrated near the center of our vision. There are three types of cones that see color: red, green and blue. The brain uses input from these cone cells to determine our color perception.

Color blindness can happen when one or more of the color cone cells are absent, not working, or detect a different color than normal. 72 Severe color blindness occurs when all three cone cells are absent.

There are different degrees of color blindness. 67 Some people with mild color deficiencies can see colors normally in good light but have difficulty in 73 dim light. Others cannot distinguish certain colors in any light. 69 The most severe form of color blindness, in which everything is seen in shades of gray, occurs when one has no working cone cell. It is uncommon. Color blindness usually affects both eyes equally and remains stable throughout life. Color blindness is usually something that you have from birth but you can also get it later in life.

70 Men are at much higher risk for being born with color blindness than women, who seldom have the problem. An estimated one in ten males has some form of color deficiency.

Color blindness can also cause safety issues. Fire hydrants and emergency equipment are often colored red or yellow to make them more visible. Someone who is color-blind may not notice bright colors that stand out to those with full-color vision.

There is no treatment for color blindness. It usually does not cause any significant disability. 70 However, there are special contact lenses and glasses that may help.

백색광은 무지개의 모든 빛깔을 내부에 숨겨서 갖고 있다. 각 색깔은 각기 다른 파장을 갖고 있다. 사물들은 각기 다른 빛의 파장을 흡수하고 반사하기 때문에 다양한 색깔로 모습이 나타난다. 딸기는 다른 빛의 파장들을 흡수하는 반면 빨간 파장을 반사하기 때문에 빨갛게 보인다.

사람들은 눈이 다양한 파장에 각기 다르게 반응하기 때문에 색깔을 볼 수 있다. 빛이 한쪽 눈에 들어가면, 이것은 망막에 초점이 맞춰진다. 망막은 안구 뒤쪽에 있는 얇은 조직막이다. 빛은 간상 세포와 원추 세포를 반응하게 한다. 이 세포들은 뇌에 신호를 보내고, 뇌는 신호를 사용해 이미지를 만든다. 간상 세포는 빛과 어둠만을 감지하며 낮은 조도에 매우 민감하다. 68 원추 세포는 색을 감지하고 우리 시야의 중앙에 집중한다. 원추 세포엔 빨간색, 녹색, 파란색을 보는 세 종류의 원추 세포가 있다. 뇌는 원추 세포에서 입력한 내용으로 우리의 색 지각을 결정한다.

색맹은 하나 혹은 그 이상의 색상 원추 세포가 없거나 작동하지 않고, 혹은 정상보다 다양한 색깔을 감지할 때 발생할 수 있다. 72 심각한 색맹은 원추 세포 3개가 모두 없을 때 발생한다.

색맹의 수준은 각기 다르다. 67 가벼운 수준의 색상 결함을 가진 일부 사람들은 빛이 밝을 땐 보통 색을 잘 보지만 73 희미한 빛일 땐 어려움을 겪는다. 다른 이들은 어느 빛에서나 특정 색깔을 식별하지 못한다. 69 모든 것이 회색으로 보이는 가장 심각한 유형의 색맹은 작동하는 원추 세포가 하나도 없을 때 발생한다. 이것은 드문 경우이다. 색맹은 보통 양쪽 눈에 동일하게 영향을 미치며, 일생 내내 변함없이 지속된다. 색맹은 일반적으로 타고나는 것이긴 하지만 살면서 나중에 발생할 가능성도 있다. 70 남성은 여성보다 색맹을 갖고 태어날 위험이 훨씬 더 높으며, 여성은 문제가 거의 없는 편이다. 한 추정치에 따르면 남성 10명 중 한 명이 색상 결함과 관련된 문제를 갖고 있다고 한다.

색맹은 안전 문제를 유발할 가능성도 있다. 소화전과 비상 장비는 보통 눈에 좀 더 잘 띄게 하기 위해 빨간색이나 노란색 색상을 지닌다. 색맹인 사람들은 총천연색 시야를 가진 사람들에겐 보이는 밝은 색상을 알아보지 못할 수 있다.

색맹엔 치료법이 없다. 이것은 보통 그 어떤 큰 장애도 유발하지 않는다. 70 하지만, 도움이 될 수 있는 특수 콘택트렌즈와 안경이 존재한다.

어휘 color blindness 색맹 wavelength 파장; 주파수 absorb 흡수하다, 빨아들이다 reflect 비추다; 반사하다 retina 망막 layer 막, 층, 겹 tissue (세포들로 이뤄진) 조직 rod cell 간상 세포 trigger 일으키다, 유발하다, 촉발하다 cone cell 원추 세포 detect 발견하다, 알아내다, 감지하다 concentrate 집중하다[집중시키다], 전념하다 perception 지각, 자각 severe 극심한, 심각한; 가혹한, 혹독한 deficiency 결핍[부족](증); 결점, 결함 dim 어둑한, 흐릿한 distinguish 구별하다; 식별하다 uncommon 흔하지 않은, 드문 equally 똑같이, 균등하게 stable 안정된; 변동 없는 estimate 추산[추정]하다 fire hydrant 소화전 visible (눈에) 보이는, 알아볼 수 있는; 가시적인, 뚜렷한 disability (신체적 · 정신적) 장애 shape 모양, 형태, 형상 tell apart 구별하다, 분간하다 corrective surgery 교정 수술 remedy 처리 방안, 해결[개선]책

67. 색맹은 무엇인가?
 (a) 그 어떤 색깔도 볼 수 없게 된 것
 (b) 형태를 식별할 수 없게 된 것
 (c) 특정 색상을 분간할 수 없게 된 것
 (d) 어둠 속에서 볼 수 없게 된 것

네 번째 단락에서 색맹은 '희미할 때 색상을 제대로 못 보는 경우, certain colors(특정 색깔들)을 식별하지 못하는 경우, 모든 게 회색으로 보이는 경우'와 같이 설명하고 있으므로 정답은 (c)이다.

68. 색상을 보는 걸 책임지는 것은 무엇인가?
 (a) 원추 세포
 (b) 간상 세포
 (c) 망막
 (d) 뇌

두 번째 단락에서 'cone cells detect color(원추 세포가 색을 감지하고)' 우리 시야의 중앙에 집중하는 세포라고 설명돼 있으므로 정답은 (a)이다. 참고로 간상 세포는 '빛과 어둠'을 감지하는 세포이다.

69. 작동하는 원추 세포가 없는 사람들에겐 무슨 일이 생기는가?
 (a) 모든 것이 회색 색조로 보인다
 (b) 어둠 속에서 색상을 식별할 수 없다.
 (c) 모든 것이 녹색 색조로 보인다.
 (d) 그 어떤 색상과 형태도 볼 수 없다.

네 번째 단락에서 'everything is seen in shades of gray(모든 것이 회색으로 보이는)' 유형의 색맹은 기능하는 원추 세포가 하나도 없을 때 발생한다고 설명돼 있으므로 정답은 (a)이다.

70. 누가 색맹에 더 많은 영향을 받는가?
 (a) 여성
 (b) 아이들
 (c) 남성
 (d) 성인

다섯 번째 단락에서 여성보다 'men are at much higher risk for being born with color blindness(남성이 색맹을 갖고 태어날 위험이 훨씬 더 높다)'고 설명돼 있으므로 정답은 (c)이다.

71. 색맹을 바로잡는 데 무엇이 사용될 수 있는가?
 (a) 교정 수술
 (b) 특수 안경
 (c) 처방된 약
 (d) 특정 가정 치료법

마지막 단락에서 색맹엔 치료법이 없지만 'special contact lenses and glasses that may help(도움이 될 수 있는 특수 콘택트렌즈와 안경)'이 있다고 설명돼 있으므로 정답은 (b)이다.

72. 글의 문맥에서, severe는 _____을 의미한다.
 (a) mild (가벼운)
 (b) extreme (심각한)
 (c) gentle (온화한)
 (d) weak (약한)

밑줄 친 severe는 '심각한, 극심한'이라는 뜻을 가진 형용사로서 보기 중 이와 일맥상통하는 것은 '(b) extreme(극도의, 극심한, 지나친, 심각한)'이다.

73. 글의 문맥에서, dim은 _____을 의미한다.
 (a) faint (희미한)
 (b) vivid (생생한)
 (c) clear (분명한)
 (d) fancy (화려한)

밑줄 친 dim은 '어둑한, 흐릿한'이라는 뜻을 가진 형용사로서 보기 중 이와 일맥상통하는 것은 '(a) faint(희미한, 약한)'이다.

74-80 (안내) 학교 폐쇄 조치에 대한 안내 서신

Dear Miss Kim,

74 75 After careful consideration, and based on guidance from the State of California, the California Department of Education, and the Student and Exchange Visitor Program (SEVP), we will be closing our school and canceling all school-related activities as of Tuesday, March 17, 2020, through Friday, April 3, 2020 for 3 weeks.

Here are steps we are taking to **79** ensure a smooth operation during this public health crisis:

1. **76** Classes will be held on our existing online platform, Canvas, on http://qis.instructure.com, starting Tuesday, March 17, 2020, through Friday, April 3, 2020.
2. We are closely monitoring information from the Center for Disease Control and Prevention (CDC), and federal, state and local agencies to help ensure actions we're taking are in line with the latest CDC recommendations and guidance and will monitor and update the school's closure accordingly.
3. **77** We are in close contact with our host families to ensure students who are staying in a host family are in good health.
4. We are committed to helping when our partners and students need us.
   a. Teachers will be **80** available online for all students during class hours and via email.
   b. Staff will be available for all agent partners and students both in person on a limited time schedule and via email/social media/phone.

78 If you have any urgent questions or requests, please contact Alvin, our Associate School Director, directly. His email is alvinb@gschool.com

We want you to know that you can continue to rely on us. We truly appreciate your patience and trust in Q international School. We are here to serve you, and we will be here when you need us.

Stay healthy and safe.

Sincerely,
Sarah Zimmer
Center Director
Q International School
1234 Fifth Avenue, San Diego CA
92090

김 씨에게

74 75 진지한 고려 및 캘리포니아 주의 지침 및 캘리포니아 교육부, 교환 학생 프로그램(SEVP)의 방침을 근거로 저희는 2020년 3월 17일 화요일부터 2020년 4월 3일 금요일까지 3주 동안 학교를 폐쇄하고 학교와 관련된 모든 활동들을 취소할 예정입니다.

저희는 이 같은 공중 보건 위기를 겪는 동안 원활한 운영을 **79** 보장하기 위해 다음과 같은 조치를 취할 것입니다.

1. **76** 수업은 저희의 기존 온라인 플랫폼 캔버스에서 http://qis.instructure.com을 통해 2020년 17일 화요일에 시작해 2020년 4월 3일 금요일까지 진행됩니다.
2. 저희는 질병 관리 예방 센터(CDC) 및 연방, 주, 지역 단체들의 정보를 면밀히 모니터링하여 저희가 취하고 있는 조치가 CDC의 최신 권고 및 방침에 맞는지 확실히 하고 있으며 이에 맞춰 학교 폐쇄에 대해 모니터링하고 정보를 업데이트할 것입니다.
3. **77** 저희는 민박 가정과 긴밀히 연락을 주고받아 민박 가정에 머물고 있는 학생들이 건강한 상태인지 여부를 확실히 보장하고 있습니다.
4. 저희는 파트너와 학생들이 저희를 필요로 할 때 돕는 것에 전념을 다하고 있습니다.
   a. 교사들은 수업 시간 및 이메일을 통해 모든 학생들에게 온라인으로 **80** 응대 가능할 것입니다.
   b. 직원들은 제한된 일정표 및 이메일/소셜 미디어/전화를 통해 직접 대리인 파트너와 학생들 모두에게 응대 가능할 것입니다.

78 긴급한 질문이나 요청이 있을 경우, 저희 측 학교 부책임자인 앨빈에게 바로 연락하시기 바랍니다. 그의 이메일 주소는 alvinb@gschool.com입니다.

귀하께서 계속 저희에게 의지하실 수 있음을 부디 알아 주셨으면 합니다. Q 국제 학교에 대해 인내심과 신뢰를 가져 주신 귀하께 진심으로 감사의 마음을 표합니다. 저희는 이곳에서 귀하를 모시고, 저희가 필요하실 때 이곳에 있을 것입니다.

건강하시고 안전하시기 바랍니다.

진심을 담아,
사라 짐머
센터 책임자
Q 국제 학교
샌디에고 CA 5번 가 1234
92090

어휘 careful 조심하는, 주의 깊은; 세심한 consideration 사려, 숙고; 배려 guidance 지도, 지침, 안내 public health crisis 공중 보건 위기 Center for Disease Control and Prevention 질병 관리 예방 센터 be in line with ~와 일치하다 closure 폐쇄; 종료, 종결 accordingly (상황에) 부응해서, 그에 맞춰 host family 민박 가정[가족] committed to ~에 전념하는 in person 직접 rely on ~에 기대다, ~에 의존하다 assign 맡기다, 배정하다; 파견하다; 배치하다 scheduling 일정 관리 conflict 갈등, 충돌 complaint 불평, 항의 ongoing 계속 진행 중인 submit 제출하다; 항복[굴복]하다 supervise 감독[지휘/지도]하다 designated 지정된 guarantee 보장[약속]하다; 보증하다 expose 드러내다, 폭로하다 edible 식용의 doable 할 수 있는 foreseeable 예측할 수 있는 reachable 닿을 수 있는

74. 이 서신의 목적은 무엇인가?
(a) 수업 일정 변경을 알리는 것
(b) 민박 가정을 배정하는 것
(c) 학교 폐쇄를 알리는 것
(d) 불법 행위를 경고하는 것

첫 단락에서 글쓴이가 'closing our school(학교를 폐쇄하고), cancelling all school-related activities(학교와 관련된 모든 활동들을 취소)'하는 것에 이야기하고 있으므로 정답은 (c)이다.

75. 학교는 왜 폐쇄하기로 결정했는가?
(a) 학교가 일정 관리 갈등을 겪고 있기 때문에
(b) 학교에서 불만 사항을 접수 받았기 때문에
(c) 주 정부가 권고했기 때문에
(d) 계속 진행 중인 공사로 인해

첫 단락에서 글쓴이가 'guidance from the State of California(캘리포니아 주의 지침)'에 따라서 학교를 3주 동안 폐쇄할 예정이라고 말하고 있기 때문에 정답은 (c)이다.

76. 수업은 어떻게 진행될 예정인가?
(a) 학생들을 일대일로 돕기
(b) 이들만의 온라인 시스템을 이용하기
(c) 소셜 미디어에서 소통하기
(d) 직접 숙제를 제출하기

세 번째 단락에서 글쓴이가 'our existing online platform, Canvas(우리의 기존 온라인 플랫폼 캔버스)'를 통해 수업이 진행될 예정이라고 설명했으므로 정답은 (b)이다.

77. 폐쇄한 학교는 왜 민박 가정에 연락을 취하는가?
(a) 이들의 학생들이 잘 있는지 확인하기 위해
(b) 불법 행위를 감독하기 위해
(c) 학생들이 밥을 먹는 걸 확실히 보장하기 위해
(d) 학생들에 대한 불만 사항을 수집하기 위해

다섯 번째 단락에서 민박 가정과 긴밀히 연락을 주고받으면서 이곳에 머물고 있는 학생들이 'are in good health(건강한 상태인지)' 여부를 확실히 보장하고 있다고 설명하고 있으므로 정답은 (a)이다.

78. 비상 상황이 됐을 경우 무엇을 할 것이 권고되는가?
(a) 민박 가정과 이야기한다
(b) 즉시 학교에 간다
(c) 사라 짐머에게 이메일 답장을 한다
(d) 지정된 사람에게 연락한다

여덟 번째 단락에서 글쓴이가 긴급한 질문이나 요청이 있을 경우 'our Associate School Director(우리의 학교 부책임자)'인 앨빈에게 연락하라고 말하고 있으므로 정답은 (d)이다.

79. 글의 문맥에서, ensure는 _____을 의미한다.
(a) guarantee (보장하다)
(b) expose (폭로하다)
(c) believe (믿다)
(d) take (취하다)

밑줄 친 ensure는 '보장하다, 확실히 하다'라는 뜻을 가진 동사로서 보기 중 이와 일맥상통하는 것은 (a) guarantee (보장[약속]하다, 보증하다)'이다.

80. 글의 문맥에서, available은 _____을 의미한다.
(a) edible (먹을 수 있는)
(b) doable (할 수 있는)
(c) foreseeable (예측할 수 있는)
(d) reachable (닿을 수 있는)

밑줄 친 available은 '이용(응대) 가능한'이라는 뜻을 가진 형용사이며, 이용 및 응대가 가능하다는 것은 '닿을 수 있고 접촉할 수 있는' 상태를 의미하므로 정답은 (d)이다.

Actual Test 05 / Vocab 주요 어휘 총정리

Actual Test 05에 등장했던 주요 어휘를 한눈에 훑어보며 정리해 보도록 합시다.
모르는 어휘가 있을 경우 박스(☐)에 체크(V) 표시를 한 뒤 재차 암기하도록 하세요.

- ☐ invent 발명하다
- ☐ aptitude 소질, 적성
- ☐ inexpensive 비싸지 않은
- ☐ affordable (가격이) 알맞은
- ☐ market (상품을) 내놓다[광고하다]
- ☐ possession 소유(물), 소지(품)
- ☐ well-suited 적합한, 편리한; 궁합이 좋은
- ☐ conceive (생각·계획 등을) 마음속으로 하다[품다]
- ☐ go public 주식을 공개[상장]하다
- ☐ resign 사직[사임]하다, 물러나다
- ☐ autobiography 자서전
- ☐ incapable ~을 할 수 없는, ~하지 못하는
- ☐ durable 내구성이 있는, 오래가는
- ☐ civilization 문명 (사회)
- ☐ emerge 나오다; 생겨나다, 부상하다
- ☐ privileged 특권[특전]을 가진; 영광스러운
- ☐ territory 지역, 영토
- ☐ conform 따르다[순응하다]; ~에 일치하다
- ☐ colonize 식민지로 만들다
- ☐ devoted to ~에 헌신하는[전념하는]
- ☐ cooperation 협력, 합동, 협동
- ☐ hospitality 환대, 후대
- ☐ live up to ~의 기대에 부응하다
- ☐ harmonious 조화로운
- ☐ orderly 정돈된, 정연한
- ☐ appoint 임명[지명]하다
- ☐ athletic (몸이) 탄탄한
- ☐ muscular 근육의, 근육질의
- ☐ ultimate 궁극[최종]적인; 최고[최상]의
- ☐ proclaim 선언[선포]하다
- ☐ invade 침입[침략]하다
- ☐ strive 노력하다, 분투하다
- ☐ disloyal 불충실한, 불충한
- ☐ unfaithful 부정직한, 부정한
- ☐ dedicated 전념하는, 헌신적인

- ☐ absorb 흡수하다, 빨아들이다
- ☐ reflect 비추다; 반사하다
- ☐ trigger 일으키다, 유발하다, 촉발하다
- ☐ detect 발견하다, 알아내다, 감지하다
- ☐ concentrate 집중하다[집중시키다], 전념하다
- ☐ perception 지각, 자각
- ☐ severe 극심한, 심각한; 가혹한, 혹독한
- ☐ deficiency 결핍[부족](증); 결점, 결함
- ☐ dim 어둑한, 흐릿한
- ☐ distinguish 구별하다; 식별하다
- ☐ uncommon 흔하지 않은, 드문
- ☐ equally 똑같이, 균등하게
- ☐ stable 안정된; 변동 없는
- ☐ estimate 추산[추정]하다
- ☐ visible (눈에) 보이는, 가시적인, 뚜렷한
- ☐ disability (신체적·정신적) 장애
- ☐ tell apart 구별하다, 분간하다
- ☐ remedy 처리 방안, 해결[개선]책
- ☐ careful 조심하는, 주의 깊은; 세심한
- ☐ consideration 사려, 숙고; 배려
- ☐ guidance 지도, 지침, 안내
- ☐ be in line with ~와 일치하다
- ☐ closure 폐쇄; 종료, 종결
- ☐ accordingly (상황에) 부응해서, 그에 맞춰
- ☐ committed to ~에 전념하는
- ☐ rely on ~에 기대다, ~에 의존하다
- ☐ assign 맡기다, 배정하다; 파견하다; 배치하다
- ☐ conflict 갈등, 충돌
- ☐ complaint 불평, 항의
- ☐ ongoing 계속 진행 중인
- ☐ submit 제출하다; 항복[굴복]하다
- ☐ supervise 감독[지휘/지도]하다
- ☐ guarantee 보장[약속]하다; 보증하다
- ☐ foreseeable 예측할 수 있는
- ☐ reachable 닿을 수 있는

어차피 제시카

G-TELP 모의고사

G-TELP | Level 2

Listening
청해 정답&해설

Actual Test 01 / 정답 & 해설
Actual Test 02 / 정답 & 해설

Listening Section
Actual Test 01

▶▶ **정답 & 나의 점수 확인**

테스트 날짜: _____월 _____일 / 테스트 점수: _____

27 (b) 28 (a) 29 (a) 30 (d) 31 (b) 32 (c) 33 (d) 34 (c) 35 (c) 36 (a) 37 (b) 38 (d) 39 (b)
40 (a) 41 (b) 42 (b) 43 (a) 44 (c) 45 (b) 46 (b) 47 (d) 48 (b) 49 (c) 50 (d) 51 (b) 52 (a)

▶▶ **출제 경향 & 흐름 파악**

지피지기면 백전백승! 출제 경향과 흐름을 한눈에 파악해 봅시다. 출제된 지문이 어떤 종류의 글이었는지, 각 지문과 관련해 어떤 종류의 문제가 출제되었는지 아래의 표를 보며 정리해 보세요.

(조언) 재정 문제에 대한 상담 및 조언	27	남성이 여성에게 한 부탁	(토론) 채식주의의 장단점에 대한 토론	40	워크샵에서 정보를 얻은 인물
	28	여성이 남성에게 한 지적 사항		41	채식주의 음식을 망설이는 이유
	29	남성이 돈에 쪼들리고 있는 이유		42	지방이 중요한 영양소인 이유
	30	남성이 시도하려 했으나 실패한 것		43	채식주의가 건강에 안 좋은 이유
	31	남성의 아파트에 대한 여성의 의견		44	채식주의자가 해야 할 행동
	32	여성이 남성에게 한 권고		45	채식주의자 아이의 특징
	33	남성이 빚진 금액이 증가한 이유		46	수잔이 다음에 하게 될 일
(안내) 항공기 이륙 전 기내 안내 방송	34	안내 방송의 목적	(소개) 명상에 대한 소개 및 센터 홍보	47	명상의 이점
	35	안전 카드를 봐야 하는 이유		48	명상에 필요한 권고 사항
	36	산소 마스크가 떨어지는 상황		49	화자가 생각하는 중요 사항
	37	산소 마스크 사용 시 권고 사항		50	명상이 힘든 이들을 위한 조언
	38	기물 파손 시 있게 될 조치		51	명상에 도움이 되는 부가 요소
	39	안내 방송 이후에 있을 예상 절차		52	문제 해결에 필요한 권고 사항

27-33 (조언) 재정 문제에 대한 상담 및 조언

27. What does John want from Mel?
28. What does Mel point out to John?
29. Why is most likely John short on money this month?
30. What did John try to do and never did?
31. What does Mel think of his studio apartment?
32. What does Mel recommend John to do?
33. Why did the amount of money John owe increase?

M: Hi Mel, I am so glad to run into you. How have you been?

F: Hi John. I've been great. Thanks. I took a trip to Greece with a couple of my friends this summer. How about you? How have you been?

M: I am doing okay, I guess. The trip to Greece sounds amazing. I haven't gone anywhere during the summer. **27** I have to ask you a favor though. Could I borrow a few bucks? I'm a little strapped for cash.

F: I guess. **28** You still owe me $500 from last month. How are things going anyway?

M: Well, not very well. I made some bad investment decisions. I've been watching the cryptocurrency markets for a few hours, and well, let's say my bank account is hurting.

F: I am sorry to hear that. I didn't know you were interested in investing. Is that why you are short on cash right now? I thought you landed a great job recently.

M: **29** Well, I do have a great job, but I've also used my credit cards to pay off a lot of things recently, but now, I can't seem to pay the money off.

F: Oh no, do you have a budget? I mean, **30** how do you keep track of your income and expenses?

M: Well, I meant to do it, but I never got around to doing it, but I guess I should have some financial plan.

F: Well, let me see if I can help you. How much money do you spend on your apartment?

M: Uh, I pay $890 on rent for the studio apartment downtown. Not including utilities and my cell phone bill, I pay around $250 for those.

M: 안녕 멜, 이렇게 만나서 반갑다. 어떻게 지냈어?

F: 안녕 존. 난 잘 지냈어. 고마워. 이번 여름에 친구들 몇 명이랑 그리스로 여행을 갔다 왔어. 넌 어때? 어떻게 지냈어?

M: 괜찮게 지내고 있는 것 같아. 그리스로 여행을 다녀왔다니 정말 멋지다. 난 여름 내내 아무 데도 안 갔거든. **27** 그나저나 나 너한테 부탁할 게 있어. 나 돈 좀 빌릴 수 있을까? 내가 현금이 부족해서.

F: 글쎄. **28** 너 지난달부터 아직도 나한테 500달러 빚진 상태잖아. 그나저나 요즘 좀 어때?

M: 그게, 썩 좋지 않아. 내가 투자를 잘 못했거든. 나 몇 시간 동안 가상 화폐 시장을 들여다보고 있었어. 뭐, 그냥 내 은행 계좌가 처참해졌다고 해 두자.

F: 그랬다니 정말 유감이다. 난 네가 투자에 관심이 있는 줄 몰랐어. 그게 지금 현금이 부족한 이유야? 난 네가 최근 좋은 직장을 구했다고 생각했는데.

M: **29** 나 좋은 직장에 다녀, 그런데 최근 이런저런 많은 것들에 돈을 갚느라 신용 카드를 썼거든. 지금 그 돈도 못 갚을 것 같아.

F: 이런. 너 예산 계획은 있는 거야? 그러니까, **30** 네 수입이랑 지출 비용은 어떻게 파악하고 있어?

M: 음, 파악하려고는 했는데, 내가 관심이 없었어. 하지만 재무 계획을 세워야 할 것 같아.

F: 내가 널 도울 수 있는지 한번 보자. 너 네 아파트엔 돈을 얼마나 쓰고 있어?

M: 시내에 있는 원룸형 아파트 집세로 890달러를 내고 있어. 공과금이랑 내 휴대폰 비용은 빼고. 여기엔 한 250달러 정도 내고 있어.

F: $890? 31 I think you're paying too much for such a small place when you could find a cheaper one somewhere outside of the downtown area?

M: Uh, I thought about moving to a bigger place outside of downtown, but I think I value my time more. I don't want to waste time commuting.

F: Well, that's fair, but I recommend you look for a cheaper place though, or since you live so close to work, maybe you can get rid of your car.

M: Oh I see. I barely use my car anyway. I can do that. I can save up on tax and parking at least.

F: How much money do you spend on food a month?

M: Hmm. I'm not really sure. I think I spend around $600. I go out to eat at least four times a week, so those expenses add up.

F: Well, perhaps you ought to eat at home more to save some money. You can eat healthier at home, you know.

M: Well, I guess I could. I always go grocery shopping thinking I would cook something nice for myself and eat healthier, but then I just end up eating out because I have no energy to cook after work. I just get deliveries or out eat. I have to throw away the food I got at the store, so I am wasting money by buying groceries.

F: I've heard enough. 32 No wonder you're having money problems. You've got to curb your spending, or you'll end up broke. Stop investing in that cryptocurrency thing as well. I suggest you either move to a cheaper place. You need to create a budget for yourself and stick to it, and start with paying off your bills, starting with me. You owe me $600 dollars.

M: $600? Wait, I only borrowed $500 from you last week. How did you come up with $600?

F: 33 Financial consulting fees. My advice is at least worth $100!

F: 890달러? 31 내 생각엔 네가 시내 외곽에 좀 더 저렴한 곳을 구할 수 있는데도 그런 작은 공간에 너무 돈을 많이 내고 있는 거 같은데?

M: 음, 시내를 벗어나서 좀 더 넓은 곳으로 이사 가는 걸 생각해 봤는데, 난 내 시간이 좀 더 소중해. 난 통근하면서 시간을 낭비하고 싶지 않아.

F: 뭐, 그렇다면 형평성에 맞긴 하네. 하지만 난 네가 좀 더 저렴한 장소를 찾는 걸 추천해. 아니면 넌 직장 가까이 살고 있으니까 차를 없앨 수도 있고.

M: 알았어. 어쨌든 난 차를 거의 안 쓰니까. 그렇게 할 수 있어. 적어도 세금과 주차에 돈을 아낄 수 있겠다.

F: 한 달에 음식에 돈은 얼마나 써?

M: 흠, 잘 모르겠어. 내 생각에 600달러 정도 쓰는 거 같아. 적어도 일주일에 네 번은 외식하러 가니까. 이 비용도 더해야 돼.

F: 너 돈을 아끼려면 집에서 더 많이 먹어야 되겠다. 너도 알겠지만 집에서 더 건강하게 먹을 수 있잖아.

M: 그렇게 할 수 있을 것 같아. 난 항상 혼자서 뭔가 좋은 걸 요리해서 건강하게 먹을 수 있을 거라 생각하고 장을 보는데, 일 끝나고 요리할 힘이 없어서 결국 외식을 하고 말아. 그냥 배달시켜 먹거나 나가서 먹지. 상점에서 산 음식을 버려야 하니까 식료품을 사는 데 돈을 낭비하고 있어.

F: 충분히 잘 들었어. 32 네가 금전 문제가 있다는 건 자명한 사실이야. 넌 소비를 제한해야 되고, 안 그러면 파산하게 될 거야. 그런 가상 화폐 같은 거에 투자하는 것도 관두고. 난 네가 좀 더 저렴한 곳으로 이사 가는 걸 추천해. 너 스스로를 위한 예산을 세워서 유지하고 청구서 요금을 내는 걸 시작해야 돼. 나랑 같이 하자. 너 나한테 빚이 600달러야.

M: 600달러? 나 지난주에 너한테 500달러밖에 안 빌렸어. 어떻게 600달러라는 생각을 하게 됐어?

F: 33 재정 상담 요금이야. 내 조언은 최소 100달러의 가치가 있으니까!

어휘 run into ~와 우연히 만나다 buck (미국·호주·뉴질랜드의) 달러 strapped 돈에 쪼들리는 owe (돈을) 빚지고 있다; 신세를 지고 있다 cryptocurrency 가상 화폐 bank account 계좌 short on ~이 부족한 pay off ~을 다 갚다[청산하다] budget 예산(안), (지출 예상) 비용 keep track of ~에 대해 계속 파악하고 있다 income 소득, 수입 expense (어떤 일에 드는) 돈, 비용 get around to ~을 할 시간을 내다[관심을 갖다] rent 집세, 방세 studio apartment 원룸형[오피스텔형] 아파트 utility (전기·가스·수도 등의) 공공 요금 commute 통근하다 barely 간신히, 가까스로; 거의 ~ 아니게[없이] add up 합산하다, 더하다 ought to V ~해야 하다 grocery shopping 장보기 throw away 버리다 curb 억제[제한]하다 stick to 굳게 지키다, 방침을 고수하다 pay back 갚다 spacious 널찍한 professional 전문가의; 전문직 종사자

---

27. 존은 멜에게 무엇을 원하는가?
 (a) 돈 관리에 있어 그녀의 조언을 얻길 원한다.
 (b) 자신에게 돈을 빌려주길 원한다
 (c) 거주할 새로운 장소를 찾아 주길 원한다.
 (d) 가상 화폐에 돈을 투자하길 원한다.

> 대화 초반에 존이 멜에게 'Could I borrow a few bucks?(돈을 좀 빌릴 수 있겠느냐?)'고 부탁하면서 자신이 현재 현금이 쪼들리는 상황이라고 설명하고 있으므로 정답은 (b)이다.

28. 멜은 존에게 무엇을 지적하는가?
 (a) 그가 이미 그녀에게서 돈을 빌렸다는 사실
 (b) 그가 그녀에게 돈을 빌리려고 했다는 사실
 (c) 돈이 많이 드는 직업을 가졌다는 사실
 (d) 가상 화폐에 돈을 투자하고 있다는 사실

> 현금이 쪼들려 돈을 빌려 달라는 존의 말에 멜이 'you still owe me $500 from last month(넌 지난달부터 아직도 나에게 500달러의 빚이 있는 상황이다)'라고 지적하고 있으므로 정답은 (a)이다.

29. 존은 왜 이번 달에 돈이 쪼들리는 것 같은가?
 (a) 버는 것보다 더 많이 쓰기 때문에
 (b) 새로운 직장을 구했기 때문에
 (c) 멜이 그에게 쓸 돈을 빌려줬다는 사실
 (d) 투자로 돈을 벌었기 때문에

> 존의 말에 의하면 자신이 좋은 직장에 다님에도 'used my credit cards to pay off a lot of things(이런저런 곳에 돈을 갚느라 신용 카드를 썼다)' 현재 그 돈도 못 갚을 것 같다고 말하고 있으므로 정답은 (a)이다.

30. 존은 무엇을 하려고 시도했다가 하지 못했는가?
 (a) 빌린 돈을 갚는 것
 (b) 시내에서 새로운 곳을 찾아보는 것
 (c) 스스로 음식을 해 먹는 것
 (d) 지출 비용과 수입을 추적하는 것

> 'how do you keep track of your income and expenses(수입과 지출 비용을 어떻게 파악하고 있느냐)'는 멜의 말에 존이 파악을 하려고 했으나 그렇게 하지 못했다고 답하고 있으므로 정답은 (d)이다.

31. 멜은 그의 원룸형 아파트를 어떻게 생각하는가?
 (a) 자신의 원룸형 아파트보다 더 좋다고 생각한다.
 (b) 시내 외곽에 더 저렴한 곳을 찾아야 한다고 생각다
 (c) 시내에서 살기에 아주 널찍하고 편리하다고 생각한다.
 (d) 그가 새로운 곳을 찾을 때 그의 아파트를 사야 한다고 생각한다.

> 존의 아파트 월세 금액을 들은 멜이 'a cheaper one somewhere outside of the downtown area(시내 외곽에 좀 더 저렴한 곳)'을 구할 수 있음에도 월세에 돈은 너무 많이 낸다고 지적했으므로 정답은 (b)이다.

32. 멜은 존에게 무엇을 하길 권고하는가?
 (a) 돈 관리를 위해 전문가와 상담하는 것
 (b) 금융 설계사로서 그녀를 고용하는 것
 (c) 예산을 세우고 불필요한 지출 비용을 줄이는 것
 (d) 모든 걸 기록하여 그가 돈을 얼마나 썼는지 알게 되는 것

> 대화 막바지에 멜이 존에게 'curb your spending(소비를 제한할 것), create a budget for yourself(스스로를 위한 예산을 세울 것), paying off your bills(청구서 요금을 낼 것)'을 권고하고 있으므로 정답은 (c)이다.

33. 왜 존이 빚진 돈의 액수가 증가했는가?
 (a) 멜이 빚을 진 다른 사람에게 돈을 갚길 원하기 때문에
 (b) 존이 멜에게 빚진 돈의 액수를 멜이 오해했기 때문에
 (c) 멜이 자신의 돈에 대한 이자를 받길 원하기 때문에
 (d) 멜이 자신의 조언에 대한 비용을 그에게 청구했기 때문에

> 대화 막바지에 빚이 왜 500달러가 아니라 600달러냐고 묻는 존의 말에 멜이 'financial consulting fees(재정 상담 요금)'이라고 하면서 자신의 조언이 100달러의 가치가 있다고 언급했으므로 정답은 (d)이다.

34-39 (안내) 항공기 이륙 전 기내 안내 방송

34. What is the purpose of the announcement?
35. Why is the speaker telling the passengers to take a look at the safety card?
36. According to the speaker, when will the oxygen mask drop?
37. What is recommended when helping others with an oxygen mask?
38. What will happen if you break the smoke detector in the restroom?
39. According to the speaker, what will happen next?

Hello and thank you for flying with Frontier America. **34** A few announcements as we begin our flight. Everyone should have a look at the safety card that is in the seat pocket in front of you. **35** Not only does it have pretty pictures, but it has important information about the location and how to operate exits, and explains other safety features of this airplane. Please keep your seat belts fastened whenever the seat belt light is on. For the 0.001% of you who have never operated a seatbelt before, it works like this: Just insert the metal end into the buckle until it clicks, and pull on the loose end to tighten and you're good to go.

There are four doors, two in the front and two in the rear. Each door has an inflation slide which inflates when the door's open. There are also four windows over the wings, also equipped with inflation slides. The slides at each door can also be detached from the airplane and be used for floatation if necessary. Each door and window and door exist is indicated by an exit sign. There is also a path of white lights along the base of the seats that lead to red lights which mark the exits. Take a moment to look around and find your closest exit. This may be behind you.

36 It is unlikely, but if the cabin pressure changes suddenly during the flight, oxygen masks will automatically drop from the compartment above your seat. If this happens, pull one of the masks down to your face and cover your nose and mouth. Slip the elastic band around your head and tighten by pulling the loose ends at each side of the mask. **37** Be sure to put your mask on before helping others and keep it on until a crew member advises you to take it off.

Also unlikely is the possibility of a water landing. But just in case, a pouch containing a lifevest is located under your seat. In first class, they're between seats at floor level. Take it out of the plastic bag and place the vest over your head. The strap goes around your waist and attaches with a buckle. Pull on the end of the strap to tighten. As you leave the aircraft, pull sharply on the red plastic handles to inflate. The vest can also be inflated by blowing into the red tubes at both shoulders.

---

34. 본 공지의 목적은 무엇인가?
35. 화자는 왜 승객들에게 안전 카드를 살펴보라고 말했는가?
36. 화자에 따르면, 언제 산소 마스크가 떨어지는가?
37. 다른 이들이 산소 마스크를 사용하는 걸 도울 때 무엇이 권고되는가?
38. 화장실에 있는 연기 탐지기를 부술 경우 무슨 일이 생기게 되는가?
39. 화자에 따르면, 다음에 무슨 일이 일어나는가?

안녕하세요, 프론티어 아메리카로 비행해 주신 것에 감사드립니다. **34** 비행을 시작하며 몇 가지 안내 말씀을 드립니다. 여러분 모두 앞쪽 좌석 주머니에 든 안전 카드를 살펴보아야 합니다. **35** 안전 카드엔 예쁜 사진만 있는 것이 아니라, 위치 및 출구 이용 방법에 대한 중요한 정보를 담고 있으며 본 항공기의 다른 안전 설비에 대해 설명하고 있습니다. 좌석 벨트 불이 들어올 때마다 좌석 벨트를 착용하십시오. 여러분 중 이전에 안전벨트를 전혀 사용해 본 적이 없는 0.001퍼센트에 해당하는 분들을 위해 설명 드리자면, 딸깍 소리가 날 때까지 금속 끝부분을 버클에 삽입하고 느슨한 끝부분을 당겨 팽팽하게 만들면 제대로 된 것입니다.

앞쪽에 2개, 뒤쪽에 2개, 이렇게 4개의 문이 있습니다. 각 문엔 문이 열릴 때 부풀어 오르는 인플레이션 슬라이드가 있습니다. 날개 쪽에도 인플레이션 슬라이드를 갖춘 창문 4개가 있습니다. 각 문의 슬라이드는 필요할 경우 문에서 분리되어 물에 뜨는 데 사용될 수 있습니다. 각 문과 창문, 출구는 유도등으로 표시됩니다. 또한 좌석을 따라 흰색 등으로 된 길이 있으며 이것은 출구를 표시하는 붉은색 등으로 이어집니다. 잠시 시간을 내 주변을 둘러보시고 가장 가까이 있는 출구를 찾으십시오. 여러분 뒤쪽에 있을 것입니다.

36 가능성은 낮지만, 객실 압력이 비행 중 갑자기 변화하는 경우 산소 마스크가 여러분 좌석 위쪽에 있는 칸에서 자동적으로 떨어지게 됩니다. 이 같은 일이 발생하면, 마스크 중 하나를 얼굴 아래로 당겨 코와 입을 덮게끔 하십시오. 머리 주변에 고무 밴드를 두르고 마스크 각 옆면에 있는 느슨한 끝 부분을 당겨 팽팽하게 만드십시오. **37** 다른 사람들을 돕기 전에 마스크를 반드시 착용하도록 하시고, 승무원이 마스크를 벗으라고 권고할 때까지 그 상태를 계속 유지하십시오.

또한 낮은 확률로 수상 착륙을 할 가능성이 있습니다. 만일에 대비해, 좌석 아래에 구명조끼가 든 파우치가 있습니다. 1등석의 경우, 바닥 쪽 좌석 사이에 있습니다. 구명조끼를 비닐봉투에서 꺼내 머리에 걸쳐 두르십시오. 끈은 허리 주변으로 가게 하여 버클로 고정시키십시오. 끈의 끝부분을 당겨 팽팽하게 만드십시오. 항공기에서 나가면, 붉은색 플라스틱 손잡이를 재빨리 당겨 부풀어 오르게 하십시오. 조끼는 어깨 양쪽 붉은색 튜브에 바람을 불어 넣어 부풀게 할 수도 있습니다.

A water-activated locator light is attached at shoulder level. Keep in mind that your seat cushion is not a floatation device so don't take it with you in case of emergency.

The airplane is one big no smoking zone. So you can't smoke in the restrooms or anywhere else on the airplane. 38 Tampering with restroom smoke detectors isn't allowed by law. And everyone is required to follow the instructions from the in-flight team and comply with information – lighted signs and posted placards.

Okay, as we get ready to take-off, please check that your seatbelts are fastened, seats and tray-tables are up and your electronics are off. 39 As the crew comes through to make a final cabin check, please let us know if you have any questions or need any help. We promise to do everything we can to make sure you have a safe, comfortable flight. Thanks.

수중 위치 탐지등이 어깨 높이에 부착돼 있습니다. 좌석 쿠션은 부유 도구가 아니니 비상 시 이를 가지고 나가지 않도록 유념하십시오.
비행기는 거대한 금연 구역입니다. 따라서 화장실이나 비행기의 그 어떤 곳에서도 흡연하실 수 없습니다. 38 화장실 연기 탐지기를 건드리는 것은 법으로 금지되어 있습니다. 그리고 여러분 모두 기내 팀의 지시에 따르고 등으로 된 표시 및 게시된 벽보에 있는 정보를 준수할 것이 요구됩니다. 이륙할 준비가 되었으니, 안전벨트를 착용했는지, 좌석 및 접이식 테이블이 위로 올라가 있는지, 전자기기의 전원은 꺼져 있는지 확인하십시오. 39 승무원이 마지막 객실 점검을 위해 지나갈 때, 질문이 있거나 도움이 필요할 경우 저희에게 알려주십시오. 안전하고 편안한 비행이 되실 수 있도록 저희가 할 수 있는 모든 걸 다하겠다고 약속드립니다. 감사합니다.

어휘 have a look at ~을 살펴보다 oxygen 산소 detector 탐지기 seatbelt 안전벨트 insert 끼우다, 넣다, 삽입하다 tighten 팽팽하게 하다, 조이다 inflate 부풀리다; 과장하다 equipped with ~을 갖춘 detach from ~에서 떨어지다[떼어 놓다] floatation (물 위에) 뜸[부유] indicate 나타내다, 표시하다, 보여주다 take a moment 잠시 시간[짬]을 내다 pressure 압박; 압력 compartment (물건 보관용) 칸 crew member 승무원 lifevest 구명조끼 attach 붙이다; 붙들어 매다; 첨부하다 aircraft 항공기 blow into ~에 입김을 불어넣다 locator 위치 탐지기 tamper with ~에 손대다, ~을 건드리다 comply with ~을 따르다[준수하다] procedure 절차, 수순 turbulence 격동, 격변; 난기류 get caught 들이다, 걸리다 fine 벌금; 벌금을 물리다[부과하다] confine to ~에 틀어박히다, ~에 국한되다 face charges 기소되다, 고발을 당하다

34. 본 공지의 목적은 무엇인가?
(a) 승객들에게 항공기의 오락 시설에 대해 말하는 것
(b) 승객들이 기내 쇼핑을 하는 데 도움을 주는 것
(c) 승객들에게 항공기의 안내 시설 및 절차에 대해 알리는 것
(d) 승객들에게 어디로 가고 얼마나 오래 걸릴지 설명하는 것

첫 단락에서 화자가 이륙 전 'have a look at the safety card(안전 카드를 살펴볼 것)'을 권고하며 여기에 위치 및 출구 이용 방법, 'safety features(안전 설비)'에 대한 내용이 담겨 있다고 했으므로 정답은 (c)이다.

35. 화자는 왜 승객들에게 안전 카드를 살펴보라고 말했는가?
(a) 예쁜 사진들이 많이 있기 때문에
(b) 쇼핑을 하는 데 필요할 것이기 때문에
(c) 중요한 정보를 포함하고 있기 때문에
(d) 안전 카드 서식을 작성해야 하기 때문에

첫 단락에서 안전 카드가 위치 및 출구 이용 방법, 그리고 비행기의 각종 안전 설비에 관한 'has important information(중요한 정보를 담고 있다)'고 설명하고 있으므로 정답은 (c)이다.

36. 화자에 따르면, 언제 산소 마스크가 떨어지는가?
(a) 객실 압력이 갑자기 변화했을 경우
(b) 항공기가 충돌하게 되는 경우
(c) 항공기가 난기류를 통과하며 이동하는 경우
(d) 객실이 너무 많은 사람들로 가득 찬 경우

세 번째 단락에서 'if the cabin pressure changes suddenly during the flight(객실 압력이 비행 중 갑자기 변화하는 경우)' 산소 마스크가 좌석 위쪽 칸에서 떨어지게 된다고 했으므로 정답은 (a)이다.

37. 다른 이들이 산소 마스크를 사용하는 걸 도울 때 무엇이 권고되는가?
(a) 자신의 마스크를 쓰기 전에 다른 사람을 도와라
(b) 다른 사람을 돕기 전 자신의 마스크를 먼저 써라
(c) 승무원에게 다른 사람들 도우라고 말하라
(d) 마스크를 어떻게 쓰는지 보여줘라

세 번째 단락에서 'put your mask on before helping others(다른 사람들을 돕기 전에 마스크를 착용하고)' 승무원이 권고할 때까지 착용한 상태를 계속 유지하라고 했으므로 정답은 (b)이다.

38. 화장실에 있는 연기 탐지기를 부술 경우 무슨 일이 생기게 되는가?
(a) 걸리게 되면 벌금을 내야 한다.
(b) 화장실을 사용할 수 없게 될 것이다.
(c) 본인의 비행기 좌석에 갇혀 있게 될 수 있다.
(d) 경찰에게 기소를 당할 수 있다.

다섯 번째 단락에서 연기 탐지기를 건드리는 것은 'isn't allowed by law(법으로 허락되지 않는다[금지되어 있다])'고 했으며, 이는 결국 법적인 기소/고발 조치를 당할 수 있음을 뜻하므로 정답은 (d)이다.

39. 화자에 따르면, 다음에 무슨 일이 일어나는가?
(a) 공지가 끝나자마자 이륙하게 될 것이다.
(b) 승무원이 이륙할 준비가 되었는지 확인할 것이다
(c) 승무원이 사람들로 하여금 안전 카드를 보게 할 것이다.
(d) 승무원이 사람들이 화장실을 이용할 수 있게 할 것이다.

여섯 번째 단락에서 'as the crew comes through to make a final cabin check(승무원이 마지막 객실 점검을 위해 지나갈 때)' 필요한 것이 있으면 알려 달라고 했으므로 방송 후 예상되는 행위는 (b)이다.

40-46 (토론) 채식주의의 장단점에 대한 토론

40. Who did Susan mainly get her information from at the workshop?
41. Why is Steve reluctant to feed his children vegan food only?
42. Why is fat an important nutrient?
43. Why does Susan say being vegan could be unhealthy?
44. Based on the conversation, what do people still have to do even if they are vegan?
45. According to Susan, what did the studies say about vegan kids?
46. What does Susan most likely do next?

M: Hello Susan, how was your healthy baby diet workshop?

F: Hi Steve, it was great! I learned a lot. **40** There was an actual pediatrician in the group, so we got to hear about health benefits of raising your kids vegan and a lot of parents seem to share similar concerns.

M: Vegan? **41** I am very interested in vegan food, but I am not sure I would want to feed my kids exclusively vegan food. I am concerned that they wouldn't get enough nutrients they need to grow up. Is It really okay for a growing baby to never eat meat, dairy, fish, or eggs?

F: Well, raising children vegan is a very popular trend right now and the doctors say you can get all the essential nutrients you need from plant-based foods. I mean for a few months, babies will need only one type of food, which is breast milk or formula.

M: That is true. I didn't even think about that. Breast Milk is technically an animal product but it is human milk made for human babies, so there are no problems.

F: That's right. All you have to do is to keep these nutrients in mind: protein, fat, and carbohydrates. For vegan babies, the right amounts of protein and fat are especially the key. You can get protein from beans, peas, tofu, nut/seed butters.

M: What can replace dairy products?

F: Well, you can drink almond, coconut, or rice milk, but these are not recommended for babies and toddlers. And the thing is you can only get something called DHA omega-3 fatty acids primarily through animals so you should think about getting a DHA supplement.

M: 안녕, 수잔, 건강한 아기 식단 워크숍은 어땠어?

F: 안녕, 스티브, 정말 좋았어! 많은 걸 배웠지. **40** 그룹 중에 실제 소아과 의사가 있어서 아이들을 채식주의자로 키우는 것의 건강상 이점에 대한 이야기를 들을 수 있었고, 많은 부모들이 비슷한 관심사를 갖고 있는 것 같아 보였어.

M: 채식주의? **41** 나도 채식주의 음식에 관심이 많긴 한데, 아이들에게 채식주의 음식만 먹이고 싶은지는 잘 모르겠어. 아이들이 성장에 필요한 영양분을 충분히 섭취 못할 게 우려되거든. 성장하는 아이들이 고기, 유제품, 계란을 안 먹는 게 정말 괜찮은가?

F: 아이들을 채식주의자로 키우는 건 현재 굉장히 인기 있는 트렌드고 의사들 말에 따르면 식물성 음식에서 필요한 필수 영양소를 모두 얻을 수 있대. 아기들은 몇 달간 모유나 유아용 유동식 같은 한 종류의 음식만 먹으면 되잖아.

M: 그건 맞아. 거기에 대해선 생각 못했어. 엄밀히 말해 모유는 동물성 제품이지만 인간 아기를 위해 만들어진 사람의 젖이니까 아무런 문제가 없지.

F: 맞아. 네가 해야 할 일은 단백질, 지방, 탄수화물 등의 영양소들을 염두에 두는 거야. 채식주의자 아이들에겐 알맞은 양의 단백질과 지방이 특히 중요하지. 단백질은 콩, 완두콩, 두부, 견과류/씨앗 버터에서 얻을 수 있어.

M: 유제품은 뭘로 대체할 수 있지?

F: 아몬드, 코코넛, 쌀로 된 우유를 마실 수 있는데 이건 아기와 유아들에겐 권장되지 않아. 그리고 중요한 건 DHA 오메가-3 지방산이라 불리는 물질은 주로 동물을 통해 얻을 수 있기 때문에 DHA 보조 식품을 구하는 걸 고려해 봐야 할 거야.

M: Yeah, of course. 42 Fat is an important nutrient for growing baby bodies and brains. You don't want to miss that.

F: I guess you have to talk with your doctor when the child is done breastfeeding to get enough nutrients for the kid.

M: Interesting. I understand that it is beneficial and climate-friendly.

F: That's what people think but being vegan is not necessarily healthy.

M: Oh, really? What do you mean?

F: The problem is that people think that eating vegan is healthy and don't really pay attention to what their nutritional needs are. 43 Parents who feed their children a vegan diet could give too much fatty or sugary food, which is a common problem among vegans.

M: 44 You mean that you still have to pay attention to what you eat even if you only eat plant-food?

F: Exactly! There are lots of sugary vegan treats.

M: Oh I see. I didn't even think that would be a problem. I just thought that being vegan is healthy.

F: Right? Me neither. 45 So the doctor said that in studies where they studied 400 kids who are fed vegan food, there were no significant differences in age-appropriate development, meaning average height and weight.

M: Right, but there haven't been any long-term studies yet.

F: That is true, but 46 I think feeding my children vegan has a lot of benefits and they might like the idea, so I am going to discuss it with my family and look into it further. I am glad that I went to the workshop. It was very informative.

M: Way to go, Susan. I would like to know more about it. Let me know if there is another opportunity like that.

M: 물론 그렇지. 42 지방은 성장하는 아기의 신체와 뇌에 중요한 영양소니까. 이걸 놓쳐선 안 되지.

F: 아이를 모유로 키워서 충분한 영양소를 얻게 하고자 할 땐 의사와 이야기해야 할 거야.

M: 흥미롭네. 이게 이로운 점이 많고 환경 친화적이라는 사실은 이해했어.

F: 사람들이 그렇게들 생각하는데, 사실 채식주의자인 게 반드시 건강하기만 한 건 아니야.

M: 아, 정말? 그게 무슨 뜻이야?

F: 사람들이 채식주의로 먹는 것이 건강에 좋다고 생각해서 필요한 영양소가 뭔지 제대로 주의를 기울이지 않는다는 게 문제야. 43 아이들에게 채식주의 식단을 먹이는 부모들은 지나치게 기름지거나 단 음식을 줄 가능성이 있고, 이건 채식주의자들 사이에서 흔히 있는 문제야.

M: 44 네 말은 식물성 음식만 먹는다 해도 계속해서 뭘 먹는지 관심을 기울여야 한다는 거지?

F: 맞아! 달콤한 채식주의자용 간식들이 정말 많거든.

M: 그렇구나. 그게 문제가 될 거라는 생각은 못했어. 난 채식주의자인 게 건강에 좋다고만 생각했거든.

F: 그렇지? 나도 그랬어. 45 의사가 말하길 채식주의 음식을 먹는 400명의 아이들을 연구한 연구에서 평균 신장과 몸무게, 즉 나이에 적합한 발달 과정에 있어 뚜렷한 차이가 없었다고 하더라고.

N: 맞아. 하지만 아직 장기적으로 진행된 연구는 하나도 없는 상황이잖아.

F: 맞아, 하지만 46 아이들을 채식주의자로 키우는 덴 장점이 많고 아이들도 이런 생각을 좋아할 것 같으니, 가족과 의논해서 이에 대해 좀 더 알아볼 계획이야. 워크샵에 가서 정말 좋아. 아주 유용했거든.

M: 잘했어, 수잔. 나도 여기에 대해 좀 더 알아보고 싶어. 그런 또 다른 기회가 있으면 내게 알려줘.

어휘 reluctant to V ~하길 주저하는 vegan 엄격한[완전] 채식주의자 nutrient 영양소, 영양분 pediatrician 소아과 의사 exclusively 배타[독점]적으로; 오로지, 전적으로 ~뿐 essential 필수적인, 본질[근본]적인 plant-based 채식 주의의, 식물성의 breast milk 모유 formula 유아용 유동식 technically 엄밀히 따지면[말하면] carbohydrates 탄수화물 keep in mind 염두에 두다, 기억하다 dairy product 유제품 toddler 걸음마를 배우는 아이, 유아 fatty acids 지방산 primarily 주로 supplement 보충[추가](물); 보조 식품 breastfeeding 모유 양육(의) beneficial 유익한, 이로운 not necessarily 반드시 ~인 것은 아닌 look into ~을 조사하다; ~을 주의 깊게 살피다 informative 유용한 정보를 주는, 유익한 deep-fried 튀긴 overeat 과식하다 multiple 많은, 다수의 from time to time 가끔 stunted 성장[발달]을 저해당한

40. 수잔은 워크샵에서 누구에게 주로 정보를 얻었는가?
 (a) 그룹 내에 있었던 의사
 (b) 아이를 채식주의자로 키우고 있던 화자
 (c) 함께 워크숍에 갔던 친구
 (d) 채식주의에 관심이 있는 스티브

여성이 워크숍에서 'there was an actual pediatrician in the group(그룹 중 실제 소아과 의사가 있었고)' 그 사람에게서 워크숍 주제에 대한 이야기를 들을 수 있었다고 했으므로 정답은 (a)이다.

41. 스티브는 왜 자녀들에게 채식주의 음식만 먹이는 걸 주저하는가?
 (a) 아이들에게 채식주의 음식을 어떻게 소개할지 몰라서
 (b) 아이들에게 필수 영양소가 부족할 것이 걱정돼서
 (c) 채식주의로 먹는 것이 건강에 좋지 않다고 믿어서
 (d) 채식주의자가 되는 것에 대한 정보가 충분치 않다고 느껴서

남성이 채식주의 음식에 관심이 있으나 'they wouldn't get enough nutrients they need to grow up(아이들이 성장에 필요한 영양분을 충분히 섭취 못할 게)' 우려되어 망설여진다고 했으므로 정답은 (b)이다.

42. 지방이 왜 중요한 영양소인가?
 (a) 근육을 형성하는 데 필요하기 때문에
 (b) 뇌 성장에 필요하기 때문에
 (c) 머리카락이 자라는 데 필요하기 때문에
 (d) 눈을 건강하게 유지하는 데 필요하기 때문에

남성의 말에 따르면 지방이 'growing baby bodies and brains(성장하는 아기의 신체와 뇌)'에 중요한 영양소라고 했고, 이는 곧 지방이 뇌 성장에 필요한 영양소라는 의미로 해석 가능하므로 정답은 (b)이다.

43. 수잔은 채식주의자인 것이 왜 건강에 안 좋을 수 있다고 말하는가?
 (a) 여전히 튀긴 음식과 단 음식을 먹을 수 있기 때문에
 (b) 배부를 때까지 과식할 수 있기 때문에
 (c) 하루에 끼니를 여러 번 먹을 수 있기 때문에
 (d) 채식주의 음식에서 필수 영양소을 얻을 수 없기 때문에

여성의 말에 따르면 아이들에게 채식주의 식단을 먹이는 부모들이 'too much fatty or sugary food(지나치게 기름지거나 단 음식)'을 줄 가능성이 있고, 이것이 흔히 있는 문제라 했으므로 정답은 (a)이다.

44. 대화에 따르면, 사람들은 채식주의자라도 여전히 뭘 해야 하는가?
 (a) 여전히 가끔씩 고기를 먹어야 한다.
 (b) 여전히 비타민과 다른 식품 보조제를 먹어야 한다.
 (c) 여전히 무엇을 먹는지에 관심을 기울여야 한다
 (d) 여전히 소아과 의사들과 상담해야 한다.

채식주의 식단의 문제점을 언급한 여성의 말에 남성이 채식주의로 먹으면서도 still have to pay attention to what you eat(여전히 뭘 먹는지에 관심을 기울여야 한다)'는 의미냐고 되물었으므로 정답은 (c)이다.

45. 수잔에 따르면, 연구에서 채식주의자 아이들에 대해 무엇을 말했는가?
 (a) 채식주의자가 아닌 아이들보다 더 활동적이다.
 (b) 채식주의자인 걸로 인해 성장이 저해된다는 성장상 징후가 없다
 (c) 채식주의자가 아닌 아이들보다 학교 생활을 더 잘한다.
 (d) 가끔 고기를 먹어 채식주의 음식에서 못 얻는 영양소를 얻는다.

채식주의자 아이들을 연구한 연구에서 아이들이 'no significant differences in age-appropriate development(나이에 적합한 발달 과정에 있어 현저한 차이가 없다)'고 했으므로 정답은 (b)이다.

46. 수잔은 다음에 무엇을 할 것 같은가?
 (a) 채식주의자인 친구 중 한 명과 이야기할 것이다.
 (b) 채식주의자가 되는 것에 대해 아이들과 이야기할 것이다
 (c) 학교에 전화해 선생님들과 이야기할 것이다.
 (d) 아이들을 병원에 데려가서 의사와 상담하게 할 것이다.

여성의 말에 의하면 아이들을 채식주의자로 키우는 것에 대해 'I'm going to discuss it with my family(가족과 의논을 할 예정)'이라고 했고, 가족엔 아이들이 포함되어 있기 때문에 정답은 (b)이다.

47-52 (소개) 명상에 대한 소개 및 센터 홍보

47. According to the speaker, what is the benefit of meditation?
48. What does the speaker advise people to do?
49. What does the speaker think is important?
50. What does the speaker recommend to people who have a hard time sitting still during the meditation?
51. According to the speaker, what kind of thing can you use to help you meditate?
52. What does the speaker want people to do when they have emotional or psychiatric problems?

Hello everybody and welcome to MindfulnessJourney. Meditation is an ancient practice that is believed to have originated in India several thousand years ago. Throughout early history, the practice was adopted by neighboring countries quickly.

Our days easily fill up with things that we have to do, and self-care is usually at the bottom of the list. But 47 a short daily meditation practice may reduce stress, anxiety and depression while improving mood, resilience, and focus and a sense of well-being. It can give you the fuel you need to accomplish your goals. Most importantly, meditation is a gift you can give yourself every day.

To begin meditating, find a place where you can sit comfortably and quietly. Then close your eyes and do nothing for a minute or so. Thoughts may come during that time, and that is okay. It is natural to have thoughts during meditation. Meditate every morning and every evening for 5 to 10 minutes. It is best to meditate before you eat.

The benefits of meditation come from meditating regularly. The benefits come naturally over time, and there is nothing you can do to make those benefits come. So 48 avoid looking for particular experiences or signs of progress or failure with your meditation because that will block you from getting the benefits of meditation. Sometimes it's that feeling that we're pushing ourselves too hard and making too much of an effort, either it's because we're so used to doing things this way all the time in our days because we're so busy and used to working so hard, or sometimes it's because we're trying so hard to project an idea of what we want our meditation to be, that we're not even giving the experience room to breathe. We're not even providing the opportunity to experience what we'd really like to experience.

Meditation can make you happier, make you feel more at ease and calmer, and it can help you get along better with others. You may notice those changes soon, or you may meditate for six months before you notice any changes. So, 49 it is important to just get in the habit of meditating

---

47. 화자에 따르면, 명상의 이점은 무엇인가?
48. 화자는 사람들에게 무엇을 하라고 권고하는가?
49. 화자는 무엇이 중요하다고 생각하는가?
50. 화자는 명상 중 가만히 앉아 있는 게 힘든 이들에게 뭘 하라고 권고하는가?
51. 화자에 따르면, 명상을 돕는 데 무엇을 사용할 수 있는가?
52. 화자는 사람들이 감정적, 정신적 문제가 있을 때 뭘 하길 원하는가?

안녕하세요, 여러분. MindfulnessJourney에 오신 걸 환영합니다. 명상은 수천년 전 인도에서 유래되었다고 여겨지는 오래된 관행입니다. 초기 역사에 걸쳐, 이 같은 관행은 이웃 국가들에게 빠른 속도로 받아들여지게 되었습니다.

우리의 삶은 해야 할 일들로 쉽게 채워지고, 자기 관리는 보통 리스트의 맨 밑바닥에 있습니다. 하지만 47 매일의 짧은 명상은 기분, 회복력, 집중, 행복감을 증진시켜 스트레스, 불안, 우울감을 줄일 수 있습니다. 이것은 목표 달성에 필요한 연료를 제공해 줄 수 있습니다. 무엇보다도 중요한 건, 명상은 여러분이 매일같이 스스로에게 줄 수 있는 선물이라는 점입니다.

명상을 시작하고자 한다면, 편안하게 조용히 앉아 있을 수 있는 장소를 찾으십시오. 그다음엔 잠시 동안 눈을 감고 아무것도 하지 마십시오. 그러는 동안 생각이 밀려올 수 있지만, 괜찮습니다. 명상을 하는 동안 생각이 드는 건 자연스러운 일입니다. 매일 아침 저녁으로 5분에서 10분간 명상을 하십시오. 식사하기 전에 명상을 하는 것이 가장 좋습니다.

명상의 혜택은 규칙적인 명상에서 비롯됩니다. 혜택들은 시간이 지나면 자연스레 찾아오고, 이 같은 혜택들을 찾아오게 하기 위해 뭔가 할 필요는 없습니다. 그러니 48 특이한 체험이나 진척의 양상을 굳이 찾으려 하지 마세요, 그렇지 않으면 이것이 명상의 혜택을 얻는 걸 방해해 명상에 실패하고 맙니다. 이것은 스스로를 심하게 채찍질하고 너무 과도한 노력을 하는 느낌과 같으며, 이것은 우리가 너무 바쁘게 열심히 일하는 것에 익숙해져 있어 살면서 이런 방식으로 뭔가를 하는 것에 너무 길들여져 있기 때문에 생기고, 혹은 명상이 어떻게 됐으면 하는지에 대한 생각을 종종 너무 열심히 하기 때문에 생기며, 따라서 우리는 체험할 수 있는 여지에 숨쉴 틈조차 주지 않습니다. 우리는 심지어 우리가 진정 체험하고자 하는 것을 체험할 기회조차 주지 않습니다.

명상은 여러분을 좀 더 행복하고 편안하게, 그리고 좀 더 평온하게 느끼도록 만들고 이것은 여러분이 다른 이들과 더 잘 어울리게 해 줍니다. 여러분은 이 같은 변화를 곧 알아챌 수도 있고, 혹은 변화를 알아채기 전 6개월간 명상을 지속하고 있을지 모릅니다. 따라서, 49 매일 두 차례 규칙적으로 명상하는 습관을 들인 다음 인내심

regularly twice every day, and then be patient. If you stop meditating, just start it back up again.

If you find that sitting quietly is difficult for you, stop meditating. Restlessness is a common problem. It can be a body that just doesn't want to sit still and keeps fidgeting or moving. We may not be able to find that place of quiet ease and comfort. Or it might be a mind that's overly active, that's overly busy, it just doesn't seem to stop chatting away to itself. 50 If so, instead of forcing yourself to meditate, try walking in nature, doing yoga, or exercising to relax.

51 You can also use sound or smell to aid your meditation. The sound focus meditation involves listening to some bell or tone, like a Tibetan singing bowl.

You can also use online resources. It is proven that online mindfulness practices may ease fear, anxiety and stress.

Finally, 52 meditation is not for solving serious emotional or psychiatric problems. So if you think you have such problems, do not try to fix them by meditating and get professional help.

Thank you for listening and hope you find inner peace with meditation. Don't forget to subscribe to our YouTube channel for free video content!

을 갖는 것이 중요합니다. 만약 명상을 멈추게 되면, 그냥 다시 시작하면 됩니다.

조용히 앉아 있는 게 힘들다면, 명상을 멈추세요. 좌불 안석은 흔한 문제입니다. 이것은 신체가 가만히 앉아 있길 원치 않고 계속 꼼지락거리거나 움직이려 하는 것일 수 있습니다. 조용한 편안함과 안락함을 주는 장소를 못 찾아서 그럴 수 있습니다. 또는 마음이 과도하게 활발하거나 바빠서 그럴 수 있고, 스스로 잡담하는 행동을 멈출 수 없어서 그럴 수 있습니다. 50 만약 그렇다면, 명상에 집중하는 대신 자연을 거닐거나 요가를 하고 긴장을 푸는 운동을 하십시오.

51 명상을 돕기 위해 소리나 냄새를 활용할 수도 있습니다. 소리에 초점을 맞춘 명상엔 티베트 싱잉볼 같은 벨 소리나 음색을 듣는 것이 수반됩니다.

온라인 자료를 쓸 수도 있습니다. 온라인 명상은 두려움, 불안, 스트레스를 완화하는 걸로 입증됐습니다.

마지막으로, 52 명상은 심각한 감정적 혹은 정신적 문제를 해결하기 위한 것이 아닙니다. 따라서 이런 문제가 있다면, 명상을 통해 고치려 하지 말고 전문가의 도움을 구하십시오.

들어 주셔서 감사하며 명상을 통해 내면의 평안을 찾길 바랍니다. 저희 유튜브 채널을 구독하셔서 무료 동영상 콘텐츠를 보는 걸 잊지 마시고요.

어휘 meditate 명상하다, 묵상하다 psychiatric 정신 의학의 originate 비롯되다, 유래하다 adopt 입양하다; 쓰다[취하다]; 채택하다 fill up with ~로 가득 차다[채우다] self-care 자기 부양, 자기 관리 resilience 탄성, 회복력 accomplish 완수하다, 성취하다, 해내다 regularly 정기[규칙]적으로; 자주 signs of progress 진척[진전]의 조짐 project 계획하다, 기획하다 push oneself 스스로를 채찍질하다 experience 경험; 여지, 기회, 가능성 get along with ~와 잘 지내다 get in the habit of V-ing ~하는 습관을 들이다 start back up 다시 시작하다 restlessness 차분[침착]하지 못함, 안절부절(증) fidget 꼼지락거리다, 가만히 못 있다 overly 너무, 몹시 chat away 지껄이다, 잡담으로 시간을 보내다 aid 도움, 원조, 지원; 돕다, 촉진하다 mindfulness 명상, 마음 챙김 therapeutic 치료(법)의; 치료의 힘이 있는

47. 화자에 따르면, 명상의 이점은 무엇인가?
(a) 사람들이 시험 점수를 올리는 걸 돕는다.
(b) 사람들이 목표를 달성하는 걸 돕는다.
(c) 사람들이 다른 이들을 이해하는 걸 돕는다.
(d) 사람들이 스트레스를 줄이고 집중을 더 잘 하게 돕는다

두 번째 단락에서 명상이 'reduce stress, anxiety, and depression(스트레스, 불안, 우울감을 줄이고), improve mood resilience, and focus(기분, 회복력, 집중을 증진시킨다)'고 했으므로 정답은 (d)이다.

48. 화자는 사람들에게 무엇을 하라고 권고하는가?
(a) 친구들과 명상 훈련을 하는 것
(b) 특이한 체험을 하려고 기대하지 않는 것
(c) 목표를 세우고 규칙적으로 진행해 나가는 것
(d) 명상을 시작하면 멈추지 않는 것

네 번째 단락에서 화자가 명상의 혜택을 누리기 위해 뭔가 특별한 걸 할 필요가 없으므로 'avoid looking for particular experience(특이한 체험을 찾으려 들지 말라)'고 조언하고 있기 때문에 정답은 (b)이다.

49. 화자는 무엇이 중요하다고 생각하는가?
(a) 조용한 장소를 찾는 것
(b) 가능한 조용한 분위기로 세팅하는 것
(c) 규칙적으로 명상하는 것
(d) 내면의 생각에 집중하는 것

다섯 번째 단락에서 화자가 'it is important to just get in the habit of meditating regularly twice every day(매일 두 차례 규칙적으로 명상하는 습관을 들이는 것이 중요하다)'고 말하고 있으므로 정답은 (c)이다.

50. 화자는 명상 중 가만히 앉아 있는 게 힘든 이들에게 뭘 하라고 권고하는가?
(a) 매일 가만히 앉아 있는 걸 연습하는 것
(b) 쿠션을 사용해 의자에 앉는 것
(c) 벽에 기대 등을 받치는 것
(d) 다른 활동에 참여하는 것

여섯 번째 단락에서 가만히 앉아 있는 게 힘들 경우 'try walking in nature, doing yoga, or exercising to relax(자연을 거닐거나 요가를 하고 긴장을 푸는 운동을 하라)'고 조언했기 때문에 정답은 (d)이다.

51. 화자에 따르면, 명상을 돕는 데 무엇을 사용할 수 있는가?
(a) 앱을 다운로드 받는 것
(b) 소리를 듣는 것
(c) 푸짐한 식사를 하는 것
(d) 전문가의 도움을 받는 것

일곱 번째 단락에서 'you can also use sound or smell to aid your meditation(명상을 돕기 위해 소리나 냄새를 활용할 수도 있다)'고 했으므로 정답은 (b)이다.

52. 화자는 사람들이 감정적, 정신적 문제가 있을 때 뭘 하길 원하는가?
(a) 적합한 전문가를 만나 이들과 상담하는 것
(b) 문제를 고치기 위해 명상하는 것
(c) 치유적 명상에 대해 좀 더 알아가는 것
(d) 명상을 더 길게 하는 것

아홉 번째 단락에서 감정적, 정신적 문제가 있을 경우 'do not try to fix them by meditating and get professional help(명상을 통해 고치려 하지 말고 전문가의 도움을 구하라)'고 했으므로 정답은 (a)이다.

Actual Test 01 / Vocab 주요 어휘 총정리

Actual Test 01에 등장했던 주요 어휘를 한눈에 훑어보며 정리해 보도록 합시다.
모르는 어휘가 있을 경우 박스(☐)에 체크(V) 표시를 한 뒤 재차 암기하도록 하세요.

- ☐ run into ~와 우연히 만나다
- ☐ strapped 돈에 쪼들리는
- ☐ owe (돈을) 빚지고 있다; 신세를 지고 있다
- ☐ short on ~이 부족한
- ☐ pay off ~을 다 갚다[청산하다]
- ☐ budget 예산(안), (지출 예상) 비용
- ☐ keep track of ~에 대해 계속 파악하고 있다
- ☐ income 소득, 수입
- ☐ expense (어떤 일에 드는) 돈, 비용
- ☐ get around to ~을 할 시간을 내다[관심을 갖다]
- ☐ utility (전기·가스·수도 등의) 공공 요금
- ☐ commute 통근하다
- ☐ ought to V ~해야 하다
- ☐ stick to 굳게 지키다, 방침을 고수하다
- ☐ pay back 갚다
- ☐ professional 전문가의; 전문직 종사자
- ☐ insert 끼우다, 넣다, 삽입하다
- ☐ equipped with ~을 갖춘
- ☐ detach from ~에서 떨어지다[떼어 놓다]
- ☐ indicate 나타내다, 표시하다, 보여주다
- ☐ pressure 압박; 압력
- ☐ attach 붙이다; 붙들어 매다; 첨부하다
- ☐ aircraft 항공기
- ☐ blow into ~에 입김을 불어 넣다
- ☐ tamper with ~에 손대다, ~을 건드리다
- ☐ comply with ~을 따르다[준수하다]
- ☐ procedure 절차, 수순
- ☐ turbulence 격동, 격변; 난기류
- ☐ get caught 들키다, 걸리다
- ☐ fine 벌금; 벌금을 물리다[부과하다]
- ☐ confine to ~에 틀어박히다, ~에 국한되다
- ☐ face charges 기소되다, 고발을 당하다
- ☐ reluctant to V ~하길 주저하는
- ☐ vegan 엄격한[완전] 채식주의자
- ☐ nutrient 영양소, 영양분
- ☐ pediatrician 소아과 의사
- ☐ exclusively 배타[독점]적으로; 오로지, 전적으로 ~뿐
- ☐ essential 필수적인, 본질[근본]적인
- ☐ plant-based 채식 주의의, 식물성의
- ☐ technically 엄밀히 따지면[말하면]
- ☐ carbohydrates 탄수화물
- ☐ keep in mind 염두에 두다, 기억하다
- ☐ dairy product 유제품
- ☐ toddler 걸음마를 배우는 아이, 유아
- ☐ primarily 주로
- ☐ supplement 보충[추가](물); 보조 식품
- ☐ beneficial 유익한, 이로운
- ☐ look into ~을 조사하다; ~을 주의 깊게 살피다
- ☐ informative 유용한 정보를 주는, 유익한
- ☐ multiple 많은, 다수의
- ☐ stunted 성장[발달]을 저해당한
- ☐ meditate 명상하다, 묵상하다
- ☐ psychiatric 정신 의학의
- ☐ originate 비롯되다, 유래하다
- ☐ adopt 입양하다; 쓰다[취하다]; 채택하다
- ☐ fill up with ~로 가득 차다[채우다]
- ☐ self-care 자기 부양, 자기 관리
- ☐ resilience 탄성, 회복력
- ☐ accomplish 완수하다, 성취하다, 해내다
- ☐ regularly 정기[규칙]적으로; 자주
- ☐ push oneself 스스로를 채찍질하다
- ☐ get along with ~와 잘 지내다
- ☐ get in the habit of V-ing ~하는 습관을 들이다
- ☐ start back up 다시 시작하다
- ☐ restlessness 차분[침착]하지 못함, 안절부절(증)
- ☐ fidget 꼼지락거리다, 가만히 못 있다
- ☐ overly 너무, 몹시
- ☐ chat away 지껄이다, 잡담으로 시간을 보내다
- ☐ aid 도움, 원조, 지원; 돕다, 촉진하다
- ☐ therapeutic 치료(법)의; 치료의 힘이 있는

Listening Section
Actual Test 02

▶▶ **정답 & 나의 점수 확인**

테스트 날짜: _____월 _____일 / 테스트 점수: _____

27 (b) 28 (d) 29 (d) 30 (b) 31 (a) 32 (a) 33 (c) 34 (a) 35 (c) 36 (d) 37 (d) 38 (c) 39 (b)
40 (b) 41 (a) 42 (c) 43 (c) 44 (c) 45 (d) 46 (a) 47 (d) 48 (b) 49 (a) 50 (a) 51 (b) 52 (d)

▶▶ **출제 경향 & 흐름 파악**

지피지기면 백전백승! 출제 경향과 흐름을 한눈에 파악해 봅시다. 출제된 지문이 어떤 종류의 글이었는지, 각 지문과 관련해 어떤 종류의 문제가 출제되었는지 아래의 표를 보며 정리해 보세요.

	27	여성이 지원한 업무 분야		40	여성이 결정하고자 하는 사항
	28	여성이 특정 분야를 가르친 이유		41	여성이 남성에게 문의하는 이유
(면접)	29	영어로 말하는 게 필요한 상황	(상담)	42	남성이 자신의 차를 좋아하는 이유
교직원 채용 관련 면접	30	여성이 미국으로 돌아온 이유	차량 구매에 대한 상담 및 조언	43	여성이 표하고 있는 우려
	31	여성이 이 일에 지원한 이유		44	남성이 생각하는 전기차의 이점
	32	여성이 이 일에 최적인 이유		45	여성이 가격에 불만을 표하는 이유
	33	남성이 여성에게 공지할 사항		46	여성이 대화 후 하게 될 일
	34	이야기의 목적		47	방송에서 진행될 내용
	35	유타 여행을 즐길 만한 대상		48	요리법이 실패 불가능한 이유
(방송) 관광지를 소개하는 방송	36	유타 주가 이기적인 이유	(방송) 가정식 요리법을 다루는 방송	49	요리에서 머스터드의 역할
	37	즐길 수 있는 관광거리		50	요리에 쓰이는 계란의 상태
	38	유타 주의 날씨		51	기름을 천천히 넣는 이유
	39	유타라는 이름의 유래		52	기름 추가 후 해야 할 일

27-33 (면접) 교직원 채용 관련 면접

27. Based on the conversation, what kind of job is Alice applying for?
28. Why did Alice also teach cooking along with English in South Korea?
29. According to Alice, when do chefs need to speak English?
30. What brought Alice back to the United States?
31. Why did Alice apply for this job?
32. Why does Alice think she is best suited for the position?
33. What is Fred going to notify Alice of on Friday?

M: Hi, thanks for coming to the interview today, Alice. I am Fred. It's nice to meet you.

F: Well, thank you.

M: To begin with, why don't you tell us a little about yourself?

F: Okay. Um, **27** I've always been interested in teaching in a language program like this, and I graduated with a degree in English and psychology eight years ago and then I landed my first job overseas in South Korea.

M: Oh wow, that's pretty impressive. I have been to Korea. I think it is very brave of you to work in a different country. What did you do there? What kind of work?

F: Well, I worked full time, for a private language school in Seoul for the first two years, and then I found a job at a community college.

M: Did you find it hard to adjust to a new environment?

F: To be honest, I did at first. I took some language classes to learn Korean and made some friends. After that, I adjusted pretty quickly.

M: Okay. You seem very friendly, so I guess making friends isn't a problem.

F: Thank you, Fred.

M: So, exactly what did you do in your work there then?

F: Well, I taught English and culinary arts.

M: You taught cooking classes?

27. 대화를 근거로 봤을 때, 앨리스는 어떤 일에 지원하고 있는가?
28. 앨리스는 왜 한국에서 영어와 함께 요리 또한 가르쳤는가?
29. 앨리스에 의하면, 셰프는 언제 영어로 말해야 하는가?
30. 무엇이 앨리스를 미국에 돌아오게 했는가?
31. 앨리스는 왜 이 일에 지원했는가?
32. 앨리스는 왜 이 직책에 자신이 최적이라 여기는가?
33. 프레드는 금요일에 앨리스에게 무엇을 알릴 것인가?

M: 안녕하세요, 오늘 면접에 와 주셔서 감사합니다, 앨리스 씨. 전 프레드입니다. 만나서 반갑습니다.

F: 네, 감사합니다.

M: 본인에 대해 간단하게 소개부터 해 보시겠어요?

F: 네. **27** 전 항상 이 같은 언어 프로그램에서 가르치는 데 관심이 있었고, 8년 전 영어와 심리학 학위를 따고 졸업한 다음 한국이라는 해외에서 제 첫 직장을 다녔습니다.

M: 와, 그거 꽤 인상적이네요. 저도 한국에 가 본 적이 있어요. 다른 나라에서 일을 하셨다는 게 정말 용기 있네요. 거기서 뭘 하셨나요? 어떤 종류의 일?

F: 처음 2년 동안은 서울에 있는 사립 언어 학교에서 정규직으로 일했고, 그 후엔 전문 대학에서 일자리를 구했습니다.

M: 새로운 환경에 적응하는 게 힘들었나요?

F: 솔직히 말씀드리면, 처음엔 그랬습니다. 언어 수업에 등록해서 한국어를 배웠고 친구도 몇 명 사귀었습니다. 이후엔, 빠르게 적응할 수 있었고요.

M: 알겠습니다. 굉장히 우호적인 성격이신 거 같아요. 그래서 친구 사귀는 덴 문제가 없겠어요.

F: 감사합니다, 프레드 씨.

M: 그럼 직장에선 무슨 일을 했나요?

F: 영어와 요리를 가르쳤습니다.

M: 요리 수업을 가르치셨다고요?

F: Well, 28 I know it sounds like an unusual combination, but I completed a program in culinary arts before I got my degree.

M: Oh, wow. You've done a lot, haven't you? So, how did you teach and what exactly did you do?

F: Well, many of my students wanted to become chefs in restaurants, or they wanted to start their own restaurants, and in our area, there were many tourist spots. A lot of tourists came to that particular area, and so 29 with English, they would be able to communicate not only with suppliers, you know things that they need for restaurant's food and so forth, but also with their customers, and so I taught them English and cooking at the same time.

M: Wow, that's pretty interesting. Why did you return to the United States? How long have you been back?

F: I've been back for probably about a year now.

M: Okay, so what brought you back then?

F: 30 31 Well, one of my friends opened a restaurant in town and he asked me to work with him.

M: So you're still working there still?

F: Right, but then I want to return to teaching.

M: You have such a wide range of experience. You know, to be honest, we have fifteen people who are applying for this position. Why don't you tell me the reasons why you would be the best person for this job?

F: First of all, 32 I understand that different students have different learning styles, and for that reason, I have used iPads, video, music, cooking, drama, role plays, and games to reach every student. I think my experience working with international students would also be a great asset to your program.

M: Good. You do have an impressive resume. We're going to have two rounds of interviews, and 33 we will contact you on Friday and let you know whether or not you'll be coming back for the second round of interviews.

F: Okay.

M: It's been really nice meeting you, and thank you for your time.

F: 28 이게 흔치 않은 조합으로 보일 수 있다는 걸 아는데, 학위를 따기 전 요리 프로그램을 이수했습니다.

M: 와, 정말 많은 걸 하셨네요. 그렇다면 어떻게, 그리고 정확히 뭘 가르치셨나요?

F: 제 학생들 대다수가 식당에서 셰프가 되거나 자신만의 식당을 차리길 원했고, 저희 지역엔 관광지가 많이 있었습니다. 많은 관광객들이 특정 지역을 찾아왔기 때문에 29 영어를 할 줄 알면 공급사 및 식당 음식에 필요한 부분 등에 있어 의사소통이 가능하고, 그뿐만 아니라 고객들과도 소통할 수 있게 되기 때문에 전 제 학생들에게 영어와 요리를 동시에 가르쳤습니다.

M: 와, 그거 정말 흥미롭네요. 왜 미국으로 돌아왔나요? 돌아온 지는 얼마나 됐나요?

F: 돌아온 지는 현재 일 년 정도 됐습니다.

M: 그렇군요. 그럼 무엇 때문에 돌아왔나요?

F: 30 31 제 친구 중 한 명이 시내에 식당을 열었는데 저에게 함께 일하자고 부탁했습니다.

M: 그럼 아직도 그곳에서 일하고 있나요?

F: 네, 하지만 교직 쪽으로 돌아가고 싶습니다.

M: 정말 폭넓은 경험을 갖고 계시네요. 아시겠지만, 솔직히 말해서 15명의 사람들이 이 직책에 지원한 상태입니다. 본인이 왜 이 일에 가장 잘 맞는 사람인지 그 이유를 저에게 설명해 보시겠어요?

F: 우선, 32 저는 다양한 학생들이 다양한 학습 스타일을 갖고 있다는 걸 알고 있고, 이런 이유로 저는 모든 학생에게 닿을 수 있도록 아이패드, 영상, 음악, 요리, 드라마, 역할극, 게임을 활용해 왔습니다. 국제적인 학생들과 일한 제 경험 또한 귀사의 프로그램에 좋은 자산이 될 걸로 생각합니다.

M: 좋습니다. 이력이 인상적입니다. 저희는 면접을 두 번 진행할 예정이고, 33 금요일에 연락해서 2차 면접을 보러 오시게 될지 여부를 알려드리겠습니다.

F: 알겠습니다.

M: 만나서 정말로 반가웠습니다. 시간 내주셔서 감사합니다.

어휘 be interested in ~에 관심[흥미]이 있다 psychology 심리학 overseas 해외에[로] impressive 인상적인, 인상 깊은 work full time 전임[정규직]으로 일하다 community college 전문 대학 adjust to ~에 적응하다 friendly 친절한, 우호적인 make friends 친구가 되다 culinary arts 요리법 unusual 특이한, 흔치 않은, 드문 combination 조합, 연합 complete 완료하다, 끝마치다; 완벽한, 완전한 tourist spot 관광지 supplier 공급자, 공급 회사 so forth ~ 등등[따위] reach 이르다, 닿다; (목표에) 미치다 asset 자산, 재산 instructor (전임) 강사, 교사 human resources (회사의) 인사부 payroll 급여 대상자 명단; 급여 지불 총액 former 예전의, 과거의; 전자의 employer 고용주, 고용인 staff member 직원 contract 계약[약정](서) extensive 아주 넓은(많은), 대규모의 get paid 봉급[월급]을 받다 a variety of 여러 가지의

27. 대화를 근거로 봤을 때, 앨리스는 어떤 일에 지원하고 있는가?
(a) 고객 서비스
(b) 언어 강사
(c) 인사부
(d) 급여 관리

여성이 자신을 소개하며 'I've always been interested in teaching in a language program like this(전 항상 이 같은 언어 프로그램에서 가르치는 데 관심이 있었다)'고 설명하고 있으므로 정답은 (b)이다.

28. 앨리스는 왜 한국에서 영어와 함께 요리 또한 가르쳤는가?
(a) 그녀의 학생들이 대부분 요리사이기 때문에
(b) 그녀의 이전 고용주가 그렇게 하라고 했기 때문에
(c) 그녀 자신이 그렇게 해야 할 것 같다고 느끼기 때문에
(d) 그녀가 요리 프로그램을 이수했기 때문에

여성이 자신이 영어와 요리를 가르쳤다고 소개하며 그렇게 할 수 있었던 이유로서 자신이 'completed a program in culinary arts(요리 프로그램을 이수했다)'고 설명했기 때문에 정답은 (d)이다.

29. 앨리스에 의하면, 셰프는 언제 영어로 말해야 하는가?
(a) 직원들을 관리할 때
(b) 새로운 음식 조리법을 배울 때
(c) 자신만의 식당을 열 때
(d) 외국인 고객들과 소통할 때

여성이 말하길 셰프가 관광객이 많은 곳에서 영어를 할 줄 알면 'suppliers(공급사들) 및 customers(고객들)과 be able to communicated(소통할 수 있게 된다)'고 설명하고 있으므로 정답은 (d)이다.

30. 무엇이 앨리스를 미국에 돌아오게 했는가?
(a) 계약이 만료되었다.
(b) 새로운 취업 기회가 주어졌다
(c) 고용주와 잘 지내지 못했다.
(d) 직장에서 해고되었다.

미국으로 돌아온 이유를 묻는 남성의 말에 여성이 친구 중 한 명이 식당을 열었는데 그가 'asked me to work with him(자신에게 함께 일하자고 부탁해서)' 돌아왔다고 설명했으므로 정답은 (b)이다.

31. 앨리스는 왜 이 일에 지원했는가?
(a) 교직으로 돌아가기 위해
(b) 해외 경험을 좀 더 쌓기 위해
(c) 좀 더 폭넓은 경력을 만들기 위해
(d) 월급을 좀 더 많이 받을 수 있는지 알아보기 위해

아직도 이전 직장에서 일하고 있느냐는 남성의 말에 여성이 아직 그곳에서 일하고 있는 중이지만 'I want to return to teaching(교직으로 돌아가고 싶다)'고 설명했기 때문에 정답은 (a)이다.

32. 앨리스는 왜 이 직책에 자신이 최적이라 여기는가?
(a) 다양한 방법을 활용하여 학생들을 도울 수 있기 때문에
(b) 학생들이 요리하는 데 도움을 줄 수 있기 때문에
(c) 다른 사람들보다 저임금으로 일할 것이기 때문에
(d) 외국어로 사람들과 소통할 수 있기 때문에

여성이 말하길 다양한 학습 스타일을 고려해 'iPads, videos, music, cooking drama, role play, and games(아이패드, 영상, 음악, 요리, 드라마, 역할극, 게임)' 등을 활용해 왔다고 설명했으므로 정답은 (a)이다.

33. 프레드는 금요일에 앨리스에게 무엇을 알릴 것인가?
(a) 그녀가 지원한 직책이 계속해서 유효한지 여부
(b) 면접에서 좋은 결과를 냈는지 여부
(c) 2차 면접을 볼 수 있게 됐는지 여부
(d) 해당 직책에 고용되었는지 여부

남성이 여성에게 금요일에 연락하여 'whether or not you'll be coming back for the second round of interviews(2차 면접을 보러 오게 될지 여부)'를 알려주겠다고 했으므로 정답은 (c)이다.

34-39 (방송) 관광지를 소개하는 방송

34. What is the purpose of the talk?
35. According to the talk, who most likely would enjoy traveling to Utah?
36. Why does the speaker say it is selfish?
37. What can people do in Park City?
38. Based on the talk, what is the weather like in the winter in Utah?
39. Where did Utah get its name?

---

34 Hi, this is Ben and today, in our show, I'd like to talk about the best places to visit in Utah. I have been to Utah a couple of times to hike or ski. Nature is just magnificent and it will take your breath away. **35** Utah is truly an outdoor lover's dream. With natural wonders— including five national parks — and small towns with many outdoor activities, Utah offers ample opportunities to reconnect with nature. I hope it helps you decide where to go for your next getaway.

36 So Utah has five national parks and it is really selfish, isn't it? They could have left some national parks for someone else, right? It has unique vistas and geology, giving them all a character of their very own. Bryce Canyon has the bright red hoodoos, the arches have… arches, and Zion is a rugged and rich mix of biodiversity and winding clear rivers.

You can take a helicopter ride at Zion Helicopter Tours – the ideal introduction to the area. You can see how vast the area is. You can see the whole thing from above. It is completely safe and a great way to enjoy the view. The next morning, go on the stunning Narrows Hike.

Nature isn't just the only thing you can enjoy in Utah. **37** If you love indie movies, check out the world-famous movie festival. Park City's Sundance Film Festival is well worth a look, too. Hosted every winter, Sundance is not only America's largest indie film fest but also has the first showings of the movies generating awards buzz. Catch one of the 200 screenings, check out a Q and A with a director or sneak into one of the many parties across the town. If you are lucky, you might be able to run into celebrities like Brad Pitt. Park City, with its chic restaurants, boutique stores, super cool coffee shops and bars, can get quite crowded.

Salt Lake City is the capital of the State of Utah and the city itself has a lot to offer. Did you know that Salt Lake City hosted the winter Olympics in 2002? It has the largest salt lake in the Western Hemisphere. It's an amazing place to watch the sunset. We can't ignore the either in Salt Lake City. **38** If you go to Utah in the winter, you can land in a frozen Salt Lake CIty, work your way down through Park City and

Midway to take in the snow sports and snake your way down to Snow Canyon, where you'll need to remove a layer or two under the bright blue skies. By the time you reach Nevada to catch the plane home from Vegas, you'll have covered at least three seasons. Isn't it amazing? Three different seasons in one trip.

You can also learn history. 39 Utah is named after the Ute People who, along with the Navajo, occupied the region millennia before any white settlers arrived. The state is packed with plenty of Native history, from remarkable petroglyphs and wondrous rock art to ancient ruins and artifacts.

Utah also has the world's most extensive hiking trails set in many cities, so if you like hiking, don't miss out on this great outdoor adventure in Utah. I hope you enjoyed our show today and thank you for listening.

수 있고 구불구불한 길을 따라 내려가 스노우 협곡까지 가면 푸른 하늘 아래에서 한 겹, 혹은 두 겹의 옷을 벗어야 하게 될 겁니다. 베이거스에서 집으로 향하는 비행기를 타기 위해 네바다에 도착할 때쯤이면, 여러분은 최소 세 개의 계절을 체험하는 것이 됩니다. 놀랍지 않나요? 한 번의 여행에 세 개의 다른 계절이 있다니 말이죠. 여러분은 역사 또한 배울 수 있습니다. 39 유타라는 이름은 백인 정착민들이 도착하기 전까지 나바호족과 함께 수천년 동안 지역을 차지해 온 우트족 사람들의 이름을 따서 명명된 것입니다. 주는 놀랄 만한 암면 조각 및 경이로운 암면 미술부터 시작해 고대의 유적 및 공예품까지, 풍부한 원주민의 역사로 가득합니다.

유타엔 세계에서 가장 큰 하이킹 코스 또한 수많은 도시에 구비돼 있으며, 따라서 하이킹을 좋아하신다면 유타에서의 멋진 야외 모험을 놓치지 마시기 바랍니다. 오늘 우리 쇼를 즐겁게 보셨기를 바라며 청취해 주셔서 감사드립니다.

어휘 magnificent 참으로 아름다운[멋진] take one's breath away 숨이 멎을 정도이다 natural wonders 자연의 경이로움, 자연 경관 ample 충분한, 풍만한 reconnect 다시 연결되다[하다] getaway 도주; (단기) 휴가 vista 경치, 풍경 geology 지질학; 지질학적 기원[역사] rugged 바위투성이의, 기복이 심한 winding 구불구불한 well worth a look 볼 가치가 충분한 showing (영화) 상영 screening (영화) 상영[방영] sneak into ~에 몰래 들어가다 chic 멋진, 세련된 Western Hemisphere 서반구 sunset 해질녘, 일몰 name after ~의 이름을 따서 명명하다 occupy (공간·지역·시간을) 차지하다 settler 정착민 petroglyph 암면 조각, 암각화 wondrous 경이로운 ruin 잔해, 폐허, 유적 artifact 인공물, 공예품 socialize 사귀다, 어울리다, 교제하다 majestic 장엄한, 위풍당당한 unpredictable 예측 불가능한 tribe 부족, 종족

34. 이 이야기의 목적은 무엇인가?
  (a) 여행 목적지를 소개하는 것
  (b) 주에 대한 정보를 제공하는 것
  (c) 주의 역사를 설명하는 것
  (d) 여행 패키지를 홍보하는 것

첫 단락에서 화자가 'I'd like to talk about the best places to visit in Utah(유타에서 방문하기 가장 좋은 곳들에 대해 이야기하고자 한다)'고 말문을 열고 있으므로 정답은 (a)이다.

35. 이야기에 따르면, 누가 유타로 여행가는 걸 즐길 것 같은가?
  (a) 몰에서의 쇼핑을 즐기는 사람들
  (b) 다른 이와 어울리는 걸 즐기는 사람들
  (c) 야외 활동을 즐기는 사람들
  (d) 오락 공연을 즐기는 사람들

첫 단락에서 화자가 'Utah is truly on outdoor lover's dream(유타는 진정 야외 활동가들의 꿈이다)'라고 설명했고, 이는 곧 유타가 야외 활동을 즐기는 사람들에게 좋은 여행지임을 뜻하므로 정답은 (c)이다.

36. 화자는 왜 이것이 이기적이라고 말하는가?
  (a) 좋은 식당과 멋진 카페가 있기 때문에
  (b) 국제적인 영화 축제가 있기 때문에
  (c) 헬리콥터 투어가 있기 때문에
  (d) 유타에 국립 공원이 많기 때문에

두 번째 단락에서 화자는 유타에 'has five national parks(국립 공원이 5개나 있고)', 다른 이들을 위한 국립 공원을 좀 남겨 줄 수도 있었을 텐데 참 이기적이라고 설명하고 있으므로 정답은 (d)이다.

37. 사람들은 파크 시티에서 무엇을 할 수 있는가?
  (a) 북미 원주민의 문화를 즐길 수 있다.
  (b) 장엄한 산맥을 즐길 수 있다.
  (c) 다양한 유형의 날씨를 체험할 수 있다.
  (d) 유명한 독립 영화를 관람할 수 있다

네 번째 단락에서 'indie movies(독립 영화)'를 좋아한다면 세계적인 영화 축제를 찾아보라고 추천하는 동시에 'Park City's Sundance Film Festival(파크 시티의 선댄스 영화 축제)'를 언급했으므로 정답은 (d)이다.

38. 이야기를 근거로 봤을 때, 유타의 겨울 날씨는 어떠한가?
(a) 예측 불가능하고 위험하다.
(b) 온화하고 쾌적하다.
(c) 장소에 따라 변화한다
(d) 매섭게 춥고 눈이 많이 내린다.

39. 유타는 어디서 그 이름을 얻게 되었나?
(a) 지역을 차지한 영국인들로부터
(b) 북미 원주민 종족으로부터
(c) 지역에 서식하고 있는 동물들로부터
(d) 지리적 특징으로부터

여섯 번째 단락을 보면 겨울에 유타에 가서 다양한 곳을 돌아다니게 되면 'you'll have covered at least three seasons(최소 세 개의 계절을 체험하는 것이 된다)'고 설명하고 있으므로 정답은 (c)이다.

일곱 번째 단락에서 유타란 이름은 수천년간 이 지역을 차지해 온 'the Ute People(우트족 사람들)'의 이름을 따서 명명되었다고 했고, 이는 곧 원주민의 이름을 따서 만들었음을 뜻하므로 정답은 (b)이다.

40-46 (상담) 차량 구매에 대한 상담 및 조언

40. What does Julie want to decide?
41. Why is Julie asking Fred about the topic?
42. What does Fred love about his car?
43. What concerns Julie about charging?
44. According to Fred, what financial benefit does an electric car have?
45. Why does Julie think electric cars are not so affordable?
46. What will Julie probably do after talking to Fred?

M: Hi Julie!

F: Hello Fred. Can I ask you something?

M: Sure, go ahead.

F: You know I am thinking of buying a car, just because mine is very old and it keeps breaking down. It just stopped in the middle of the road yesterday, and I really think it is not safe to drive my car anymore.

M: Oh, really? I am sorry to hear that, so what did you do?

F: I just called the insurance company and they took care of it but now I don't have a car. I have to take the bus for a while. Well, anyhow, **41** I am just debating what kind of car I should buy next.

M: **41** I think you should go electric. I recently purchased a new electric car and I love it. Carol and I were thinking about it for a long time and as soon as the new Ion came out, we just got it.

F: Well, what do you like about electric cars?

M: Well, I have had this car for three months. **42** First of all, you wouldn't believe how smoothly and quietly it runs. Once you get used to driving an electric car, you will never want to drive anything that runs on gas.

F: Oh wow, hmm. I've driven one before and that is also my favorite part. Well, how long does it take to charge and can you find the charging stations easily?

M: It takes approximately 20 minutes to several hours to fully charge the car depending on whether you're using a rapid charger or a home-based plug-in system. If you live in the city, finding a charging station wouldn't be a problem.

---

40. 줄리는 무엇을 결정하고자 하는가?
41. 줄리는 왜 프레드에게 본 주제에 관해 묻고 있는가?
42. 프레드는 자신에 차와 관련해 무엇을 좋아하는가?
43. 줄리는 어떤 우려를 제기하고 있는가?
44. 프레드에 따르면, 전기차가 가진 재정상의 이점은 무엇인가?
45. 줄리는 왜 전기차 가격이 적절치 않다고 보는가?
46. 줄리는 프레드와 대화 후 무엇을 할 것 같은가?

M: 안녕, 줄리!

F: 안녕, 프레드. 나 뭐 좀 물어봐도 될까?

M: 물론이지, 한번 해 봐.

F: 내 차가 너무 오래돼서 계속 고장이 나는 바람에 새 차를 살 생각 중이거든. 어젠 길 한복판에서 멈추기까지 했고, 이젠 내 차를 모는 게 더 이상 안전하지 않다는 생각이 들어.

M: 정말? 그랬다니 유감이다. 그래서 어떻게 했어?

F: 보험 회사에 전화해서 처리해 줬는데, 지금 현재는 차가 없어. 당분간은 버스를 타야만 하고. 뭐, 어쨌든, **40** 다음엔 어떤 종류의 차를 사야 할지 곰곰이 생각해 보고 있어.

M: **41** 내 생각에 전기차로 하는 게 좋을 것 같아. 내가 최근에 전기차 한 대를 샀는데 너무 좋거든. 캐롤이랑 난 긴 시간 동안 심사숙고했고, 신형 아이온이 출시되자마자 바로 샀어.

F: 음, 넌 전기차의 어떤 점이 좋은데?

M: 3개월 동안 차를 사용 중이거든. **42** 우선, 차가 얼마나 부드럽고 조용하게 달리는지 믿기 힘들 거야. 일단 전기차를 모는 데 길들여지게 되면 휘발유로 달리는 차는 절대 몰고 싶지 않게 될 거야.

F: 와, 나도 전에 한번 몰아본 적이 있는데 그 점이 내가 제일 좋아하는 부분이야. 충전하는 데 얼마나 걸리고 충전소는 쉽게 찾을 수 있나?

M: 고속 충전기를 사용하는지, 혹은 집에서 쓰는 플러그인 시스템을 사용하는지 여부에 따라 차를 완전히 충전시키는 데 거의 20분에서 수시간 정도 걸려. 네가 도시에 산다면 충전소를 찾는 건 문제가 안 될 거야.

F: **43** But then what about when you go outside of the city and have to drive through rural areas or on a long-distance road trip?

M: Yeah, I have to admit, it would be challenging. We're taking a long trip soon for the holiday so we will find out soon I guess. We're planning to find charging stations ahead of time and plan our trip accordingly.

F: And I still think it takes too long to fully charge the car. If I drive a gasoline powered car, it will just take a few minutes, but recharging an electric car would take forever. You know what I mean?

M: Well, the government is building more infrastructure for electric cars by 2025, so I am counting on that, but what you are saying also makes sense.

F: Yeah, I don't know what I need to do while it is charging. Since more people are buying electric cars, the city has to build more charging stations and I think this kind of problem can be solved pretty easily.

M: That's right. **44** Also charging an electric car is much cheaper than gassing up. I only have to spend 10 bucks whereas other people would spend 100 dollars to fill a tank. You can also get tax benefits for your car and discounts in parks and public parking lots. I think that's a good deal.

F: Right. That was what I thought at first, but electric cars still cost a lot of money. Of course you save a lot of money by fuel cost savings and tax credits but **45** the upfront price of most electric cars is so much more than that of comparable gas-powered vehicles. I am not really sure electric cars are actually cheaper.

M: Wow, Julie. You're really weighing your options. I didn't even think of that, but that is a choice you have to make. What do you value more? Initial cost or maintenance cost? It all depends how much you drive and where you drive. Are you going to mostly drive in the city or in the rural areas? I think you just have to consider all the things and make the right choice for you.

F: I guess. I am still not sure. **46** Maybe I should go and test drive a few of the models I like. Thanks for your input. I really appreciate it.

F: **43** 하지만 도시 외곽으로 나가서 시골 지역을 운전해 지나가거나 장거리 여행을 하는 경우엔 어떤데?

M: 힘들 거라는 점은 인정해. 우리가 곧 휴가 때 장거리 여행을 할 예정이라 조만간 찾을 거거든. 사전에 빨리 충전소를 찾아서 그에 맞춰 여행 일정을 짜려고 계획 중이야.

F: 그리고 차를 완전히 충전하는 데 너무 오래 걸린다는 생각이 계속 들어. 휘발유 자동차를 운전하면 단지 몇 분 정도 걸리는데, 전기차 충전은 너무 오랜 시간이 걸리잖아. 내 말이 무슨 뜻인지 알지?

M: 정부에서 2025년까지 전기차를 위한 기반 시설을 좀 더 많이 만들 예정이고, 난 그렇게 될 거라고 확신하지만 네 말도 일리가 있어.

F: 맞아, 차가 충전되는 동안 뭘 해야 할지 모르겠어. 더 많은 사람들이 전기차를 사고 있으니 시에선 충전소를 더 많이 지어야 할 거고, 내 생각엔 이런 문제가 꽤 쉽게 해결될 수 있다고 봐.

M: 맞아. **44** 그리고 전기차 충전은 휘발유를 넣는 것보다 훨씬 더 저렴해. 다른 사람들이 기름 탱크를 채우려고 100달러를 쓸 때 난 10달러만 쓰면 되니까. 또한 차량 관련 세금 혜택 및 주차와 공영 주차장에서 할인도 받을 수 있어. 난 이게 꽤 좋다고 봐.

F: 맞아. 그게 바로 내가 처음에 생각한 점이지만, 전기차는 여전히 돈이 많이 들어. 물론 연료 비용 절감이나 세액 공제로 돈을 많이 절약하게 되지만 **45** 대부분의 전기차 선불 가격이 이와 유사한 휘발유 자동차 가격보다 훨씬 더 나가니까. 난 전기차가 실질적으로 더 저렴한 게 맞는지 확신이 안 들어.

M: 와, 줄리. 너 정말 요모조모 따지는구나. 난 그렇게는 미처 생각 못했는데, 하지만 네가 내려야 하는 결정이니까. 어떤 걸 더 따져 볼래? 초기 비용이나 유지 비용? 이건 전부 네가 얼마나 많이, 어디로 운전하는지에 달려 있어. 주로 도시, 아니면 시골 지역에서 운전할 거야? 내 보기엔 모든 걸 다 고려해서 너에게 맞는 선택을 내려야 한다고 봐.

F: 글쎄. 아직도 확신이 안 서. **46** 아마도 가서 내가 좋아하는 모델로 운전해 봐야 할 것 같아. 의견 줘서 고마워. 정말 감사하게 생각해.

어휘 break down 고장 나다; 실패하다 insurance company 보험 회사 take care of ~을 돌보다 debate 논의[토의/논쟁]하다; 곰곰이 생각하다, 숙고하다 purchase 구입, 구매; 구입[구매]하다 get used to ~에 익숙해지다 approximately 거의 (정확하게), ~ 가까이 rural area 시골 지역 challenging 도전적인; 힘든, 간단하지 않은 ahead of time 시간 전에, 예정보다 빨리 recharge 충전하다[되다], 재충전하다 take forever 엄청난[오랜] 시간이 걸리다 infrastructure 사회[공공] 기반 시설 count on ~을 믿다[확신하다] make sense 타당하다, 말이 되다 tax credit 세액 공제 upfront 솔직한; 선불의 comparable 비슷한, 비교할 만한 weigh 무게를 달다; 저울질하다, 따져 보다 value 소중하게 생각하다; (가치·가격을) 평가하다 maintenance 유지; 관리, 보수 test drive 시운전하다 dealership (특히 승용차) 대리점

40. 줄리는 무엇을 결정하고자 하는가?
(a) 원하는 차량 브랜드
(b) 사고 싶은 차종
(c) 좋은 중고차를 얻을 수 있는 방법
(d) 새 차를 구매해야 하는 시기

여성이 남성에게 'I am just debating what kind of car I should buy next(다음엔 어떤 종류의 차를 사야 할지 곰곰이 생각해 보고 있다)'고 문의하고 있으므로 정답은 (b)이다.

41. 줄리는 왜 프레드에게 본 주제에 관해 묻고 있는가?
(a) 그가 최근 전기차를 구매했기 때문에
(b) 그 역시 새 차를 살 생각 중이기 때문에
(c) 줄리에게 자신의 차를 팔고 싶어 하기 때문에
(d) 자동차 회사에서 일하기 때문에

차량 구매에 대해 문의하고 있는 여성에게 남성이 'I recently purchased a new electric car and I love it(최근에 전기차 한 대를 샀는데 너무 좋다)'고 설명하고 있는 것을 봤을 때 (a)가 답임을 유추할 수 있다.

42. 프레드는 자신에 차와 관련해 무엇을 좋아하는가?
(a) 그의 오래된 차보다 저렴하다.
(b) 그의 오래된 차보다 훨씬 더 빠르다.
(c) 운전할 때 매우 조용하다
(d) 호화로운 내부 디자인을 가지고 있다.

남성이 자신의 전기차에 내해서 'how smoothly and quietly it runs(얼마나 부드럽고 조용하게 달리는지)' 믿기 힘들 거라고 설명하며 장점을 어필하고 있기 때문에 정답은 (c)이다.

43. 줄리는 어떤 우려를 제기하고 있는가?
(a) 충전을 자주 할 충분한 시간이 없다는 것
(b) 차를 충전하는 동안 불만을 제기하는 사람들
(c) 시골 지역에서 충전소를 찾는 것
(d) 가정용 충전기 설치에 돈을 많이 들여야 하는 것

도시에 산다면 충전소 찾는 것은 문제가 안 된다고 말하는 남성에게 여성이 'outside of the city(도시 외곽), rural areas(시골 지역)'에서 운전할 땐 어떻게 되는 거냐고 우려를 표하고 있으므로 정답은 (c)이다.

44. 프레드에 따르면, 전기차가 가진 재정상의 이점은 무엇인가?
(a) 공영 주차장에서 무료로 주차하는 것
(b) 장기적으로 봤을 때 낮은 관리 비용
(c) 휘발유에 비해 합리적인 충전 비용
(d) 더 저렴한 전기차 가격

남성의 말에 의하면 'charging an electric car is much cheaper than gassing up(전기차를 충전하는 것이 휘발유를 넣는 것보다 훨씬 더 저렴하다)'고 했으므로 정답은 (c)이다.

45. 줄리는 왜 전기차 가격이 적절치 않다고 보는가?
(a) 정부 장려금이 조만간 종료되기 때문에
(b) 값비싼 부품을 필요로 하기 때문에
(c) 유지하는 데 훨씬 더 많은 비용이 들기 때문에
(d) 일반 차량보다 가격이 더 나가기 때문에

여성이 'upfront price of most electric cars is so much more than that of comparable gas-powered vehicles(전기차 선불 가격이 이와 유사한 휘발유 자동차 가격보다 훨씬 더 나간다)'고 했으므로 정답은 (d)이다.

46. 줄리는 프레드와 대화 후 무엇을 할 것 같은가?
(a) 결정을 내리기 전 차량을 시운전하러 갈 것이다
(b) 차를 시운전하기 전에 전문가와 이야기할 것이다.
(c) 대리점에 가기 전 광범위한 조사를 한다.
(d) 차를 사기 전에 가족과 이 문제를 논의한다.

대화 마지막 부분에서 여성이 'I should go and test drive a few of the models I like(가서 내가 좋아하는 모델로 운전해 봐야 할 것 같다)'고 말했으므로 정답은 (a)이다.

47-52 (방송) 가정식 요리법을 다루는 방송

47. What does Homie food try to do in the show?
48. Why does the speaker say it is fail-proof?
49. What does mustard do in mayonnaise?
50. How do the eggs have to be when used in making mayonnaise?
51. Why does the speaker say to add oil slowly in tiny drops?
52. What does the speaker tell people to do after adding oil?

47 Hello everybody and welcome to Homie food, the show that tries to make simple homemade food, including the stuff we normally buy at a store. Homemade versions of kitchen staples are cheaper and healthier than their store-bought counterparts and they taste much better, too. Last time we made spinach basil pesto. Many people said that they made the pasta or used it as a spread.

Today, we are going to try to make mayonnaise in 10 minutes using whole eggs instead of just the yolk. **48** It makes this homemade mayonnaise recipe practically fail-proof and extra easy.

I've used this mayonnaise recipe more times than I can count. If you've never tried homemade mayonnaise, then you are in for a treat. Homemade mayo is very creamy and so much more flavorful than anything you can buy at the store.

The ingredients to make mayo are simple – we bet you even have them in your kitchen right now. You will need eggs, mustard, vinegar or lemon juice and oil. How simple is that?

49 Mustard adds a bit of flavor, but it also helps to keep the mayonnaise stable. If you use mustard, your mayo will not be runny. It gives consistency to the mayo. You don't want to use oil that has a strong flavor like olive oil. Use an oil that is light in flavor like canola.

50 Room temperature ingredients are best when making mayonnaise at home. Don't pull an egg out of your refrigerator and try to make mayo with it. You might get lucky and it will work, but chances are it won't. If you're not able to wait for the egg to come to room temperature, submerge it in lukewarm water for a couple of minutes. And a lot of people are concerned about eating raw eggs. I think a person is more likely to come into contact with salmonella by eating a celery stalk than they are a raw egg. But if you don't feel comfortable eating raw egg, don't worry. It's super easy to pasteurize an egg at home.

An egg is pasteurized and considered safe to eat when it reaches an internal temperature of 58 degrees, so just boil some water and keep the eggs in there for 3 minutes and drain the water and cool the eggs in cold water and that's it. Add an egg to the bowl of your food processor and process for about 20 seconds. Add mustard, vinegar, and salt then process for another 20 seconds. Here comes the most important part: adding oil. Slowly add the oil, in tiny drops, until about a quarter of the oil has been added. Adding the oil slowly is really the key. When you begin, the oil should be poured in the tiniest stream. Once the mayonnaise begins to thicken, you can pour the oil a little faster. **51** If you were to dump it all in at once, you'd have mayonnaise soup. I have made that mistake so many times so be careful. **52** Taste the mayonnaise and adjust with additional salt and vinegar or lemon juice.

You can use your homemade mayonnaise in many different ways. You can make potato salad, coleslaw or broccoli salad or simply drizzle it on your salad and use it as a salad dressing. Thank you so much for listening and I hope you enjoy your homemade mayo.

기름을 추가하세요. 기름의 4분의 1이 들어갈 때까지 기름을 천천히, 작은 방울로 넣으십시오. 기름을 천천히 넣는 것이 매우 중요합니다. 시작할 때, 기름이 가장 가는 다란 줄기 상태로 투입되어야 합니다. 마요네즈가 굳기 시작하면, 기름을 좀 더 빠른 속도로 넣을 수 있습니다. **51** 기름을 한꺼번에 쏟아 넣으면, 마요네즈 수프를 보게 될 겁니다. 저도 이전에 이런 실수를 많이 했으니 주의하세요. **52** 마요네즈 맛을 본 후 소금과 식초 혹은 레몬 주스를 추가적으로 넣어서 맛을 조절하십시오.

여러분은 집에서 만든 마요네즈를 다방면으로 사용할 수 있습니다. 감자 샐러드, 코울슬로 혹은 브로콜리 샐러드를 만들거나 그냥 샐러드에 부어서 샐러드 드레싱으로 사용할 수도 있습니다. 들어 주셔서 감사하며 집에서 만든 마요네즈를 즐기시기 바랍니다.

어휘 staple 주요 산물; 기본 식료품 counterpart 대응 관계에 있는 사람[것] whole egg 전란 yolk 노른자 practically 사실상, 거의; 현실적으로, 실제로 in for a treat 즐길 수 있는, 기대해도 좋은 flavorful 풍미 있는, 맛 좋은 ingredient (특히 요리 등의) 재료[성분] stable 안정된, 안정적인 runny 너무 무른; 콧물[눈물]이 나는 consistency 굳기, 단단함, 견고함; 일관성 room temperature 상온, 평상시 온도 submerge 물[액체] 속에 넣다[잠그다] lukewarm 미지근한; 미온적인 come into contact with ~와 접촉하다[만나다] pasteurize 저온 살균하다 drain 물[액체]을[이] 빼내다[빠지다] food processor 믹서기 pour 붓다, 따르다 stream 개울, 시내; (액체, 기체의) 줄기 thicken 걸쭉해지다 adjust 조정[조절]하다 drizzle (액체를) 조금 붓다 mess up 엉망으로 만들다, 망치다 mixture 혼합물; 혼합 재료

47. 호미 푸드는 쇼에서 무엇을 하려고 하는가?
　　(a) 사람들에게 정찬을 만드는 법을 가르치는 것
　　(b) 사람들에게 무엇을 요리할지 제안하는 것
　　(c) 이들이 파는 음식 제품을 홍보하는 것
　　(d) 가게에서 사는 대신 가정식을 만드는 것

첫 단락에서 화자가 'show that tries to make simple homemade food(간단한 가정식을 만들어 보는 쇼)'에 온 걸 환영한다는 말로 방송을 시작하고 있으므로 정답은 (d)이다.

48. 화자는 이것이 왜 실패가 불가능하다고 하는가?
　　(a) 많은 사람들이 이를 엉망으로 해 왔기 때문에
　　(b) 이것이 별로 복잡하지 않기 때문에
　　(c) 좋은 요리법을 사용하기 때문에
　　(d) 쇼에서 방송으로 나가기 때문에

두 번째 단락에서 방송에서 소개하는 마요네즈 요리법이 집에서 마요네즈를 만드는 걸 'fail-proof(실패하지 않게)', 그리고 'extra easy(매우 쉽게)' 만들어 준다고 했으므로 정답이 (b)임을 유추할 수 있다.

49. 머스터드는 마요네즈 안에서 무엇을 하는가?
　　(a) 머스터드는 재료들을 서로 붙여 놓는다
　　(b) 머스터드는 하는 일이 전혀 없다.
　　(c) 머스터드는 마요네즈에 색을 더한다.
　　(d) 머스터드는 기름의 강한 맛을 제거한다.

다섯 번째 단락에서 머스터드가 약간의 맛을 더하면서도 'keep the mayonnaise stable(마요네즈를 견고하게 유지하여)' 무른 상태가 되지 않도록 만든다고 했으므로 정답이 (a)임을 유추할 수 있다.

50. 마요네즈를 제조에 계란을 쓸 때 계란은 어떤 상태가 돼야 하는가?
　　(a) 상온 상태가 되어야 한다
　　(b) 물에 담가져야 한다.
　　(c) 냉장고에 보관되어야 한다.
　　(d) 특정 종류여야만 한다.

여섯 번째 단락에서 'room temperature ingredients(상온 상태의 재료)'가 마요네즈를 만들 때 좋다고 하면서 냉장고에서 계란을 꺼내서 쓰지 말라고 조언하고 있으므로 정답이 (a)임을 유추할 수 있다.

51. 화자는 왜 기름을 작은 방울로 천천히 넣으라고 하는가?
(a) 강한 맛을 더해 줄 것이기 때문에
(b) 걸쭉해지지 않을 것이기 때문에
(c) 제대로 된 맛이 나지 않을 것이기 때문에
(d) 믹서기를 파손시킬 것이기 때문에

일곱 번째 단락에서 기름을 천천히 작은 방울로 넣으라고 조언하면서 'dump it all in at once(한꺼번에 모두 쏟아 넣으면)' 결국 'mayonnaise soup(마요네즈 수프(액체))'가 된다고 경고했으므로 정답은 (b)이다.

52. 화자는 사람들에게 기름 추가 후 뭘 하라고 하는가?
(a) 샐러드에 넣어서 내 간다
(b) 믹서기에 다시 한번 넣는다
(c) 혼합된 재료에 계란을 추가로 넣는다
(d) 맛을 보고 재료를 좀 더 추가한다

일곱 번째 단락에서 기름을 넣은 후 'adjust with additional salt and vinegar or lemon juice(소금과 식초 혹은 레몬 주스를 추가적으로 넣어서 맛을 조절하라)'고 했으므로 정답은 (d)이다.

Actual Test 02 / Vocab 주요 어휘 총정리

Actual Test 02에 등장했던 주요 어휘를 한눈에 훑어보며 정리해 보도록 합시다.
모르는 어휘가 있을 경우 박스(□)에 체크(V) 표시를 한 뒤 재차 암기하도록 하세요.

- ☐ be interested in ~에 관심[흥미]이 있다
- ☐ psychology 심리학
- ☐ overseas 해외에[로]
- ☐ impressive 인상적인, 인상 깊은
- ☐ work full time 전임[정규직]으로 일하다
- ☐ friendly 친절한, 우호적인
- ☐ make friends 친구가 되다
- ☐ unusual 특이한, 흔치 않은, 드문
- ☐ combination 조합, 연합
- ☐ complete 완료하다, 끝마치다; 완벽한, 완전한
- ☐ tourist spot 관광지
- ☐ supplier 공급자, 공급 회사
- ☐ reach 이르다, 닿다; (목표에) 미치다
- ☐ asset 자산, 재산
- ☐ instructor (전임) 강사, 교사
- ☐ human resources (회사의) 인사부
- ☐ payroll 급여 대상자 명단; 급여 지불 총액
- ☐ former 예전의, 과거의; 전자의
- ☐ employer 고용주, 고용인
- ☐ staff member 직원
- ☐ contract 계약[약정](서)
- ☐ extensive 아주 넓은[많은], 대규모의
- ☐ get paid 봉급[월급]을 받다
- ☐ a variety of 여러 가지의
- ☐ magnificent 참으로 아름다운[멋진]
- ☐ take one's breath away 숨이 멎을 정도이다
- ☐ ample 충분한, 풍만한
- ☐ reconnect 다시 연결되다[하다]
- ☐ getaway 도주; (단기) 휴가
- ☐ geology 지질학; 지질학적 기원[역사]
- ☐ well worth a look 볼 가치가 충분한
- ☐ sneak into ~에 몰래 들어가다
- ☐ name after ~의 이름을 따서 명명하다
- ☐ occupy (공간·지역·시간을) 차지하다
- ☐ settler 정착민
- ☐ ruin 잔해, 폐허, 유적
- ☐ artifact 인공물, 공예품
- ☐ socialize 사귀다, 어울리다, 교제하다
- ☐ majestic 장엄한, 위풍당당한
- ☐ unpredictable 예측 불가능한
- ☐ break down 고장 나다; 실패하다
- ☐ take care of ~을 돌보다
- ☐ debate 논의[토의/논쟁]하다; 숙고하다
- ☐ purchase 구입, 구매; 구입[구매]하다
- ☐ get used to ~에 익숙해지다
- ☐ approximately 거의 (정확하게), ~ 가까이
- ☐ challenging 도전적인; 힘든, 간단하지 않은
- ☐ recharge 충전하다[되다], 재충전하다
- ☐ take forever 엄청난[오랜] 시간이 걸리다
- ☐ infrastructure 사회[공공] 기반 시설
- ☐ count on ~을 믿다[확신하다]
- ☐ make sense 타당하다, 말이 되다
- ☐ comparable 비슷한, 비교할 만한
- ☐ weigh 무게를 달다; 저울질하다, 따져 보다
- ☐ value 소중하게 생각하다; (가치·가격을) 평가하다
- ☐ maintenance 유지; 관리, 보수
- ☐ counterpart 대응 관계에 있는 사람[것]
- ☐ practically 사실상, 거의; 현실적으로, 실제로
- ☐ flavorful 풍미 있는, 맛 좋은
- ☐ ingredient (특히 요리 등의) 재료[성분]
- ☐ stable 안정된, 안정적인
- ☐ runny 너무 무른; 콧물[눈물]이 나는
- ☐ consistency 굳기, 단단함, 견고성; 일관성
- ☐ submerge 물[액체] 속에 넣다[잠그다]
- ☐ drain 물[액체]을[이] 빼내다[빠지다]
- ☐ pour 붓다, 따르다
- ☐ thicken 걸쭉해지다
- ☐ adjust 조정[조절]하다
- ☐ mess up 엉망으로 만들다, 망치다
- ☐ mixture 혼합물; 혼합 재료